Hidden Secrets in the Hebrew

Volume 2 (Book 2 of 2)

2024 First Printing
© 2024 by Hannah Nesher, Voice for Israel
All rights reserved. No part of this book may be reproduced or reprinted in any form or by any means, electronic or mechanical, including photocopying, recording, or by any information storage and retrieval system, without permission in writing from the publisher.

For information regarding permission to reprint materials from this book, please send your request to the author at the address below or e-mail your request to: nesher.hannah@gmail.com

Cover Design & Book Layout by Colette Scharf
info@shineonline.ca
Shine Communications
9813-152 St. Edmonton, AB
T5P 1X2 Canada

Voice for Israel
313 – 11007 Jasper Ave.
Edmonton, AB
T5K 0K6 Canada
www.voiceforisrael.net

ISBN: 9798323421671

Acknowledgements

I would first and foremost want to give all the honor, glory and praise for the creation of this book to the Most High God, El Elyon אל עליון, Lord of Hosts, Yehovah Tzeva'ot יהוה צבאות. Without His faithful guidance, direction, and inspiration - along with a whole army of ministering angels, this book would never have been completed, proving that there is 'No chance at all if you think you can pull it off yourself, but with God all things are possible.' (Matthew 19:26 MSG) Todah rabah Abba![1]

There are also a few angels in human form that I would like to acknowledge:

Thank you (todah rabah) to Sue Socci, my faithful and diligent 'eagle eye' editor, who spent countless hours reading and re-reading each chapter over and over again for the umpteenth time, in order to catch all the little details that make for excellence. Thank you so much, to you and also to your husband Jim, for leading our Zoom Torah studies in such beautiful, anointed worship music.

Thank you (todah rabah) to my friend, Lisa Swensen, fellow sojourner and animal lover, who has cheered me on all the way, prayed for and with me, being an ever present, daily source of encouragement. Your joy and enthusiasm is contagious! And yes, I agree, we are 'so excited to see what the Lord is going to do!'

Thank you to my webmaster, Colette Scharf (Shine Communications), who has done such a great job with formatting this book and with the cover design. Your technical support has been invaluable over the years. You are a blessing!

Thank you to all my family, my Dad (may he live to 120), my sisters and brother, my cousins, and all my children and grandchildren who have been a steadfast source of love, support and prayer through all of our mountains and valleys. Todah rabah!

And lastly, thank you to my spiritual family, the Body of Messiah around the world - Zoomers and ministry supporters - who have continually lifted me, my family and my ministry up to the Throne of Grace. You have truly made a difference for the Kingdom!

I love and appreciate each and every one of you and pray that God will richly bless you and faithfully keep you safe under the shelter of his great wings.

---

[1] Todah rabah Abba means Thank you very much Father (Dad)

Endorsements for Hidden Secrets in the Hebrew

5.0 out of 5 stars   "Worth its weight in gold."

"Hidden secrets in the Hebrew is a gem of a book, and probably Hannah's best yet! Both volumes 1 and 2 are packed with insights into the Hebrew language bringing the bible to life and drawing us deeper into the heart of God. They are both a study book and an easy-read devotional at the same time. You can dip in and out of chapters, which all stand alone, or read from start to finish, whichever suits your style. A masterpiece and a treasure trove!

Hannah's rich knowledge of the Hebrew language and her deep personal life experiences combine in this beautiful collection of teachings. Hidden gems are uncovered to inspire and uplift, leading us to better know God's heart through His divine, holy language.

Each chapter is rich in wisdom, prophetic insight and practical application, bringing strength, comfort and encouragement for our daily walk with the Lord. Certainly a treasure to read, re-read and meditate upon."

- Sue Socci, Editor, Worship leader with her husband, Jim Socci, U.K.

"Hannah is a gifted and inspirational writer and it is a joy to experience another great book from her which so powerfully touches my heart. It's difficult to express the magnitude, authenticity, and stunning revelation Hannah seems to capture. I can almost imagine a picture of God as an artist painting a wonderful landscape and Hannah sitting beside Him, painting with him, copying His every brushstroke; capturing His expression through her words. Stunning!

Hannah has a wonderful gift of drawing out the deeper meaning of the bible through insights from the Hebrew meaning of words and then applying them to our ordinary lives. This could be her best yet - a masterpiece in my opinion. Truly wonderful!"

- Tania McNeil, Co-Pastor of Adore Church with her husband, David McNeil, U.K.

"Hidden Secrets in the Hebrew reveals powerful treasures in the original Scriptures of the Bible through Hannah's unpacking of these amazing Hebrew word studies. Her personal stories and impactful biblical truths will encourage you in your faith as Hannah shares honestly and from the heart."

- Liat Whelan, Light to the Nations https://www.light-tothenations.com/

"This book is so needed for today! It has made God's word come alive for me as never before! Coming from a traditional Christian background and now beginning to understand the layers and depth of the Hebrew language is like going from seeing God in black and white for so long - to seeing Him in full Technicolor.

It's as if I've been paying expensive tickets to attend the symphony only to hear the clarinet play a solo. But now that I'm coming to discover the richness of the Hebrew words, it's like I can hear the entire symphony playing its heavenly music in a beautiful harmony. After learning these truths, there is no going back. It has catapulted my understanding of God's word to a whole new level and I will never be the same again."

- Lisa Swensen, MN, promotional manager Voice for Israel Ministries

"I cannot express in words how much I LOVE the Hebrew because it has opened up a whole new world to me. It provides a more complete picture of God's Word and has added a whole new side to the Bible for me. Congratulations Hannah! I speak God's richest blessing over the release of your book. May it touch as MANY others just as it has touched me and even more so."

- Sharon Benade, South Africa

"Thank you, thank you, thank you, Hannah, for these amazing new books! I have been teaching Hebrew for many years and have loved learning about the Hebrew treasures hidden in God's holy language. (Over the years, many of them came from Hannah Nesher's Biblical commentaries.)

I can't tell you my joy at hearing Hannah was publishing two books chock full of these hidden gems! These treasures have drawn me into a deeper relationship with our heavenly Father and have shown me so much more about God's love for me. Hannah's new books will touch your heart in a new and powerful way. Well done, Hannah!"

- Joy Carroll, Hebrew with Joy https://hebrewwithjoy.com/ USA

"I am so excited I just received my Hidden Secrets in the Hebrew Volumes 1 & 2 by Hannah Nesher. Hannah brings you along a journey of opening up the scriptures in the Hebrew Language and I love how Hannah includes her personal life stories through the journey. I personally have been awakened to a greater depth of love and intimacy with Yeshua the Living Word. I highly recommend you add both volumes to your daily bible study. You will be enlightened and excited to go deeper."

- Kathy Church, Canada

Table of Contents

Hidden Secrets in the Hebrew Volume 2 (Book 2 of 2)

1. Patience Through Suffering - Savlanut 12
2. Who is the King of Glory? Melech HaKavod 25
3. Oil of Joy - Shemen Sasson 38
4. The Mighty Men of King David - Giborim 60
5. The Power of Words - D'varim 72
6. Turning Trouble into Hope - The Valley of Achor 90
7. The Maternal Nature of God - El Shaddai 106
8. Trusting in the Lord - B'tach 116
9. Walking in the Wilderness - Midbar 131
10. When Comfort Becomes a Handicap - Necheh 148
11. As Iron Sharpens Iron - Yachad 160
12. What is His Name? Mah Shmo 172
13. Called by a New Name - Hephzibah 184
14. Building with Wisdom & Understanding - Binah 203
15. An invitation to Rest - Shabbat 220
16. Leaving Egypt - Mitzraim 238
17. Watchmen on the Walls - netzer 252
18. A Right Heart - Lev Nachon 262
19. The Almond Tree - Shaked 271
20. Get in the Ark - Tevah 280
21. Preparing for the Bridegroom - Elul 291
22. Blow the Shofar in Zion 298
23. When a Kiss is a Weapon - Neshek 312
24. Going Lower to go Higher - Humility - Anavah 318
25. The Early and Latter Rains - Geshem 332
26. The Lord Our Banner - Yehovah Nissi 346
27. Wells of Satisfaction - Sheva 361
28. I will Arise and Return to the Father - Hozer 380

Introduction

Hebrew - Tongue of the Prophets, Language of Today

Hebrew is no ordinary language! The mere fact that it has, against all odds, defied extinction, and exists today as a modern language in daily use by millions of people in Israel and Jewish communities around the world is an absolute miracle!

By all human reason and logic, Hebrew should have died out two millennia ago when it ceased to be the everyday language spoken by the Jewish people. It is the only language that ever became extinct and was then resurrected to modern day usage.

The prophet Jeremiah foretold the restoration of the Hebrew language: **"Thus says the LORD of hosts, the God of Israel: 'They shall again use this speech in the land of Judah and in its cities, when I bring back their captivity.'"** (Jeremiah 31:23)

After the destruction of the Second Temple and the exile of the Jewish people from the Land of Israel, Hebrew gradually ceased to be a living, spoken language. Two thousand years of wandering throughout Yemen, Morocco, Spain, Germany, Poland, Russia and all the nations to which the Jewish people were scattered, had relegated Hebrew to a written language, used primarily in the synagogues for the sole purpose of prayer.

Before the exile, however, Hebrew was the language spoken by the common people in the Land of Israel. In the fourteenth year of the reign of Hezekiah, King of Judah, Sennacherib, king of Assyria, came up against all the fortified cities of Judah.[1]

The commander of the Assyrian army, Rabshakeh, boasted of their power and might, while attempting to undermine the faith of the people of Judah in the God of Israel.

Eliakim, the son of King Hezekiah, along with other leaders of the Israelites said to Rabshakeh, commander of the Assyrian army, **"Please speak to your servants in Aramaic, for we understand it; and do not speak to us in Hebrew in the hearing of the people who are on the wall."** (Isaiah 36:11)

---

[1] Isaiah 36:1

Ignoring Eliakim's pleas, Rabshakeh called out <u>in a loud voice in Hebrew</u>, saying, ***"Hear the words of the great king, the king of Assyria! Thus says the king: 'Do not let Hezekiah deceive you, for he will not be able to deliver you; nor let Hezekiah make you trust in Yehovah יְהוָה ...'"*** (Isaiah 36:13-15)

What does this show us? It demonstrates that although the higher class people of Judah may have learned Aramaic, the everyday language of the people was Hebrew. The son of King Hezekiah did not want the Hebrew-speaking people of Israel to hear the enemy's foul lies! But the enemy knew that in order to be understood by the people of Judah, he needed to speak to them in their native tongue – which was Hebrew!

Preservation of Jewish Identity

We can see in another Biblical example how important it was to the people of Judah to preserve the Hebrew language – and to teach it to their children. After Nehemiah rebuilt the walls of Jerusalem, he began to institute reforms among the people. It was not only the walls of Jerusalem that had been broken down, but also the faith of the people.

Among other sins, they had profaned the holiness of God by buying and selling their goods on the Sabbath day. Nehemiah also witnessed intermarriages with pagan women, which was strictly forbidden in the Mosaic law. ***"In those days I also saw Jews who had married women of Ashdod, Ammon, and Moab."*** (Nehemiah 13:23)

What disturbed him even more, however, was that half of their children spoke foreign languages and could not even speak Hebrew! ***"And half of their children spoke the language of Ashdod, and could not speak the language of Judah, but spoke according to the language of one or the other people."*** (Nehemiah 13:24)

Nehemiah cursed them, struck them, and even pulled out their hair![2] His reaction admittedly appears extreme, but such was his deep revulsion toward the people of Judah for turning to paganism, even with regards to their language.

Hebrew has been an important part of preserving our Jewish identity. Many Jewish children, even in the diaspora,[3] as well as those in mixed marriages, are still being taught Hebrew. I, myself, was sent to Talmud Torah, a Jewish Hebrew day school in Canada, where I not only learned the customs, history and traditions of our people, but also our language. Little did I know that years later, I would be writing a book about Hebrew!

---

[2] Nehemiah 13:25
[3] The diaspora is a word used to refer to people scattered away from their homeland.

Lashon Hakodesh

Hebrew has been called *'Lashon Ha'kodesh'* (*The Holy Tongue*). It is a language that contains no curse words except for those that are imported from other languages. The only word that even comes close to a curse is the word *'azazel'* which refers to the *scapegoat* of Yom Kippur who took the sins of the people of Israel onto Himself and was then sent into the wilderness. When I watched an English movie with Hebrew subtitles, as the character uttered a curse word, it showed up on the Hebrew subtitle as 'azazel'.[4]

The restoration of this holy language is a fulfillment of biblical prophecy: *"**For then I will restore to the peoples a pure language, that they all may call on the name of Yehovah** יְהוָֹה."* (Zephaniah 3:9)

We are all indebted to the Jewish people who have preserved, virtually intact, the original holy Scriptures in the very language that God used to speak with Abraham, Isaac and Jacob in ancient times.

Hebrew was the language that God used to communicate with Moses and to speak to the children of Israel at Mount Sinai. In fact, it has been said that *if Moses were to return today, he would likely understand the modern Hebrew that is spoken in Israel today!*

The finger of God etched the Ten Commandments onto the tablets of stone in Hebrew.[5] Similarly, Yeshua the Messiah likely etched Hebrew letters in the dirt with his finger when the Pharisees brought to him a woman caught in adultery.[6]

Each letter of the Hebrew aleph bet (alphabet) contains a richness of meaning that nourishes the soul and shines with the light of divine revelation. These very letters were used in combination to speak the entire creation into existence! God spoke and the universe was created.[7] Selah (pause and think about that!).

---

[4] Yeshua, as the 'azazel' became the scapegoat for us all by taking our sins upon himself. As it is written, "Behold the lamb of God who carries away the sins of the world." (John 1:29) He who knew no sin became a curse for us so that we could be called the righteousness of God. (2 Corinthians 5:21)
[5] Exodus 31:18
[6] John 8:6-9
[7] Psalm 33:6-9

Eliezer Ben-Yehudah

It was largely as a result of the fanatical efforts of Eliezer Ben-Yehudah, that Hebrew was revitalized as a spoken language during the late 19th and early 20th centuries.

Born **Eliezer Yitzhak Perlman** (January 7th 1858 – December 16th, 1922), he was a Russian-Jewish linguist, lexicographer, and journalist. Ben-Yehuda was the primary driving force behind the revival of the Hebrew language in the modern state of Israel.

Ben-Yehudah served as the lexicographer of the first Hebrew dictionary and also as the editor of Jerusalem-based *HaZvi*, one of the first Hebrew newspapers published in the Land of Israel.
As a child, he studied Hebrew and the Tanach from the age of three, as was customary among the Jews of Eastern Europe.

Front page of *HaZvi* Hebrew newspaper 1884

In 1881, Ben-Yehudah joined the first aliyah to Israel and settled in Jerusalem. Rejecting the lifestyle of the diaspora exile, he set out to develop a language which would replace Yiddish, as well as uniting the various people groups immigrating to Israel. He realized that, like the Tower of Babel, without a common language we would not be able to build the Land of Israel.

Ben-Yehudah raised his son, Ben-Zion (meaning 'son of Zion') entirely in Hebrew and did not allow anyone to speak any other language around him. Thus Ben-Zion became the first native Hebrew speaker of Israel in modern times. People said he would become a 'dim-witted idiot' but his father persevered even in the face of criticism.

Many opposed Ben-Yehudah, accusing his work of being fanciful or even blasphemous. They considered Hebrew too holy a language to be spoken by common people in a secular context. Even Theodor Herzl declared that the thought of Hebrew becoming the modern language of the Jews was ridiculous. But Ben-Yehudah persevered in his sacred mission, being radically committed to reviving Hebrew as the spoken language of the modern state of Israel, and today we continue to enjoy the fruit of his labors.

Hebrew is the KEY

A question which may arise is this: "*What relevance does Hebrew have for Christians?*" First of all, we need to acknowledge that Hebrew is the language of our Messiah and Saviour. When Yeshua went to the synagogue in Nazareth on the Sabbath day, He read from the scroll of Isaiah in Hebrew.[8]

Although mainstream Christianity seems more focused on the study of Greek, assuming that the original New Testament was written in Greek, there is evidence indicating that at least the Gospel of Matthew was originally composed in Hebrew. After all, the writers of the New Testament (with the exception of Luke) were all Hebrew speaking Jews.

In fact, the entirety of the New Testament is highly Hebraic. Its writers are Hebrews, the culture in which Yeshua and His followers lived was Hebrew, the religion of Judaism is Hebrew, the traditions are Hebrew, and the whole context of the Scriptures is Hebraic.

The Old Testament comprises 78% of Biblical text. Less than 1% of the Old Testament (portions of Ezra and Daniel) is written in Aramaic; the rest is written in Hebrew. The New Testament comprises 22% of the entire Bible; however highly Hebraic portions of the New Testament include the gospels of Matthew, Mark, Luke, the book of Hebrews and Acts (43% of the New Testament).

In addition, 176 quotations in the New Testament are derived from the Old Testament Hebrew, leaving less than 10% of the Bible written in Greek and over 90% written in Hebrew! This alone should be reason enough for students of the Word of God to want to learn the Hebrew language. It is the KEY to our understanding of Scripture!

"If any additional advances are to be made, especially in better understanding the words of Jesus, the concentration must shift to the study of Hebrew history and culture, and above all, the Hebrew language."
- ROY BLIZZARD ('UNDERSTANDING THE DIFFICULT WORDS OF JESUS')

---

[8] Luke 4:16-19

The Treasure Chest is Open

It is my hope and prayer that this book will serve as a catalyst to your desire to learn Hebrew and to discover the vast richness of the treasures that this beautiful, sacred, supernatural language contains. I see a treasure chest full of gold, silver and precious jewels which has been kept locked up for many years, inaccessible and hidden away from the Body of Messiah.

But now, the treasure chest is open and its hidden secrets are being revealed to all who are searching for fresh, new spiritual revelation of truth. I hope that while reading these chapters, you will have many '*aha*' moments and '*wow!*' insights as you delve into these hidden secrets in the Hebrew.

Even more than just acquiring more head knowledge, however (as fun as that may be), my heart's desire in writing this book is that you would come to embrace God's love and compassion for you personally, in the deepest part of your being; that you would find the peace, rest and healing that your soul has been longing for in a dry and thirsty land.

God wants to speak to you through the pages of this book. I've often felt, while writing, like a simple secretary taking dictation, but I hope that I've been able to adequately express God's heart and His thoughts – which are so much higher than our own.

Thank you for the honor and privilege of sharing this book with you. I pray that you will be blessed, encouraged and inspired to continue walking in faith with our good and gracious God. In Yeshua's name. Amen.

To assist you in your journey of discovery, we have **on-line Hebrew courses** with the tools you need to read, write and speak in basic Hebrew. Shalom Morah I includes a study on the names of God, and Shalom Morah II includes a study on wisdom in the Hebrew Aleph-bet.

Register here: https://voiceforisrael.thinkific.com
Each course comes with a downloadable workbook.
Use the code **SHALOM10** to receive a 10% discount on either course – available exclusively with the purchase of this book.

Shalom & Blessings,

Hannah Nesher
www.voiceforisrael.net

Patience Through Suffering - Savlanut סבלנות

"My brethren, count it all joy when you fall into various trials, knowing that the testing of your faith produces patience. But <u>let patience have its perfect work</u>, that you may be perfect and complete, lacking nothing." (James 1:2-4)

One of the first Hebrew words I learned upon making aliyah (immigrating to Israel) was '*savlanut*' סבלנות – which means '<u>patience</u>'. Because everything in Israel requires 'savlanut': the traffic jams, the long line ups in banks, grocery stores, or government offices – but most of all – the people! Oye vey! How we need patience with people! Right? Of course right.

Hidden within the Hebrew word for patience, <u>savlanut</u> סבלנות, is the root word, '<u>sevel</u>', סבל which means '<u>suffering</u>'. Yes, patience and suffering are actually inseparable. The word lisbol לִסְבּוֹל means 'to suffer'. We use this word when we say we can't tolerate, endure, bear with or stand something anymore. In other words, we have no more patience for this situation or person.

Patience is one of the fruits of the Spirit – and oh how we long to walk in the Spirit continually, demonstrating patience; but there are some situations or people who just get on our very last nerve and then we just lose it! Been there, done that and got the T-shirt (quite a few of them in fact).

Marriage and parenting can sometimes seem to bring out the very worst in us. I remember praying my heart out in my morning devotional time to be patient with my husband and kids; and then finding myself screaming like a banshee at them later in the day.

At one point, I think that I even threw a carrot juicer at my (then) husband's head! He got out just in time to escape injury; and I wept bitterly as I watched the carrot slush slither down the closed door. I can laugh at it now; but it was definitely not funny at the time. Being patient under stress, pressure or extreme aggravation can be a tremendous struggle!

Here are some definitions of patience:

"The bearing of provocation, annoyance, misfortune, or pain, without complaint, loss of temper, or irritation."

"The ability to remain calm when dealing with a difficult or annoying situation, task, or person."

"The capacity to accept or tolerate delay, trouble, or suffering without getting angry or upset."

Patience When Delayed

Tolerating delay patiently (with savlanut) is never easy. It almost always involves some degree of suffering (sevel). I vividly remember driving to my son's swearing in ceremony for the IDF (Israeli Defense Forces). He had qualified for an elite combat unit and this was a VERY important ceremony!! To see your beloved son vowing on the Bible, to devote himself to defending the people of Israel, even with his life if called to do so, is not something that I would have missed for the world!

And there we were – stuck in traffic – for hours!! We gave ourselves lots of time to get there according to Waze, but the longer we drove, the more time kept being added to our drive due to the notorious Israeli traffic jams; and so there we sat in the car, fuming, as the minutes and hours ticked by….

IDF Nahal Brigade special forces unit swearing in ceremony (photo taken by someone else :(

When the realization hit me that we would completely miss the entire ceremony and there was absolutely nothing we could do about it, I broke down and sobbed. I knew my son would understand; but my heart was breaking with the realization that I would not be there to see this historic event in person. He is the only one in our family who has ever served in the IDF and to miss it seemed so unfair. We finally arrived just after the ceremony ended; but all the while stuck in the car I seriously suffered – I ranted and raved about the traffic; and at the time it sure didn't seem like I was learning patience at all.

With my 2 daughters, Courtney & Liat, & my son, Avi-ad in IDF

Another situation with the Israeli army that required great patience was with my daughter's application for an exemption from military service. Due to severe back pain, she was not physically able to serve in the IDF. Not only could she not do any strenuous exercise, she could barely stand or even sit for any period of time. When she was called in for her initial interview, she actually had to lay down on the sofa in their coffee room to ease the pain while waiting.

Even though she had a stack of letters, documents, and test results testifying to her disabling condition, the army kept sending her to more doctors and more tests. At one point we had to drive down to Eilat and stay in a hostel overnight in order to get an MRI done (which was set up in a bus – only in Israel!).

Liat could not leave the country until receiving this official letter of exemption; and she was anxious to go visit Canada to meet with a certain young man she was quite fond of. They had been facetiming on their phones daily; and were ready to spend time 'in person' to see if the relationship could lead to something more serious (it did!). But being involved in a long distance relationship definitely tested their patience.

As the weeks and months dragged on and on, schlepping from one appointment and doctor to another, my daughter's patience was wearing thin (as was mine). She would go for an x-ray and they would x-ray the wrong body part; or the hours posted were incorrect and the clinic was closed when we arrived – and on and on it went… Did I mention that one needs mega-patience to live in Israel??

After over a year, she finally got the green light; and only three months after flying to Canada (I think they were done with patience by this time), they were married under the chuppah[1] in a beautiful wedding ceremony. And this one I made sure I didn't miss!!

When Moses was Delayed on the Mountain[2]

The opposite of patience is impatience – and being impatient can drag us deep into dangerous territory. We read in the Book of Exodus that when Moses was delayed in returning from the mountain, the people of Israel grew impatient and turned from God to an idol – a golden calf.

"Now when the people saw that Moses delayed coming down from the mountain, the people gathered together to Aaron, and said to him, 'Come, make us gods that shall go before us; for as for this Moses, the man who brought us up out of the land of Egypt, we do not know what has become of him.'" (Exodus 32:1)

When God is delayed in fulfilling His promises to us; when we don't see our dreams coming to pass or when our lives seem to be on hold – do we wait in faith and patience? Or do we turn to an idol – putting our trust in something we can see, feel, or touch?

Like the Israelites said of Moses, we may say during times of delay, "*As for this God… the one who brought us up out of the Kingdom of Darkness, we don't know what has become of Him.* Perhaps I need to look elsewhere for my salvation."

---

[2] See Blog Post https://www.voiceforisrael.net/post/when-moses-is-delayed-on-the-mountain

Praying to gods Who Cannot Save

If we are not looking to God to save and heal and deliver; then we are looking in the wrong direction. *"**Woe to those who carry their carved images and pray to a god who cannot save.**"* (Isaiah 45:20).

Money cannot save us; no amount of gold or silver can save us from the wrath of God. Relationships cannot save us; no matter how hard we seek that special someone who will swoop down and rescue us from the pain and trials of this life.

But God always hears us when we cry out to Him. He sees trouble and grief. He is a God who cares for His children. We can trust in His goodness.

We must not think, "*Well, I prayed yesterday and still don't see the answer, so maybe God doesn't love me; or maybe He doesn't answer prayer.*" No, God is faithful; but at times it seems like He is delayed. To live a life of faith we need patience. It is by faith and patience that we inherit the promises.

"Do not become sluggish (lazy), but imitate those who through faith and patience inherit the promises." (Hebrews 6:12)

Instead of turning to idols – the work of our own hands – we need to stay in faith, reminding ourselves that God has a right and perfect timing for everything; and it is not always 'our time'. The word of God tells us to write the vision and make it plain; to wait for it – even if it tarries (even if it is delayed).

"Write the vision and make it plain on tablets, that he may run who reads it. For the vision is yet for an appointed time; but at the end it will speak, and it will not lie. Though it tarries (is delayed), wait for it (patiently); because it will surely come." (Habakkuk 2:2-3)

Even if the manifestation of our vision is delayed – when all we see is sand dunes in the wilderness instead of the milk and honey of the Promised Land – we need to stay in faith and trust that it will surely come to pass. But it will happen in God's timing and not necessarily on our time table.

Becoming Discouraged (short) Along the Way[3]

The Israelites were headed to the Promised Land; they had a vision of a land flowing with milk and honey – but they became discouraged along the way….

"Then they journeyed from Mount Hor by the Way of the Red Sea, to go around the land of Edom; <u>and the soul of the people became very discouraged along the way</u>.

וַתִּקְצַר נֶפֶשׁ-הָעָם, בַּדָּרֶךְ.

And the people spoke against God and against Moses: 'Why have you brought us up out of Egypt to die in the wilderness? For there is no food and no water, and our soul loathes this worthless (in Hebrew it reads kulkal – rotten) bread.'

בַּלֶּחֶם הַקְּלֹקֵל.

So the Lord sent fiery serpents among the people, and they bit the people; and many of the people of Israel died." (Numbers 21:4-6)

In Hebrew, it uses an interesting word to describe their discouragement: **T'katzer** תקצר. This comes from the root word: **Katzar** קצר which means '**short**'. In other words, their patience ran short – they became <u>impatient</u> which caused them to start

---

[3] Co-written with Liat Nesher

complaining – a sin which led many to their deaths. If we are not careful, our soul (nefesh) can become discouraged to the point where we experience spiritual death.

- This word also means '**_short circuit_**' as in to cause electrical power outage. Becoming impatient 'short circuits' our connection with the power of God.

- Another word for patience is long-suffering – which basically means to suffer for a long time without becoming impatient, angry, discouraged or upset.

What ultimately led to the Israelites' destruction was impatience. God was taking them somewhere good, and faithfully providing for them in the wilderness but the Israelites grew impatient and couldn't wait for God's promises to come to pass, so they never saw the good that God had for them. WOW!

Hoping for something to happen and having our hope delayed indefinitely can actually cause us to become heartsick.

"Hope deferred (delayed) makes the heart sick, but a longing fulfilled is a tree of life." (Proverbs 13:12)

How Long, O Lord?

Like the Psalmist, we may cry out, "**How long O Lord?** *How long, O Lord? Will You forget me forever? How long will You hide Your face from me? How long shall I take counsel in my soul, having sorrow in my heart daily?*" (Psalm 13:1-2)

We may ask God, "*How long will I be single and lonely? When will I ever meet that special someone? How long do I have to stay stuck in this job I hate? How long until my financial breakthrough comes? How long until my child turns around? How long until my health improves? How long, O Lord?...*"

Rejoicing in Suffering

Waiting for something we really want, or being stuck in a place where we really don't want to be, can feel like our souls are in agony. The Word of God, however, actually tells us to 'rejoice' when we suffer because it is training us to be patient.

"And not only this, but [with joy] let us exult in our sufferings and rejoice in our hardships, knowing that hardship (distress, pressure, trouble) produces patient endurance; and endurance, proven character (spiritual maturity); and proven character, hope and confident assurance [of eternal salvation]." (Romans 5:3-4)

Patience is working on our character – causing us to grow up spiritually – but there have been plenty of times I cried out to God, *"I don't care about my character, Lord, I just don't want to suffer anymore!"* But, as has often been said, *"God is more interested in our character than our comfort."* Ouch!

Rest in the Lord

Waiting can cause us to be anxious as we worry about our future but it doesn't have to be that way. God extends an invitation for us to rest in Him as we simultaneously wait on Him.

"Rest in the Lord, and wait patiently for Him, cease from anger and forsake wrath, do not fret, it only causes harm." (Psalms 37:7-8)

Anger, fretting and hastiness are other negative side effects of impatience. When my daughter, Liat, moved out to her own apartment, we gleefully embarked on a wonderful shopping spree to IKEA (practically the only place to get furniture at a decent price in Israel).

The thing which we all know about IKEA, however, is that you take the furniture home in these neat, compact boxes but then have to assemble them with the aid of some rather sketchy instructions. Not having the patience to wait for her brother to help with this daunting task, Liat took it upon herself to assemble her furniture. Let's just say this did not end well… furniture assembly not being her strength. All she had to show for her impatience was extreme frustration and a broken vase.

Hannah & her daughter, Liat, shopping at IKEA

Having learned her lesson the hard way, Liat called upon her brother, Avi, to help assemble the furniture. But he also, for some reason, did not have that particular fruit of the spirit flowing that day and simply did not have the patience to complete the task. Not only did he screw the drawer in backwards and upside down; but the fruit of his impatience was a huge argument ending with a broken pot – given to her by her beloved. It was a cute little pot for an aloe plant that said, "*Aloe you very much!*" (Get it?)

Yes, impatience leads to hastiness which leads to anger which can lead to broken things – even broken relationships.

"The patient in spirit is better than the proud in spirit. Do not hasten in your spirit to become angry, for anger rests with fools." (Ecclesiastes 7:8-9)

What kind of spirit are we carrying around? Are we patient in spirit? Gentle, kind, and loving? Or are we irritated? Hasty? Stressed? Rushed? Angry? Annoyed? This is the contrast between our flesh and God's Spirit as we wait upon Him and rest in Him.

Our flesh wants to doubt God when He seems to be taking too long, feel sorry for ourselves, complain, get upset, be annoyed and angry with everyone, taking our frustration out on them.

But the fruit of the Holy Spirit is love, joy, peace, **patience…**

If God is love (1 John 4:7) and love is patient (1 Corinthians 13:4) then we cannot fulfill the greatest commandment in the entire bible, which is to love, if we do not learn to have patience. This is how important the lesson of patience is – and why it's worth it to endure the suffering we go through to learn patience.

Pride says, "*I'm not going to wait on God, He's taking too long, I can do this myself.*" Humility says, "*I will wait on God because I trust He has a good plan for my life and He is going to come through for me whatever this season looks like right now.*"

When we try to take things into our own hands and do things in our own strength, we carry a weight we were never meant to bear. Just like elevators have a weight limit, we also have a weight limit given to us by our manufacturer (God).

When we put that kind of pressure on ourselves that we were never meant to carry, at some point we will break. We need to rely on God's grace, and rest in Him as we do our best, and then trust Him with the rest of the things we're waiting for.

"He has made everything beautiful <u>in His time</u>." (Ecclesiastes 3:11)

A good 'bad example' of impatience is Sarah, who grew impatient, waiting for God's promise of a son to come to pass and took matters into her own hands. She suggested that her husband sleep with Hagar, her maidservant (it must have seemed a good idea at the time).[4]

Soon, Hagar became pregnant and did indeed give birth to a son but it was out of God's will and out of God's timing and it resulted in 'Ishma'el' who was a 'wild donkey of a man – always in strife with his brothers.[5]

If we don't want to live with constant strife and frustration, then we need to learn the art of patience and wait on God for His timing. Peace and patience dwell side by side.

As we become more and more patient (long-suffering), we will also enjoy more and more peace (shalom) in our lives. And even this alone would make all the suffering we go through so worth it!

"Therefore as God's chosen people, holy and dearly loved, clothe yourself with compassion, kindness, humility, gentleness and patience. And over all these virtues put on love, which binds them all together in perfect unity. Let the peace of Yeshua rule in your hearts." (Colossians 3:12-15)

No one likes suffering; but it is a part of life here on earth. God may allow suffering in our lives for many reasons: to prepare us, teach us, test us, humble us, draw us close to Him, and discipline or correct us when we get off course.

But of this we can be assured – God can bring good out of any suffering (sevel) we are going through if we will just keep a right attitude, stay in faith and be patient (have savlanut). In the meantimes, James tells us what to do while we are waiting and suffering – PRAY!

"Is anyone among you suffering? Let him pray." (James 5:13)

---

[4] Gen. 16:1–16; 21:8–21
[5] Genesis 16:12

When too much patience is just too much

Of course, like in most things, there is a balance to this issue of patience as well. Sometimes we think we are being long-suffering when in fact, we are just being long-silly; as it has been said, *"If the horse has been dead for years, perhaps it's time to dismount"*.

Can there ever be a time when patience becomes less of a virtue and more of a hindrance? Yes, we may sometimes use 'patience' as an excuse for passivity, laziness or fear. Instead of taking action to deal with an intolerable situation, we say we are patiently 'waiting upon the Lord'.

I have a family member who is extremely talented and gifted; but he has been working on a drama film series for possibly two decades! They keep hoping and praying to sell it to Netflix or the equivalent. Every week, month, and year, the situation seems just on the verge of a breakthrough – but the problem is that it just never materializes…

Meanwhile, his family sinks deeper and deeper into debt and despair. It feels like someone is holding the carrot in front of the donkey – close enough to keep going but always far enough away to never reap the reward. When does patience and faith morph into passivity and foolishness? How long is long enough??

It causes me to wonder if there are times or situations where we can be simply too patient – times when we should say enough is enough… change needs to happen now! This is not giving up; it is having the courage to confront.

I know of parents who are way too patient with their offspring. They tolerate all kinds of sass and disobedience in the name of 'patience'. They get off looking like they have the patience of Job; but meanwhile their kids are totally out of control. I don't know about you, but when I see this I feel like saying, *"Stop being so patient and give that kid a good patchkie!"* [6]

---
[6] A patchkie is a little smack with a flexible rubber stick that is used for disciplining children

Just as is written: For everything there is a time and a season; there is a time for patience; and a time to set good, healthy boundaries with situations or people. For this we need wisdom from above. The good news is that God promises to give wisdom to those who ask and seek for wisdom.

"Now if any of you lacks wisdom, he should ask God, who gives generously to all without finding fault, and it will be given to him." (James 1:5)

What Promises are you still waiting on God for? Are you becoming impatient? Angry? Discouraged?

Or are you resting in Him and patiently waiting for Him to bring it to pass?

"Therefore do not cast away your confidence, which has great reward. For you have need of endurance (patience), so that after you have done the will of God, you may receive the promise." (Hebrews 10:35-37)

Prayer: *Dear God, so much of life seems to be a waiting game – waiting to hear Your voice, to receive Your direction or to know Your timing. We are waiting upon You to see the changes that so desperately need to happen in our lives, our families, and our nations. Help us to have the patience we need, even when it involves suffering. Just as You are long-suffering with us, Lord, help us to have this kind of long-suffering patience with the people and the situations in our lives – and even with ourselves.*

Thank You that patience is doing a good work in us. We trust that You are at work in our lives, and we trust in Your timing, even if it seems to be taking forever, because Your ways are not our ways and Your thoughts are so much higher than our own. Help us not to become discouraged or impatient along the way to our Promised Land. In Yeshua's name. Amen v'Amen!

Who is the King of Glory? Melech HaKavod
מֶלֶךְ הַכָּבוֹד

"Lift up your heads, O ye gates, and be lifted up, you everlasting doors;
that the King of glory (Melech Hakavod) may come in. Who is this King of glory?
Yehovah יְהוָה strong and mighty, Yehovah יְהוָה mighty in battle.
Lift up your heads, O you gates! Lift up, you everlasting doors (pitchei olam –
eternal openings פִּתְחֵי עוֹלָם) and the King of glory shall come in.
Who is this King of glory? The Lord of hosts (Yehovah Tzeva'ot), He is the King
of glory. Selah" (Psalm 24:7-10)

When we are facing any kind of battle, we want to know that we have someone powerful on our side – we need the help of a strong and mighty ally in order to emerge victorious. This Scripture uses two of the most powerful Hebrew names of God: Melech Hakavod מֶלֶךְ הַכָּבוֹד (King of Glory) and Yehovah Tzeva'ot יְהוָה צְבָאוֹת (Lord of Hosts).

In Hebrew, the Lord of Hosts (Yehovah Tzeva'ot) יְהוָה צְבָאוֹת comes from the word 'tzavah' צָבָא, which means '<u>army</u>'. My youngest son, Avi, served in the 'tzavah' of the IDF (Israeli Defense Forces) as a combat medic. Being a soldier in the 'tzavah', he operated under the orders of his commander; and his commander is under his commander; and so on… all the way up the line of authority to the highest commander of all – the **<u>Commander-in-Chief</u>** (Lieutenant General) **<u>Rav Aluf</u>** .

Called the 'rosh hamateh haklali', Hebrew: רֹאשׁ הַמַּטֶּה הַכְּלָלִי (abbreviated Ramatkal –רמטכ"ל), he is the **supreme commander and head** of the Israel Defense Forces. Aviv Kochavi was serving as the Commander in Chief of the IDF at the time of this writing.[1]

Rav Aluf Aviv Kochavi

We are all serving in the 'army of the Lord' and are exhorted to **'endure hardship as a good soldier'**.[2] God is the highest, most supreme Commander in Chief of an entire army (tzavah) of ministering angels who seek to do His will. **"Are they not all ministering spirits sent forth to minister for those who will inherit salvation?"** (Hebrews 1:14)

When my daughter, Liat, and her husband, Yanai, found themselves stranded for three days in the Istanbul airport en route to Israel due to a severe blizzard, the situation became so tense in this Muslim country that the passengers began to riot!

---

[1] January 2019 - January 2023
[2] 2 Timothy 2:3

Conditions were terrible – people were sleeping on the freezing concrete floor with no blankets; and hotel rooms were not available. Food was scarce, all flights had been canceled, and everyone just wanted to go home!

To restore peace and order, the airport authorities called in the Turkish police. Liat and Yanai watched from above as the forces stood at attention, completely focused on their commander in chief, awaiting his orders.

As they watched this volatile scene, they could envision Yehovah Tzeva'ot, the Lord of Hosts, dispatching a whole host of angels who stood at attention, totally focused on their Commander in Chief. These angels stood by to guard and protect them. Even throughout this storm, they had perfect peace (shalom) knowing that Yehovah Tzeva'ot was with them.

Turkish police stand guard at Istanbul airport

"The Lord of hosts (Yehovah Tzeva'ot) יְהוָה צְבָאוֹת *is with us;*
The God of Jacob is our refuge. Selah" (Psalm 46:7)

We can call upon the name of Yehovah Tzeva'ot at any time – 24/7 – to come to our aid and command His troops on our behalf in every battle. Who can stop the Lord Almighty? No one!

"The LORD of Heaven's Armies (Yehovah tzeva'ot) יְהוָה צְבָאוֹת *has spoken –*
who can change His plans? When His hand is raised, who can stop Him?"
(Isaiah 14:27)

Open the Gates

The other name used in this Scripture from Psalm 24 is **'Melech Hakavod'** (King of Glory). The Psalmist is asking, who is this coming through the <u>gates (she'arim)</u>, the everlasting doors? In Hebrew, the words used for 'everlasting doors' are **'pitchei olam'**, which means an **opening into eternity.**

Psalm 118 uses this same terminology: *"Open to me the <u>gates of righteousness</u>; I will go through them, And I will praise the Lord. <u>This is the gate of the Lord</u>, through which the righteous shall enter."* (Psalm 118:19-20)

Incredibly, Yeshua proclaimed Himself to be **the gate (sha'ar)** through which His sheep <u>enter into eternal salvation</u>!

"<u>I am the gate</u>. If anyone enters by Me, he will be saved, and will go in and out and find pasture." (John 10:9)

Yeshua is not only the King of Glory coming through the gate – He *is* the gate – the opening into eternal life!

Honor and Glory - Kavod כָּבוֹד

The Hebrew word, **Kavod**, כָּבוֹד means both '<u>glory' and 'honor</u>'. The Hebrew root word is '**kaved**' כָּבֵד which can also mean '<u>heavy' or 'weighty</u>'. It is this word which is used in the Commandment to *"<u>honor (kabed) your father and your mother</u>."* (Exodus 20:12)

כַּבֵּד אֶת-אָבִיךָ, וְאֶת-אִמֶּךָ

The same word (kaved) is used in the Scripture to *"Honor God (kabed et Yehovah)* כַּבֵּד אֶת-יְהוָה *with your wealth."* (Proverbs 3:9)

By using the same word, kabed, the Torah compares the honor you are to give your father and mother to the honor you give to the Almighty. The corresponding New Testament verse attaches a promise to honoring one's mother and father – that it will go well with you….

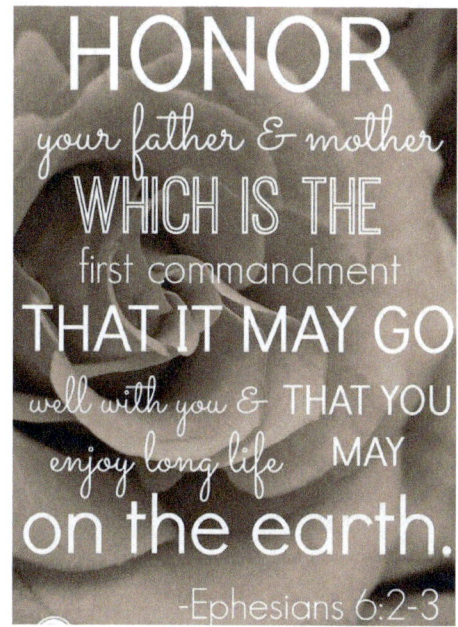

Could it be that it is just never going well for some people who don't realize the root cause being their disrespect for their parents?

We have an example of this in Noah's sons: Shem, Ham and Yafet. After the flood, Noah planted a vineyard and apparently drank a little too much of the fruit of the vine because he became drunk – so much so that he passed out buck naked in his tent.[3]

One son, Ham, saw his father's state and ran out to tell his two brothers; but Shem and Yafet took a garment, laid it on both their shoulders, and went backward and covered their father. They turned their faces away, so that they did not see their father's nakedness.

Love covers a multitude of sins.[4]

Love is a beautiful expression of honor. We don't honor our mother and father because they are perfect; but because God commands us to do so and promises it will go well with us if we do. The opposite is also true. If we dishonor our mother or father there can be dire consequences:

"Whoever curses his father or his mother, his lamp will be put out in deep darkness." (Proverbs 20:20)

"The eye that mocks his father, and scorns obedience to his mother, the ravens of the valley will pick it out, and the young eagles will eat it." (Proverbs 20:17)

When Noah awoke and found out what had happened, he cursed the lineage of Ham, father of the Canaanites, who eventually became enemies of Israel. A grandson of

---

[3] Genesis 9:18-21
[4] 1 Peter 4:8

Ham, Nimrod, built the Tower of Babel as well as Nineveh – both were established as centers of rebellion against God.

While Noah cursed the lineage of Ham, he blessed his sons, Shem and Yafet, who showed such honor (kavod) to their father.[5] When we show honor כָּבֵד to someone, we treat them like they have value – as if they are of a weighty substance (kaved) כָּבֵד – they matter, and are not to be treated lightly or frivolously.

The Weighty Glory of God

The glory (kavod) of God is also a weighty presence; so much so that those ministering in the Temple could not even stand under the weight of His glory, which often appears as a cloud.

> **"And the temple, the house of the LORD, was filled with a cloud <u>so that the priests could not stand there to minister because of the cloud; for the glory of the LORD (kvod Yehovah)</u>** כְּבוֹד־יְהוָה **<u>filled the house of God. (Beit Elohim)</u>"** (2 Chronicles 5:14)

Moses also could not enter the Tent of Meeting (Tabernacle) once it was completed because the glory of the Lord filled the tabernacle.

> **"Moses was unable to enter the Tent of Meeting because the cloud had settled on it, and the <u>glory of the LORD</u> filled the tabernacle."** (Exodus 40:35)

---

[5] Genesis 9:26-27

Show me Your Glory (Kavod)

What really is the glory of God? And how is it related to being 'weighty'? Glory is feeling the whole weight (the splendor, riches, dignity, reputation) of who God really is.

Glory (K'vod Adonai) is the physical manifestation of the presence of God. It may be easier to 'see' God's glory than to explain it. We can see the glory of God in the beauty and wonder of nature, a glorious sunset, an exquisite musical performance or even an act of kindness, love or heroism. I clearly remember being in a tent meeting and asking God to show me His glory. As I walked outside, I saw children playing and laughing together in the sunshine and I heard God say, *"There is My glory."*

When Moses went up to Mount Sinai to meet with God and receive the Ten Commandments, He experienced the glory of God; not only as a cloud but as FIRE!

"Then Moses went up into the mountain, and a cloud covered the mountain. Now the glory of the Lord (k'vod Yehovah) כְּבוֹד־יְהוָה *rested on Mount Sinai, and the cloud covered it for six days. And on the seventh day He called to Moses out of the midst of the cloud. The sight of the glory of the Lord (k'vod Yehovah)* כְּבוֹד־יְהוָה *was like a <u>consuming fire</u> on the top of the mountain in the eyes of the children of Israel."* (Exodus 24:15-17)

A Consuming Fire!

The glory of God often appears as a consuming fire! When Aaron and his sons sacrificed the sin offering and burnt offering as God had commanded: ***"Then <u>the glory of the Lord appeared to all the people</u>, and fire came out from before the Lord and consumed the burnt offering and the fat on the altar. When all the people saw it, they shouted and fell on their faces."*** (Leviticus 9:23-24)

Experiencing the glory of the Lord must, therefore, be something awesome and spectacular that would cause us to literally fall on our faces. That same fire that demonstrated the glory of God to the people, however, later consumed the sons of Aaron for offering up 'strange fire' that God had not commanded them, ***"and they died before the Lord."*** (Leviticus 10:2)

The fire that keeps us warm and cooks our food can also burn down our house and kill its inhabitants. We must be careful with the glory of God; and not treat it lightly. It is a weighty presence of the Almighty God.

As a result of being in contact with the glory of God for forty days and forty nights, Moses' face shone so intensely that he was required to cover his face with a veil when he spoke with the people of Israel. ***"So when Aaron and all the children of Israel saw Moses, behold, the skin of his face shone, and they were afraid to come near him."*** (Exodus 34:30)

In the Hebrew, it says that Moses' face <u>sent forth rays or beams of light</u>! Wow! What a powerful light must the glory of God be if Moses face absorbed all that radiance just from being close to it. The mere AFTERGLOW OF GOD'S GLORY was so intense that the people could not tolerate it.

A Greater Glory

The apostle Paul spoke of the greater glory of the New Covenant: ***"But if the ministry of death, written and engraved on stones, was glorious, so that the children of Israel could not look steadily at the face of Moses because of the glory of his countenance, which glory was passing away, how will the ministry of the Spirit not be more glorious?"*** (2 Corinthians 3:7-8)

Although God placed a veil over the eyes of His people in order that salvation could come to the Gentiles,[6] that veil is removed in the Messiah, and we are being transformed – from glory to glory.

---

[6] Romans 11:11

"But we all, <u>with unveiled faces</u>, beholding as in a mirror <u>the glory of the Lord</u>, are being transformed into the same image <u>from glory to glory</u>, just as by the Spirit of the Lord." (2 Corinthians 3:18)

God spoke to Moses face to face – like talking to a friend;[7] and yet even though Moses had experienced a measure of the glory of God on Mt. Sinai, he still asked to see God's glory (Exodus 33:18). Is the glory of God something that, once we have experienced it, we can't get enough of it?? What was Moses asking for more of? He was asking to see God for who He really is… and isn't this something that our hearts long for as well?

We long to see His greatness, splendor, majesty, holiness, mercy and goodness… and this is not a light thing! How did God reply to Moses' request? He proclaimed His name and His attributes of goodness, favor and mercy.

The Lord replied, *"I will make all My goodness pass before you, and I will proclaim My name Yehovah יְהוָה. I will show favor to those I show favor and mercy to those I show mercy. But you may not see My face, for man may not see Me and live. However, stand here on this rock beside me. <u>And when my glory passes by</u>, I will put you in the cleft of the rock and cover you with my hand until I have passed. Then I will remove my hand, and you shall see my back but not my face."* (Exodus 33:19-23)

If we cannot directly see God's glory, then how may we perceive it? We see it in the face of His son, the Messiah Yeshua:

"For it is the God who commanded light to shine out of darkness, who has shone in our hearts to give the light of the <u>knowledge of the glory of God in the face of Yeshua Hamashiach (the Messiah)</u>." (2 Corinthians 4:6)

---

[7] Exodus 33:11

Glorifying God on Earth - Finish the Work!

God is jealous of His glory and will not give it to another.[8] And yet He has given all power, honor (glory) and dominion to His son.[9] Yeshua glorified God on this earth. He said, *"**I have glorified You on the earth. I have finished the work which You have given Me to do.** And now, O Father, glorify Me together with Yourself, with the glory which I had with You before the world was."* (John 17:4-5)

And this same glory that He received from God, He has now given to all those who believe in Him: *"And the glory which You gave Me I have given them, that they may be one just as We are one (echad)."* (John 17:22)

How can we also glorify God on the earth? It is by finishing the work which God has given us to do! The glory did not manifest at the beginning of Yeshua's ministry; but once He had finished the work! The glory of God did not manifest in the wilderness tabernacle when they began its construction, but when they had completed the work – as the Lord commanded.

*"**So Moses finished the work.** Then the cloud covered the meeting and the glory of God filled the tabernacle."* (Exodus 40:33-34)

We each have a God-given purpose, a work to finish, a race to run – and we are called to press on with endurance… to fight the good fight of faith;[10] and to finish our course with joy![11]

Israel was created to glorify God; *"And He said to me, 'You are My servant, O Israel, in whom I will be glorified.'"* (Isaiah 49:3,7) In this mission, she has fallen short of the glory of God – as have each and every one of us. And yet God still loves us and showed us mercy in sending His Son, Yeshua – **a light to the Gentiles and the glory of His people Israel**.[12]

---

[8] Isaiah 42:8
[9] Daniel 7:14
[10] 1 Timothy 6:12
[11] Acts 20:24
[12] Luke 2:32

Ichabod - The Glory has Departed

It is a terrible thing when the glory of God departs from the Land. Israel had suffered a devastating defeat at the hands of the Philistines – they slaughtered 30,000 Israeli foot soldiers including Eli the priest's two sons. Worst of all was that the Philistines had captured the ark of the covenant, which represented the glory of God.

"And the ark of God was taken; and the two sons of Eli, Hophni and Phinehas, were slain." (1 Samuel 4:11)

When Eli heard the tragic news, he fell over, broke his neck and died. Eli's daughter-in-law, Phinehas' wife, was pregnant; and when she heard that her father in law as well as her husband had died, she went into labor.

Just before she died in childbirth, she named her son Ichabod אִי-כָבוֹד, which means <u>without glory</u>: ***"And she named the child Ichabod אִי-כָבוֹד, saying: 'The glory (kavod כָבוֹד) has departed from Israel'."*** (1 Samuel 4:21)

When the glory of God departs from our land, we suffer death, defeat and destruction; but it is time for the glory of God to be restored on this earth.

Restoring the Glory (Kavod)

Through repentance and returning to God in holiness, we can hasten the restoration of the glory of God upon this earth – and the glory of the latter house shall be even greater than the former:

"'The glory of this latter house shall be greater than the former', says the LORD of hosts: 'and in this place will I give peace', says the LORD of hosts." (Haggai 2:9)

God is shaking everything that can be shaken; He is purifying His Bride and faithfully completing the good work He has started in us.

May we be strong and of good courage; for the Lord our God is with us. Let us arise and shine – for the glory of the Lord has risen upon us! Halleluyah!

As the darkness upon the earth grows darker, we can be encouraged to know that one day, perhaps sooner than we think, the whole earth will be filled with His glory!

"For the earth will be filled with the knowledge of the glory of the Lord (k'vod Yehovah) כְּבוֹד יְהוָה*, as the waters cover the sea."* (Habakkuk 2:14)

Prayer: *Dear God, we praise You, Melech Hakavod, King of Glory. You deserve all the honor and glory and praise for all You have done, are doing, and will do in our lives. Show us Your glory, Adonai. Reveal to us how to honor and glorify You on this earth. Help us to show honor to the people in our lives, especially our parents, the elderly, and those to whom honor is due.*

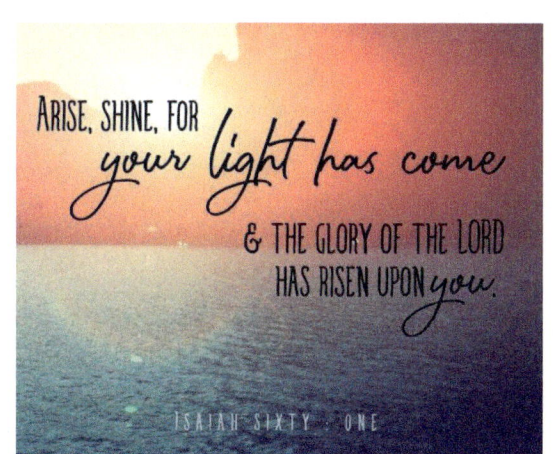

Let Your glory arise upon us, O God, that we may shine as lights in the darkness of this world. In Yeshua's name. Amen v'Amen.

Oil of Joy - Shemen Sasson שֶׁמֶן שָׂשׂוֹן

God has set you above your companions by anointing you with the oil of joy.
Hebrews 1:9

"Therefore God, Your God, has anointed You with the oil of joy (shemen sasson) more than Your companions." (Psalm 45:7)

The Joy of Special Celebrations

The Hebrew Scriptures use several different words to express the emotion of 'joy'. One of them is 'simcha' שִׂמְחָה which means *'happiness, gladness, gaiety, or exhilaration'*. A joyous or festive occasion such as a wedding or Bar Mitzvah may be called a 'simcha'. We may feel joy at a special celebration; and at festivals such as Purim or Sukkot, when we are commanded to 'feast and rejoice'.

To be 'happy' is the Hebrew word 'sameach' שָׂמֵחַ; so when wishing someone a happy festival, we say, "Chag Sameach" חג שמח. But our joy need not be confined to only special times – we can experience joy in our ordinary, everyday life as well.

The Joy of New Discoveries and Revelation

Another Hebrew word for joy is 'gilah' גילה which is the word used in the popular Jewish folk song, "*Hava Nagila*",[1] הבה נגילה "Let us rejoice". This word, gilah, may also mean 'revelation' or 'discovery'. When God reveals to us a new and wonderful discovery about His character, or a fresh insight from His Word, we can feel joyful – or even exhilarated! We want to share with someone the new and wonderful things we have learned!

The root word, גל is related to the word 'gol' גל or גוֹל which means 'roll', as in:

"Roll (gol) גוֹל your works upon the Lord, trust also in Him and He will bring it to pass." (Psalm 37:5)

"Roll (gol) גל your works upon the Lord, and your thoughts will be established." (Psalm 16:3)

It is by 'rolling' the whole burden of our cares and concerns upon the Lord, trusting also in Him, that we can find the grace to be joyful, even in the midst of trouble.

These two words, simcha and gilah, are closely related and are often written side by side in Scripture, for example:

"When God turned the captivity of His people, let Jacob rejoice (yagel) יָגֵל, and let Israel be glad (yismach) יִשְׂמַח." (Psalm 53:7)

The Joy of Salvation

There is another Hebrew word for joy and that is 'sasson' שָׂשׂוֹן which means 'joy, delight, or merriment'. King David used this word, sasson, when asking God to restore to him the 'joy (sasson) of His salvation' שְׂשׂוֹן יִשְׁעֶךָ.[2]
"Restore unto me the joy of Thy salvation." (Psalm 51:12)

---

[1] Hava Nagila is a popular Jewish folk song traditionally sung and danced in a circle at Jewish celebrations. It means, "come and let us rejoice".
[2] Psalm 51:12

David had lost his joy because of his unconfessed sin with Batsheba. The quickest way to lose our joy is to try and cover up or hide our sin.

"He who covers his sins will not prosper, but whoever confesses and forsakes them will have mercy." (Proverb 28:13)

If we sincerely desire for God to restore to us the joy of our salvation, then we must be willing to 'come clean' and 'fess up'. If we will repent and turn away from our sins, then we will find mercy – and a restoration of our joy!

The Joy of Discipline

These three words for joy, 'simcha', 'gilah' and 'sasson', are sometimes combined all together in Scripture. King David also prayed to God, ***"Make me to hear joy and gladness (sasson and simcha)*** שָׂשׂוֹן וְשִׂמְחָה***; that the bones which You have broken may rejoice (tagelna)*** תָּגֵלְנָה***."*** (Psalm 51:8)

The Hebrew uses an interesting word, (dakitah) דִּכִּיתָ to describe the breaking of King David's bones. It can mean broken; but this word may also mean 'crushed' or 'oppressed'; and is the root word of 'depression' (dika'on) דִּכָּאוֹן.

What do we do when life leaves us feeling 'crushed', oppressed and depressed? When joy seems nowhere to be found? It could be a result of our sin, like King David's trespass in the matter of Batsheba – or it could just be a result of living in this fallen world outside of the Garden of Eden.

CRUSHED

M'doo-khah

But He was pierced for our transgressions,

He was crushed for our iniquities.

Isaiah 53:5a

In recent years, I went through a period of time which I now call my '*season of broken bones*.' First, my left hip bone was broken off in order to insert a new man-made hip joint; and then the right hip bone was broken off and replaced the following year.

For twenty years prior, I had been limping around in pain, with limited mobility from severe osteoarthritis; and although I was looking forward to walking freely and pain free again, I had to first endure the suffering of the surgeries.

Even Yeshua had to endure the cross; but it was <u>for the joy that was set before Him</u> that He had the grace and strength to go through the suffering the cross required.

"Looking unto Yeshua, the author and finisher of our faith, who <u>for the joy that was set before Him endured the cross</u>, despising the shame, and has sat down at the right hand of the throne of God." (Hebrews 12:2)

We may go through difficulties, trials, and suffering; but we can endure these by knowing by faith that there is going to be 'joy' on the other side! Hallelujah!

In between these two hip replacements, we made plans to return to Israel from Canada where we had been temporarily stuck during Covid. Two weeks before flying back to Israel, however, I fell down the stairs and broke (actually shattered) my left elbow, requiring yet another surgery. The stitches came out just one day before our flight; and I returned home with my arm in a sling.

Return to Israel, at Yad Hashmona, January 2019 with Liat & Avi

What I have learned through this experience is that the first thing we need to do when a bone has been broken is to immobilize it so that we don't do further damage. I wonder if this is why there are times when we just feel completely stuck! We try to move forward but there seems to be no way; the doors are all closed and our way is blocked. All we can do is sit and wait upon the Lord, being completely still and knowing He is Yehovah God.

"Be still, and know that I am God." (Psalm 46:10)

Just when I thought I could start 'running the race' again, I began experiencing painful fractures of my pelvic bone due to osteoporosis. My bones seemed to be just disintegrating all on their own. Thankfully someone put me onto a uniquely Israeli supplement that helped with the healing and strengthening of my bones;[3] but in order to heal properly, I needed plenty of *'being still'* time, which I found tiresome and to be honest – boring. I know there are people who just love days upon weeks of 'alone time with God'; but it seems I haven't reached this level of spiritual heights as yet. God have mercy!

During these times of quietness and rest, we can remember that it is God who wounds; but also God who binds us up. We are wise if we accept and do not despise the correction, chastening and discipline of the Lord.

"Blessed indeed is the man whom God corrects; so do not despise the discipline of the Almighty. For He wounds (crushes) but He also binds up; He strikes, but His hands also heal (make whole)." (Job 5:18)

Discipline seems almost a 'dirty word' to many of us – it reeks of eating one's peas instead of pizza. But what makes this pill go down smoother is the realization that there is going to be an 'afterward' that we are so going to enjoy – if we will just submit to the discipline of the Lord.

"Now no chastening (discipline) seems to be joyful for the present, but painful; nevertheless, afterward it yields the peaceable fruit of righteousness to those who have been trained by it." (Hebrews 12:11)

> The Hebrew word for discipline, mishma'at, משמעת contains the root word, 'shma' שמע which means to 'hear' or 'listen'. We need to hear God's voice, heed His correction, and submit to His discipline in order to have a joyful, peaceful, life.

---

[3] A calcium supplement made in the Arava called Density

God's dealings with us, His children, are always redemptive. Sometimes we have to be broken first before we can be healed. I have heard that a shepherd will actually break the legs of a young lamb and carry it around its neck if the wayward creature persists in running off, getting itself into troublesome and dangerous predicaments.

Now, I'm not one hundred percent sure that this is actually true; but it does make sense. Perhaps if we persist in our rebellious ways, the Good Shepherd may have no choice but to break us in order to make us His own.

"Before I was afflicted, I went astray; but now I keep Your word." **Psalm 119:67**

God does not willingly afflict the sons of men,[4] but there are times when God knows it is necessary – just as a good father will discipline His son, so does our Abba Father correct the ones He loves.[5]

"Come, let us return to the LORD. For He has torn us to pieces, but He will heal us; He has wounded us, but He will bind up our wounds." (Hosea 6:1)

The Joy of the Anointing (Meshichah) מְשִׁיחָה

This word, 'sasson', is often associated with oil (shemen), as in the 'oil of joy' (shemen sasson) 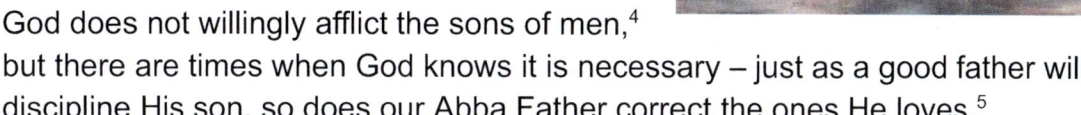שֶׁמֶן שָׂשׂוֹן. Oil often represents anointing; and the original Hebrew meaning of the Messiah (Mashiach) מָשִׁיחַ is the 'anointed one'.

"The kings of the earth stand up, and the rulers take counsel together, against YHVH יְהוָה, and against His anointed one (His Messiah; meshicho) מְשִׁיחוֹ."
(Psalm 2:2)

---

[4] Lamentations 3:33
[5] Hebrews 12:6, Proverbs 3:12

The prophet Samuel anointed young David to be the future King of Israel:

"Then Samuel took the horn of the oil (shemen) שֶׁמֶן*, and anointed him (va'yimashech oto)* וַיִּמְשַׁח אֹתוֹ*."*

(1 Samuel 16:13)

From this time on, the Spirit of God came mightily upon David. The anointing gives us power, through the Holy Spirit, to do incredible mighty exploits that we would never be able to do in our own strength.

We are each anointed for the special assignment God has ordained for us; and there are few joys that can compare to operating in our God-given anointing. I know that when I am flowing in my anointing to share and teach the Word of God, I feel vibrant, alive, exuberant and filled with joy! People will say, "*You were absolutely glowing!*" That's not 'me' – that's the anointing of the Spirit of God moving through me.

God has given each one of us gifts, talents and unique abilities in order to carry out His will on earth. If we are not using these for His glory, then we are going to feel dull, lethargic and stagnant; but if we will '<u>stir up the gifts</u>' [6] God has placed within us, then we will truly come alive and experience abounding joy!

One of the reasons we may be living without joy is because we are not tapping into the anointing of God to use our gifts and talents. If we are still alive, then God still has a purpose for our life. We need to confess and declare every day,

"I have been anointed with fresh oil to carry out my God-given assignment. I shall flourish like the palm tree; I will be fruitful, fresh and flourishing, even in my latter years!"

Yeshua was also anointed for a specific assignment – to glorify God on the earth and bring salvation to all mankind. The ancient Hebrew prophet, Isaiah, foretold of One who would be anointed by God to heal the broken-hearted and proclaim liberty to the captives.

---

[6] 2 Timothy 1:6

This 'anointed one' would also **"comfort those who mourn in Zion, to give them beauty for ashes, <u>the oil of joy (shemen sasson) for mourning</u>, and the garment of praise for the spirit of heaviness."** (Isaiah 61:1-3)

Yeshua stood up in a synagogue in Nazareth one Shabbat, as was his custom, and read these scriptures from the scroll in Isaiah, proclaiming Himself to be the Messiah – 'anointed one' – who came to fulfill this prophetic word.[7]

God wants us to be anointed with the 'oil of joy' (shemen sasson); this is a primary purpose of Yeshua's mission. I remember coming back to Israel after the devastating loss of my firstborn son who passed away after a lengthy illness at the age of thirty-six.

We had spent three years back in Canada, hoping and praying for his healing; but after a nightmare of suffering it ended in death and defeat. *"How could I ever experience joy again*?" I wondered.

Shortly after our return to Israel, we attended the Bat Zion (Daughters of Zion) women's conference, where the speaker shared a testimony of healing from the loss of miscarriage. She proclaimed these very Scriptures from Isaiah 61; and the Lord

ministered healing and comfort to me in a deep and powerful way.
How can we find joy again after a crushing disappointment, loss, or seeming failure? If we further explore '<u>oil of joy (shemen sasson)</u>', we can find a hidden secret in the Hebrew.

---

[7] Luke 4:16-21

This was the name of the Messianic congregation we attended in Jerusalem – 'Shemen Sasson' (Oil of Joy). During a congregational retreat one year, we visited the Biblical Gardens at Yad Hashmona.[8]

There, our knowledgeable guide showed us a model of an ancient olive press and explained the process of turning olives into olive oil by crushing the olives under a heavy rock.

Model of ancient olive press at Yad Hashmona Messianic Village

Even today, some people still make their own olive oil from the olive trees in Israel. I once walked into a friend's apartment in the Galilee where she had some olives sitting in a bowl under a huge, heavy rock. When I asked what she was doing, she explained that she was pressing the bitter liquid out of the olives so that she could use them.

Sometimes trials and tribulations come into our lives to 'press' and 'squeeze' this bitterness out of us. We may wonder, *"Why do I have all this pressure on me? I feel like I am being crushed by the stress of it all!"*

I have, at times, felt that I had a huge weight sitting on my back; and that the oppression of the enemy had become too 'heavy' for me to bear, as the Psalmist lamented,

"I will say to <u>God my Rock</u>, why have You forsaken me? Why do I go about <u>mourning</u> because of the <u>oppression of the enemy</u>?" (Psalm 42:9)

---

[8] **Yad Hashmona** is a vibrant community of Messianic believers in Israel. It is a moshav (communal village), located in the Judean hills close to Jerusalem. The Garden includes an ancient wine press, an olive oil press, a "Mikve" (ritual bath), a burial cave, an agricultural watchtower, a Galilean-type synagogue, and a Bedouin tent.

One of the names of God is _Tzuri (My Rock)_. If we will allow God's heavy 'rock' to sit on us for a while and do its work, we may find that when the uncomfortable time of pressing and squeezing is over (and only God knows when enough is enough), then we will be purified of the defiling bitter juices and can shine again for God's glory.

Olives straight off the tree are so bitter, they are inedible. They must go through a process of being 'hard-pressed' in order to squeeze out all the bitter juices. The pressing is not the end for the olive; it is just the beginning of its usefulness.

So too with us – we need to be 'hard-pressed' in order to squeeze all the bitterness out of our heart and soul. This is not to crush us; but to transform us into a vessel of purity that can be used by God. It is a lengthy and painful process to be cured of bitterness; but on the other side is holiness, freedom and joy!

The Joy of Trials (Nisayon) ניסיון

God wants to give us the oil of joy instead of mourning; but we may need to endure a bit of crushing first. The Lord knows just how much time and pressure it will take to accomplish His good purposes in us. It seems that when we have 'passed' one test, He just takes us to a higher level which means more advanced testing.

Isn't that great news?! We can never fail God's tests, we just get to 'try' and try again until we pass, finally coming to the place where we count it all joy when we fall into various trials and tests, knowing this is God refining our character.

"My brethren, count it all joy when you fall into various trials, knowing that the testing of your faith produces patience. But let patience have its perfect work, that you may be perfect and complete, lacking nothing." (James 1:2-4)

The Hebrew word for test or trial is nisayon ניסיון which shares its root with 'to try' (l'nasot) לְנַסוֹת. This is the same root as in the word (Hitnasut) התנסות 'experience' – we need to pass tests to get more experience to do the work God is calling us to do. One more word coming from this same root is (Nes) נס 'miracle'. We might not believe that we can pass the tests God gives us; but with God all things are possible!

From Olives to Pure Olive Oil

Olive oil production in Israel is an interesting process. Several years ago, when we lived in the Galilee, our Christian Arab neighbors asked if they could come and harvest our olives from the trees on our property. We were happy to oblige, since they were just going to waste left on their own. We had no idea how to turn olives into pure olive oil.

The workers came and spread big sheets out under the trees and then using sticks, they beat the branches until the olives fell. These were gathered in the sheets and made into pure olive oil.

We were so blessed when they gave us our very own bottles of olive oil from our own trees.

Taking a Beating

It took a serious beating to get those olives off the branches and sometimes it feels like we are taking a beating in life; but in the end, if we will be patient and not give up hope, we will end up with enough of the pure olive oil to keep our lamps lit until the break of day.

Hanah and Osnat with olives harvested from our trees in the Galilee

"The path of the righteous is like the shining sun, that shines ever brighter unto the perfect day." (Proverbs 4:18)

Anointed to Suffer

It was in the place of the oil press that Yeshua received the anointing to suffer the crucifixion. In English, we know this place as *Gethsemane*; but in actuality, it had a Hebrew name – *Gat Shemanim* גת שמנים – which means 'oil press'. Shemen is the word for oil.

This name suggests that the garden where Yeshua prayed before his crucifixion was a grove of olive trees, in which was an oil press. It was located just outside Jerusalem on the Mount of Olives.

Gethsemane (Gat Shemanim)

Here, Yeshua was so deeply distressed by the knowledge of what lay ahead of him that he said, **"The sorrow in my heart is so great that it almost crushes me."** (Matthew 26:38)

The Gospel of Luke tells us that after Yeshua knelt down and prayed, surrendering His own will to the will of His Abba Father, an angel came to strengthen Him.[9]

In the olive press, Yeshua was strengthened to face his own death by crucifixion with faith and courage. Few of us will ever endure the suffering that Yeshua went through, but we also need to be anointed by the Spirit of God to persevere through loss, disappointments and various trials with our faith in God intact.

The Joy of the Lord is our Strength

What can strengthen us to walk through this life with faith, hope, and love? **Joy**! Nehemiah told the people not to be grieved (sad), because **"the joy of the Lord is your strength."** (Nehemiah 8:10)

If there is one thing the enemy is after, it is our joy; because if he can steal our joy, then we are left weak, helpless and ineffective – which is right where the devil wants us to be – powerless and ineffective for the Kingdom of God.

If we are going to have the strength to endure, especially through tough times, then we need to be full of joy; because it is the joy of the Lord that will see us through to the end.

---

[9] Luke 22:42-43

There is actually a sect of Judaism that believes sadness to be a sin. They take the exhortation to *'rejoice in the Lord always'* to an extreme. One can often see them driving up and down the streets of Israel with their vans blaring joyful music out of loudspeakers.

Every so often, the men will stop the van, jump out and begin dancing spontaneously in the streets – probably much like King David danced.

These guys really understand the power of joy!

Chassidic Breslov Jews dance in the streets of Tel Aviv

We've simply got to get our joy back! After an appropriate time of grieving, we need to get up, dust ourselves off, and get back in the game. We need to say, *"I refuse to live my whole life mourning over what was or was not or never will be! I will not dwell in the shadow of regret all my life. I trust that God has a plan for my life and I'm going to step into it with faith and courage. I let go of the past. What's done is done; and I believe that even what the enemy meant for evil, God can turn for good. Therefore, I am going to live whatever time I have left with joy!"*

The Healing Power of Joy!

There is actually tremendous healing power in joy! The wisest man on earth said that, **"A merry heart does us good like medicine."**[10] We need to take our medicine every single day!

If life has become dull, monotonous and gloomy, we need to do whatever it takes to get our joy back – since our very lives may depend on it! Norman Cousins made a remarkable recovery from a severe and life-threatening disease of the connective tissue called degenerative collagen illness by watching funny movies and laughing![11]

One of the best ways to stay joyful is to avoid morose, negative, 'Eeyore'[12] type people; and find some happy, optimistic people to hang around with. Both joy and negativity are highly contagious! Maybe it's time to make some new friends that we can laugh and have fun with. Just saying…

One of the things we Jewish people like to do is to eat – and no better place to eat than at a smorgasbord where we can heap up our plates and feast to our heart's delight.

The Bible says that living with joy is like being at a continual smorgasbord:
"All the days of the afflicted are evil, but he who is of a merry (happy, cheerful, joyful) heart has a continual feast." (Proverbs 15:15)

So come with a merry, joyful heart and feast at the Lord's table; drink from His river of pure joy! **"They feast on the bounty of Your house; You let them drink from Your river of pure joy."** (Psalm 36:8)

The Joy of Fruitfulness

One of the ways we can lose our joy is by becoming idle and unfruitful. We need to ask ourselves if we are actively engaged in life; or if we have become passive spectators?

"You did not choose Me, but I chose you and appointed you that you should go and bear fruit." (John 15:16)

---

[10] Proverbs 17:22
[11] His story chronicles in "Anatomy of an Illness as Perceived by the Patient."
[12] Eeyore is a depressive character from Winnie the Pooh

When I became an empty nester, much of my purpose in life flew away with my family. I knew it was good and right for my children to grow up and try their wings; but it left me feeling quite at a loss…

I started to spend too much of my time sitting in a recliner, watching movies or scrolling through my phone. Life began to feel joyless and dull. God has created us to bear much good fruit for His glory; and to continue bearing fruit even in our old age.[13] After over forty years of caring for my family, I needed to re-discover what God-inspired activities would bring me joy.

What gives us joy? Is it singing or composing music? Dancing like nobody's watching? Painting a beautiful watercolor? My daughter receives joy from all of the above. She loves making anything beautiful and has become an accomplished musician, photographer, videographer, graphic artist and blogger![14]

Are we overdue for an adventure? Some people love traveling luxuriously in first class; others love to spend time in nature with a backpack and tent, cooking over an open fire. Do we like cooking gourmet meals for a table full of dinner guests or creating amazing themed birthday cakes for children? My eldest daughter loves doing both of these and she pulls it off with supernatural grace. She is also a naturopathic doctor and absolutely loves learning about natural health and helping people feel better.

We are each different in what gives us joy. Some people like working with their hands or tinkering with machinery. My youngest son used to get tremendous joy from taking apart airsoft rifles and putting them back together again. When he was serving in the IDF military, he carried around a big rifle – this time for real.

My middle son is an engineer, and even as a child it gave him great joy to build things from Leggo. As a teenager, we sent him on a long-term mission trip to Australia and when he came back, he said that his greatest experience there was when someone showed him how to put together a lock on a door! Go figure….

So what gives you joy? Could you indulge in these activities more often? How may we be more active, alert, engaged and fruitful in life? It is when we become idle, sluggish and stagnant, that we lose our freshness; and begin to deteriorate – physically, mentally and also emotionally. Engaging in God-inspired, balanced activity will keep us from becoming idle and unfruitful.

---

[13] Psalm 92:14
[14] https://www.light-tothenations.com/

The Joy of Answered Prayer

One of the ways we experience joy is through answers to our prayers. Yeshua said, ***"Until now you have not asked for anything in My name. Ask and you will receive, so that your joy may be complete."*** (John 16:24)

Hannah in the Bible was barren for a long time; and she felt humiliated especially by Peninah, her husband's other wife, who taunted her for not having children. But when God answered her prayer for a son (Samuel), she rejoiced with great joy! **At that time Hannah prayed: *"My heart rejoices in the LORD in whom my horn is exalted. My mouth speaks boldly against my enemies, for I rejoice in Your salvation."***
(1 Samuel 2:1)

If we have not been receiving an answer to our prayers, it could be that we are double minded about what we are asking for and therefore cannot receive it;[15] or it may be out of God's will or not yet in His timing. God is not a slot machine that we can put in a token and out pops the answer to our prayer. Sometimes the answer may even be 'no' or 'not yet' – or my favorite answer to my kids' requests, "We'll see...." :)

Or it could be that we just need to get more specific in what we are asking for. When Yeshua encountered Blind Bartimaeus, He asked him, "What do you want me to do for you?" I'm thinking, "*Isn't it obvious?!*" But Yeshua wanted him to verbalize specifically what he wanted – to receive his sight – and his request was granted.[16]

When my daughter and her husband were stranded in the Istanbul airport in Turkey, trying to enter Israel without the required documents and against all odds, I wrote down my specific prayer request: *"God I ask You to make a way where there is no way, so that my daughter and her husband can enter the Land together today! In Yeshua's name!"*

I folded up this piece of paper and placed it in my prayer box; then did a Jericho march – I marched around it seven times and shouted and praised God for the answer. (I would have blown a shofar but can't squeeze a note out of mine.)

By faith, I drove to the Ben Gurion airport that evening, through a torrential rain, thunder and hailstorm, not even knowing if they got through or not. When they came out and I saw with my own eyes the reality of God's miraculous answer to our prayers, we sang and danced for joy! "Shouts of joy and victory resound in the tents of the righteous..."

---

[15] James 1:7
[16] Mark 10:51

The Joy of Giving Your Life Away

Often, we become self-focused in our striving to achieve our goals and find happiness in life; but one of the keys for living with joy is to give our life away! We need to seek for opportunities to do good and show kindness to those around us.

Truly it is better to give than to receive; and there will always be opportunities to be a blessing to someone around us. It may be a conversation with a lonely elderly widow; or volunteering at an animal shelter or soup kitchen.

There is always someone who could be blessed by something we have to give; and it is in balanced giving that we find unexpected joy.

"If you extend your soul to the hungry and satisfy the afflicted soul, then your light shall dawn in the darkness, and your darkness shall be as the noonday. The Lord will guide you continually, and satisfy your soul in drought, and strengthen your bones; you shall be like a well watered garden, and like a spring of water, whose waters do not fail." (Isaiah 58:10-11)

The Joy of God's Presence

We may experience joy in many different ways; but in order to experience true, abiding joy – there is no other place to find it than in the presence of God.[17]

If we are not experiencing joy, then we have somehow become disconnected from the presence of God. Being stressed out,

---
[17] Psalm 16:11

worried, or offended can all cause us to disconnect from God's presence.

My laptop computer is great – except for one thing – the battery doesn't work, so unless I connect it to a power source, it will slowly but surely die down. Sometimes I forget to plug it in, and then wonder what in the heck is wrong with it? I get all frustrated and flustered that the functions aren't working – until I realize that I left it unplugged (again).

We too need to connect with God in order to experience joy and function well in life. If we will just turn our focus from ourselves and all of our problems and concerns onto our Heavenly Father who loves us, praising Him for who He is and thanking Him for all He has done for us, then we will reconnect with His presence and be refreshed with joy!

Life is just going to get all around better when we live with joy! But it's not going to happen all on its own. If the water pump is going strong, it doesn't take much effort to keep it going; but it's going to take a whole lot of effort to get it going once it has stopped. Likewise, if the wells of joy have run dry, it may take a bit of doing to fill them up again – but it is 'doable' if we try.

One of the best ways to fill up our dry, empty wells with the living waters of joy is through offering the sacrifice of praise and thanksgiving – for *"**God inhabits the praises of His people.**"* (Psalm 22:3)

Sacrifice of Thanksgiving - Zevach Todah זֶבַח תּוֹדָה

One of the best ways to find joy is to live with an attitude of gratitude. We take so many blessings in our life for granted that not everyone has the privilege of enjoying: clean water, enough food, a safe place to sleep at night and blankets to keep us warm, indoor plumbing, and even the ability to get out of bed in the morning – just to name a few.

Sometimes, we just need to start offering up a 'sacrifice of praise', called in Hebrew a 'zevach todah', giving thanks to His name.[18] In the Psalms, God says that He doesn't want the people's sacrifices and burnt offerings – what He really wants is their gratitude through sacrifices of thanksgiving.

"Offer unto God the <u>sacrifice of thanksgiving</u> *(zevach l'Elohim Todah)* זֶבַח לֵאלֹהִים תּוֹדָה ...Whoever offers the sacrifice of thanksgiving (zevach todah) זֶבַח תּוֹדָה honors Me." (Psalm 50:14,23)

---

[18] Hebrews 13:15

When Nehemaiah and the people of Israel finished building the walls of Jerusalem, they celebrated the dedication ***"with gladness, both with thanksgivings and singing, with cymbals and stringed instruments and harps."*** (Nehemiah 12:27)

They actually appointed two 'thanksgiving choirs' to stand in the house of God and sing loudly – and there was 'great joy'! ***"Also that day they offered great sacrifices, and rejoiced, for God had made them rejoice with great joy (simcha g'dolah); the women and the children also rejoiced, so that the joy of Jerusalem was heard afar off."*** (Nehemiah 12:43)

Never underestimate the power of singing songs of praise and thanksgiving! Can people hear our joy? Can they see it on our faces? Or do we sound like Eeyore and look like we've been sucking sour lemons?

We should be the happiest people on earth! Even though we may have troubles here on earth, we know that in the end we are 'Heaven bound'. If we have nothing else to rejoice about, at least we can rejoice that our names are written in Heaven.[19]

We can rejoice that God is with us, that we are His sons and daughters; and that Yeshua is coming back soon to dwell with us forever.

Sorrowful and Yet Rejoicing

But let's get real here – sometimes stuff happens – and it can seem as if life sucks. It's not all fun & games, parties and merry-making. There are times of suffering, of being crushed by sorrow; and feeling pressured even beyond our ability to bear. We may feel lousy physically and no one can seem to figure out why. The bank account may be dwindling and the debt increasing. It may look as if nothing good is happening in our lives at all and it's hard to just put a smile on our face and pretend to be happy.

I still remember the times when, as a brand new believer, I was trapped in an abusive marriage; and I would go to church. There, I would see everyone looking so happy, and hear everyone singing songs of praise and thanksgiving. But instead of joining in, I would run into the bathroom and hide while I cried my eyes out.

Here's what I have since discovered – we can be sorrowful and yet still be rejoicing.[20] It is possible to be joyful even in the midst of sorrow and suffering. Not necessarily with simcha (happiness) – bouncing around in a frivolous, fake, annoyingly bubbly way; but

---
[19] Luke 10:20
[20] 2 Corinthians 6:10

rather with sasson and gilah – a deep abiding joy. Even if we are going through hell, we can rejoice that God is bringing us through it safely to the other side. He will never abandon us or leave us as orphans.

What do we do when we can see no good fruit from all of our most valiant efforts? When we have prayed until our pray-er is plain worn out and we still don't have an answer? What then? We can still rejoice in the Lord and be joyful in the God of our salvation.

"Though the fig tree does not bud and no fruit is on the vines, though the olive crop fails and the fields produce no food, though the sheep are cut off from the fold and no cattle are in the stalls, yet I will rejoice in the LORD! I will be joyful in the God of my salvation!" (Habakkuk 3:17-18)

We may look at Paul as an example. He went through more pain and hardship than any of us will likely suffer in a lifetime: shipwrecked, beaten and left for dead, suffering hunger and deprivation for the gospel… and yet he never carried around the gloom of a cemetery.

He said, *"But even if I am being poured out like a drink offering on the sacrifice and service coming from your faith, I am glad and rejoice with all of you."* (Phlipians 2:17)

The apostle Paul is the one who exhorted us: *"Rejoice in the Lord always; and again I say rejoice!"* (Philipians 4:4)

What is extraordinary about this is that he penned these words while being imprisoned for preaching the gospel in Rome.

Whining and complaining about our pain or troubles will never do anyone any good – instead, let us harness the power of joy – and see God do miracles! We are all going to deal with difficult situations – that's the reality of life – but no matter what is going on around us, God wants us to experience His supernatural joy!

<u>Prayer</u>: *Abba Father thank You that despite all the challenges that I face, You have promised that I can walk in fullness of joy in Your presence. I praise You and thank You for who You are and all that You have done, are doing, and will do in my life. Thank You for Your joy that gives me the strength to endure whatever may come – both now and in the future.*

Help me to see with eyes of faith the joy that is on the other side of whatever I am going through right now. Grant me a merry heart that will bring healing to my body, mind, soul and spirit – that I may have a continual feast. Thank You for answers to my prayers – that my joy may be complete. In Yeshua's name. Amen.

The Mighty Men (Giborim) גִּבֹּרִים of King David

"David's Mighty Men"
By James Tissot (1836-1902)

"And everyone who was in distress, everyone who was in debt, and everyone who was discontented gathered to him. So he became captain over them. And there were about four hundred men with him." (1 Samuel 22:2)

Four hundred men gathered to David as he fled to the cave of Adullam to escape King Saul's murderous persecution. These were men in distress, men in debt, and discontented men. In Hebrew it actually reads, 'mar-nefesh' מַר-נֶפֶשׁ which means 'bitter of soul'.

This doesn't sound even remotely like a 'mighty band of warriors' does it? And yet these unqualified men with serious emotional, financial, and mental health issues, eventually became known as David's Mighty Men.

In Hebrew they are called 'Giborim', גיבורים.

"These are the names of the mighty men (Ha Giborim) הַגִּבֹּרִים whom David had." (2 Samuel 23:8)

Special Forces

The International Standard Version of the Bible calls them David's 'special forces'. My youngest son, Aviad, served in a 'special forces' unit of the Israeli military known as Sayeret Nahal. They risk life and limb to defend the nation of Israel from our enemies.

Israel Defense Forces - Camouflage training of the infantry Nahal brigade, CC BY 2.0, https://commons.wikimedia.org/w/index.php?curid=34368270

These special forces soldiers are trained to use advanced weaponry and reconnaissance technology for strategic intelligence gathering; as well as to become experts in hand-to-hand combat (krav maga). They are the ones involved in counterterrorism and hostage rescue operations even beyond Israel's borders.

Israel Defense Forces - Officers from the Nahal Infantry Brigade, CC BY-SA 2.0, https://commons.wikimedia.org/w/index.php?curid=34369524

Trust me, speaking from the experiences of my son, I know that these young men are pushed to the outermost limits of human endurance in order to become the fastest, strongest and most courageous of all soldiers! They are the best of the best of the best – Israel's military 'cream of the crop'.

It takes amazing leadership to transform these young 18 year old guys, fresh out of high school into a team of highly disciplined, obedient, courageous soldiers; and I imagine that David was this kind of an extraordinary leader. He took four hundred troubled men and turned them into a band of mighty warriors!

We, as followers of our leader, Yeshua, are also a sort of 'rag tag' group – a 'Motley Crew' of men and women, many of us in distress, in debt and yes, even at times, bitter of soul. And yet, we have each been called to serve in the army of Adonai, led by the Lord of Hosts – Yehovah Tz'eva'ot – Captain of angelic armies of Heaven.

The Least Likely to be Chosen

We may seem the least likely to be chosen to serve as soldiers in the army of the Lord; but He has chosen us anyway. We did not choose Him but He chose us;[1] and even while we were yet sinners, Yeshua died for us.[2]

The Word of God tells us that God chose us even before the foundations of the world were set into place!

"He chose us in His love before the foundation of the world, that we should be holy and set apart for Him, having predestined us to adoption as sons and daughters by Yeshua the Messiah, according to the good pleasure of His will, to the praise of the glory of His grace, by which He made us accepted in the Beloved." (Ephesians 1:4-6)

I remember receiving a surprising phone call out of the blue one day from an 'old flame'. Graham and I had dated briefly before I became a believer. I knew that he had grown up in Kenya as the son of Christian missionaries, but had backslidden in his faith (as evidenced by the fact that he was dating me!).

We had broken up years earlier; and since that time, I had come to faith in Yeshua as my Messiah – a bonafide 'born again' believer. When I shared about this amazing miracle, he was absolutely shocked! He said, *"You are the LAST person in the world that I would ever have expected to be born again!"*

Yes, we may be the *last person in the world* that people consider qualified to serve the Lord; but it is the weak and foolish of this world that God calls, not the strong and wise.[3]

As has been said, *"God doesn't call the qualified; He qualifies the called."*

The Least of the Least

The way we see ourselves may not be at all the way God sees us. We may see ourselves as grasshoppers (like the Israelites did after witnessing the giants in the Land).[4] We perceive ourselves to be the 'least of the least'; but God sees our potential for greatness and calls us 'mighty' (Gibor).

When the angel of the Lord appeared to Gideon, he called him a mighty warrior, **"The Lord is with you, mighty warrior (Gibor hachayil)** גִּבּוֹר הֶחָיִל**."** (Judges 6:12)

---

[1] John 15:16
[2] Romans 5:8
[3] 1 Corinthians 1:27
[4] Numbers 13:33

What was Gideon's response? When the Lord told him to go and save Israel from the Midianites, he said, *"You've got to be kidding me! I think you've got the wrong guy! I'm no mighty warrior; I'm the least of the least of the least."* (Hannah's paraphrase)

What he actually said was, **"Pardon me, my lord, but how can I save Israel? My clan is the weakest in Manasseh, and I am the least in my family."** (Judges 6:15)

Gideon saw himself through his past; and as others perceived him; but God saw him as 'gibor' גִּבּוֹר – a mighty man who would save all of Israel!

El Gibor - Mighty God

The word Giborim גִּבֹּרִים is plural for Gibor גִּבּוֹר, which is one of the names of the Messiah. **El Gibor** means **'Mighty God'**.

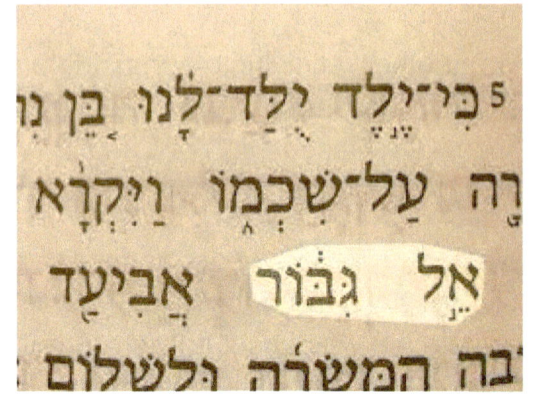

"For unto us a Child is born, unto us a Son is given; And the government will be upon His shoulder. And His name will be called Wonderful Counselor, Mighty God (EL GIBOR) אֵל גִּבּוֹר*, Everlasting Father, Prince of Peace."* (Isaiah 9:6)

The Hebrew word **gibor** גִּבּוֹר means strong, mighty or powerful. It is also the Hebrew word used for **'hero'**. This word is used to describe heroes like Nimrod who was a **"mighty warrior… a mighty hunter before the Lord."** (Genesis 10:8-9)

A related word, 'g'vurah' גְּבוּרָה means **'heroism'**. Yehovah is our ultimate hero!

"Therefore, behold, I will cause them to know… My hand and My might (g'vurati) גְּבוּרָתִי*; and they shall know that My name is Yehovah* יְהוָה*."* (Jeremiah 16:21)

This word, gibor, depicts bravery, courage and daring action. These are all qualities of our mighty God (El Gibor) who is a courageous warrior, fighting our battles and bringing us through to triumph.

We don't often think of God in military terms; but the truth is that God is not only a God of love; but also a Mighty Warrior. He is Adonai **strong and mighty (gibor)** גִּבּוֹר – 'Gibor Milchamah' – גִּבּוֹר מִלְחָמָה – mighty in battle (Psalm 24:8).

We may grow weary from all the battles of life; and the enemy is waging an all out assault in these last days to *'wear out the saints of the Most High (Elyon)'*.[5] This is when we need to call upon El Gibor – Mighty God – to come and fight our battles for us.

When Pharaoh and his armies pursued the Israelites after they had been set free from slavery in Egypt, they found themselves trapped in front of the Red Sea. Terrified, they cried out to the Lord and Moses said to them not to fear: ***"The Lord will fight for you, and you shall hold your peace (shalom)."*** (Exodus 14:14)

There are times when we are simply too exhausted to fight anymore; but then all we need to do is stay in peace (shalom) for the battle is the Lord's.

When God brought them through the Red Sea and gave them victory over their enemies, Moses and the children of Israel sang a song of triumph, proclaiming:

***"Yehovah is a man of war (Ish Milchamah)** אִישׁ מִלְחָמָה."* (Exodus 15:3)

There will come a day when God will reveal His might, His power and His name to the whole earth: Yes, God is a warrior, Mighty God, El Gibor, mighty in battle. Yeshua the Messiah was given this name, El Gibor, and although we may think of him more as a humble lamb of God led meekly to the slaughter, He also demonstrated His mighty power – over sin, over sickness and disease; over demons and over death itself! When He returns, it will not be as a gentle lamb, but as the mighty Lion of Judah!

What is a Man? A Gever

The Hebrew word, gibor, גִּבּוֹר comes from the root word, 'gever', גבר and is one of the modern day Hebrew words used for 'man'. One might say, "Hey gever!" like "Hey Dude!"; or even *"Eize gever!"* – "What a man!" ☺

---
[5] Daniel 7:25

Public toilets in Israel may have a sign on the door which reads גבר (gever) signifying it as the men's bathroom. From this root word for man, we derive the word gibor, גיבור which means *mighty, strong, a warrior or even a hero!*

Aren't these the qualities that many women are looking for in their 'ideal' man; and the type of male character we read about (and perhaps sigh over in romance novels or movies) – a mighty hero? A knight in shining armor who will swoop in and rescue us damsels from all of our distress?

Sometimes it seems that men are being asked to apologize these days for being a 'man' (gever); and to become a softer, gentler, more sensitive version of masculinity. There is a wicked agenda, growing in strength and popularity, to emasculate and feminize our men. But God, in His infinite wisdom, has created men to be mighty, strong, courageous heroes.

It is only when men use their power to abuse or control the weak and defenseless instead of to protect and defend them, that the creation of man is marred from God's original design.

We see this in the Bible in the example of Samson, who was called 'Shimshon Ha'Gibor', a man endowed with great physical strength; but an accompanying fatal flaw. Samson seemed to lack inner integrity; he demonstrated a pathetic lack of wisdom and discernment when it came to women. This moral weakness almost cost Samson his destiny to deliver Israel from the Philistines, and it eventually cost him his life!

Samson: The Strongest Man In The Bible (You Tube)

A true 'gever' will have the moral character to accompany his physical strength. He is a man who will use his power to save, rescue and deliver the weak and the helpless. He is a faithful provider and fearless protector, whose strength is expressed in humility.

More Than Conquerors

The first time this word גבר is mentioned in the Bible is in the book of Genesis (Breisheet). The flood waters 'prevailed' (va'yigbaru) over the earth. **"And the waters prevailed, (וַיִּגְבְּרוּ הַמַּיִם) and increased greatly upon the earth; and the ark went upon the face of the waters."** (Genesis 7:18)

Modern Hebrew still uses this word to communicate the quality of prevailing over or overcoming an obstacle or challenge. To overcome in Hebrew is 'l'hitgaber' לְהִתְגַּבֵּר.

Whether male or female, we are all called to prevail over our circumstances – to overcome the many challenges we face in life. Both men and women in the special forces battalion of the Lord need to be strong and courageous.

What do we do when we feel weak and powerless? We may not be strong or mighty in and of ourselves; but we can be strong in the Lord and in the power of His might.[6] **"For God has not given us a spirit of fear; but of power, of love and of a sound mind."** (2 Timothy 1:7)

---

[6] Ephesians 6:10

Just as the mighty men of David were tough and strong physically, we are also called **'more than conquerors'** through the Holy Spirit who empowers us (Romans 8:37). However, the weapons of our warfare are not carnal; but rather spiritual attributes such as love, peace, joy, patience, kindness, faithfulness, gentleness and self control.[7]

King Solomon wrote that a man who rules over his own spirit and is slow to anger is more mighty (gibor) גִּבּוֹר than one who takes a whole city! (Proverbs 16:32). Wow! That means that if we demonstrate patience and self-control over our emotions, we are mightier than the great warrior Joshua who conquered Jericho! Selah (pause and think about that!).

Even Yeshua spoke about a different kind of greatness to which we are called. To be mighty in God's Kingdom is to become the least – a servant of all. (Matthew 20:25-26).

What can we learn from David's mighty men?

1. David's Giborim were <u>teachable</u>; they grew in character while going through all their wilderness trials. At first, they were quick to suggest that David take vengeance upon Saul when he had his chance; but David taught them that vengeance belongs to the Lord.

He said to his men, **"'The LORD forbid that I should do such a thing to my master, the LORD's anointed, or lift my hand against him; for he is the anointed of the LORD.' <u>With these words David rebuked his men and did not allow them to attack Saul.</u>"** (1 Samuel 24:6-7)

David's Giborim learned from their leader that they dare not touch the Lord's anointed, no matter how he treated them, but to leave the matter in God's hands. They came to see David demonstrate Kingdom principles in the crucible of their daily lives.

Similarly, we can look to Yeshua for how to live out the Kingdom of God in our lives: seeking to serve and not to be served; endeavoring to love and forgive even those who mistreat, hurt, betray or persecute us; leaving vengeance to the Lord, honoring and

---

[7] 2 Corinthians 10:4-6

respecting God-given authority; and obeying the commands of our Father in Heaven, seeking to do His will.

2. <u>David's mighty men were patient and loyal</u>. They needed to be extremely patient until they saw the promises of God come to pass. From the time that the prophet Samuel (Shmuel) anointed the young David to be king until actually reigned upon the throne of Israel, 15-20 years had passed.

During this time, David and his men lived constantly on the run, in poverty and lack, suffering hunger and ever present dangers; and yet these Giborim were willing to pay the price in order to remain loyal to their leader.

We may also suffer reproach, lack and persecutions while staying faithful to Yeshua. We must be willing to go to Him outside the camp and bear His disgrace (Hebrews 13:13). We may be living on the run, hiding in caves, enduring a long waiting period and seeing nothing change; but this is not the end of the story! Even as we wait upon the Lord, we can be growing in character.

If we will be patient, staying loyal to Yeshua as His Giborim, then there will come a day when we will see God's promises fulfilled. Yeshua will sit on the Throne of His Father David to which He is destined, as foretold of the Messiah by the Prophet Isaiah.

"Of the greatness of His government and peace there will be no end. He will reign on David's throne and over his kingdom, establishing and upholding it with justice and righteousness from that time on and forever." (Isaiah 9:7)

"...and the Lord God will give Him the throne of His father David. And He will reign over the house of Jacob forever, and of His kingdom there will be no end." (Luke 1:32-33)

3. David's 'Giborim' were <u>willing to endure hardship but remain faithful</u>. They suffered many trials and tribulations throughout their long years together with David in the wilderness, but they remained faithful to their leader; and when David finally took his destined place as King of Israel, his 'Giborim' were exalted right along with him.

We may also suffer hardship, trials and persecutions during these long years in the wilderness en route to the Promised Land; but when Yeshua returns to sit on the throne of His Father David, we who have been faithful unto the end will be raised up to rule and reign alongside Him.

Wake up the Mighty Men

At the time of this writing, the shofar (ram's horn) is being blown all over the land of Israel and in the nations of the world on Yom Zikaron Tru'ah (Feast of Trumpets). The shofar is blown for several reasons, one of which is to act as an alarm – to awaken us to the realization that the day of the Lord is at hand!

The shofar also calls God's people to assembly to prepare for war! God spoke through the prophet Joel,

"Proclaim this among the nations: *Prepare for war! Wake up the mighty men* (Ha'Gibborim) הַגִּבּוֹרִים…**'"**

(Joel 3:9)

God is, in this hour, awakening His Gibborim – mighty men and women of faith – to prepare for the end time battle with principalities and powers of darkness that we are now facing.

So now, **"Let the weak say, 'I am strong.'"** (Joel 3:10)

IDF Spokesperson's Unit, CC BY-SA 3.0, https://commons.wikimedia.org/w/index.php?curid=89222000

Let each of us take up our positions as good soldiers in the army of Yehovah, mighty men and women of God, willing to endure hardship,[8] and ready to give our lives for the sake of our King.

"Be faithful even unto death, and I will give you the crown of life."
(Revelation 2:10)

Yeshua the Messiah is going to set up His throne in Jerusalem and make it His Millennial capital! And from there He will rule and reign over all the earth, and we who are His Giborim (mighty overcomers) shall rule and reign with Him!

---

[8] 2 Timothy 2:3

"To him who overcomes, I will give the right to sit with me on my throne, just as I overcame and sat down with my Father on His throne." (Revelation 3:21)

What a glorious day we have to look forward to! Come soon, Adonai Yeshua.

Prayer: *Dear God, at times we feel that we are the least qualified to serve in the 'army of the Lord' under Your command. We may even be discontented, distressed or deeply in debt – and yet You have called us to Your side.*

Thank You that even when we feel weak, we can say, by faith, "I am strong in the Lord and in the power of His might". We choose to believe that You call us 'Gibborim', and that You have a vital position for us in Your Kingdom.

Help us, son of David, to be loyal to You, brave, and willing to endure hardship as good soldiers. Strengthen us to become more than conquerors – overcomers who walk in a spirit of power, love and discipline. In Yeshua's name. Amen.

The Power of Words - D'varim דְּבָרִים

"These are the words (אֵלֶּה הַדְּבָרִים) which Moses spoke unto all Israel beyond the Jordan; in the wilderness." (desert - midbar) בַּמִּדְבָּר (Deut. 1:1)

Let There be Light

The words we speak are incredibly important; they carry an amazing creative power and authority. God created the entire universe with His words: He spoke….and it was accomplished. He said,

"Let there be light.. And there was light."

He didn't just think it; He spoke it. Since we are created in the image and likeness of God, we can actually speak things into existence.

This secret is hidden in the Hebrew language itself.

Words & Things

> The Hebrew word for 'word' is 'davar' דבר
>
> The Hebrew word for 'thing' is 'davar' דבר

We can see that Hebrew uses the exact same words for 'word' and 'thing' (davar) דבר. What does this mean to us? Our words can actually create 'things' (substance – visible reality).

We have been given the gift of creative power in our words, and therefore we need to use this ability wisely. Like fire that can either keep us warm or burn down our house; we can use our words for good or for evil, to bless or to curse. The Word of God tells us that the power of life and death is in the tongue.[1]

Everything we speak should be to edify, bless, impart grace, inspire, and encourage, as it is written: **"Let no corrupt word proceed out of your mouth, but what is good for necessary edification, that it may impart grace to the hearers."** (Ephesians 4:29)

Abra Cadabra

Although any form of magic, witchcraft, or sorcery is strictly forbidden in Scripture. We have all likely seen the image of the magician pulling a rabbit out of a hat saying the 'magic words': 'abracadabra'; but did you know that this is actually a Hebrew phrase??

You may be surprised to find out that this phrase actually comes from the Hebrew:

> 'ABRA' אברא means 'I will create' and 'K'DABRA' כ'דברה means 'as has been spoken'. Together, it means that I will create as I have spoken. Wow!

---

[1] Proverb 18:21

The Word Becomes Visible Reality

Yeshua is the perfect example of the Word becoming physical reality: *"The 'Word' (davar) became flesh (basar) and dwelt amongst us."* (John 1:14)

The phrase 'to preach the gospel' is '*l'vaser et ha'besorah*'.

It also means 'to bring the good news', as in, *"How beautiful on the mountains are the feet of those who bring good news, who proclaim peace, who bring good tidings, who proclaim salvation, who say to Zion, 'Your God reigns!'"* (Isaiah 52:7)

It is from this Scripture, that we receive the name of a city in Israel, Mevaseret Zion. מבשרת ציון

This word, mevaser, מְבַשֵׂר means *to bring a message*, which comes from the root word, 'basar' בָּשָׂר which means 'flesh' or 'meat'.

"And man said, 'This time, it is bone of my bones and flesh of my flesh. This one shall be called ishah (woman) because this one was taken from ish (man). Therefore, a man shall leave his father and his mother, and cleave to his wife, and they shall become <u>one flesh (basar echad)</u> בָּשָׂר אֶחָד.'" (Genesis 2:23-24)

The gospel (or good news) in Hebrew is called the 'besorah' בשורה. This word, besorah, also contains the root word 'basar' (flesh).

Originally, the word 'besorah' was used to describe the report of victory in battle. (2 Samuel 4:10.) Through Yeshua, our Messiah, we have victory over our enemies. God always causes us to walk in triumph!

To preach the gospel is to herald a message of good news, that a Savior has been born – the Word has become flesh (basar) and dwelt among us, born as a baby in Bethlehem. Halleluyah!

You Shall Have What You Say

The idea that we human beings, created in the image of God, have power to create reality with our words, however, is not 'magical' but Biblical. Yeshua said, **"You shall have what you say."** (Mark 11:23)

We have a miracle sitting right under our noses through which we have the power to create life or death, as it is written,

"Death and life are in the power of the tongue, and those who love it will eat its fruit." (Proverbs 18:21)

We can literally 'eat our words'. Our physical bodies are impacted by the words we speak. It has been proven by scientific experiments that even the cells of our body hear the words we speak about it and respond accordingly.

Hidden Messages in Water

Masaru Emoto, who wrote, The Hidden Messages in Water, conducted experiments involving exposing glasses of water to various words, pictures or music, then freezing the water and examining the frozen crystals under a microscope.

He concluded that water exposed to positive speech and thoughts created visually "pleasing" ice crystals, and that negative words yielded "ugly" ice formations. Since our bodies are made up of 75% water, obviously our words can have a tremendous impact.

Life-giving words of love, hope and faith create health patterns in the body; but negative words create chaos and destructive patterns.

Speaking Blessings

If we constantly speak words such as, *"I'm so ugly, I'm so fat, I'm looking so old! I feel so tired and weak, everything hurts"*, then the cells of our body will produce after the words we have spoken. But if we intentionally say words such as, *"I am fearfully and wonderfully made. I am created in the image of God. He is restoring my health, my youth and my beauty. I am strong in the Lord and in the power of His might"*, then we can create better physical health and vitality.

We can speak forth those things we hope for but do not yet see, since the just live by faith and not by sight (appearances): *"And now, let the weak say, 'I am strong'; let the poor say 'I am rich' because of what the Lord has done for me."* [2]

It is important that we speak a blessing over the food we eat and the water we drink, so that it will be a blessing to our bodies. We need to break the bad habit of speaking negative words; and replace them with faith-filled, life-giving words of blessing.

Negative words release toxins that can short circuit our nervous system and cause all kinds of physical issues. Words of criticism and condemnation either towards ourselves or others can cause arthritis, release stress hormones and have all sorts of destructive physiological effects on our bodies.

Miriam's accusatory words against her brother Moses caused her to be afflicted with leprosy. Only Moses' merciful pleas brought her healing; and only after a week of being shut outside of the community of Israel.[3]

We must be extremely careful of the sin of Lashon harah (evil tongue): slander, accusation and gossip; for it brings the judgment of God. We can renounce a critical, judgmental spirit and speak blessing instead; for as Yeshua warned us, ***"Judge not, that you be not judged."*** (Matthew 7:1)

---

[2] Joel 3:10
[3] Numbers 12

And the one who curses another is in danger of hell fire.[4] If we don't want to be judged harshly, then we must not judge others. This is the law of giving and receiving in action. If we give grace, mercy, compassion and forgiveness, we will receive these back in kind. But if we give out criticism, condemnation and judgment, this is also what we will receive in return. Whatsoever we want to receive – that shall we give.

Fresh Water and Salt Water Don't Mix

When I was a young girl, I loved tropical fish; and this became my passionate hobby. I loved choosing fish for my aquariums and watching them swim by in their array of colors. I don't know if the love of fish can be inherited, but my late son, Clayton, also loved fish and even had a business taking care of office aquariums.

But his passion was salt water aquariums. Setting up a saltwater tank with its beautiful corals and colorful species of sea life was too complex and finickity of a task for me; but Clayton's was a true work of art and a testament to the glory of God's infinite creativity. I would have loved to keep some of his beautiful saltwater fish in my own fresh water tank, but the fact is that salt water and fresh water just don't mix!

This is what the author of the book of James meant when he wrote that blessing and cursing should not be coming out of the same mouth.

"With the tongue we bless our Lord and Father, and with it we curse men, who have been made in God's likeness. Out of the same mouth come blessing and cursing. My brothers, this should not be! <u>Can both fresh water and salt water flow from the same spring?</u> " (James 3:10 Berean Study Bible)

---

[4] Matthew 5:22

Justified or Condemned by Our Words

Most of us (myself included) tend to be quite careless with the words we speak, oftentimes indulging in meaningless chit chat just to fill in the empty spaces in a conversation. But Yeshua said that we will be required to give an account for every idle (careless) word we have spoken.

"But I tell you that men will give an account on the day of judgment for every careless word they have spoken. For by your words you will be justified, and by your words you will be condemned." (Matthew 12:36- 37)

This is another indication that we are to understand the incredible power contained in our words. We must not speak carelessly but become mindful of what we are saying. If we have a problem in our life, the source could be 'right under our nose'.

In times of trial or frustration, we say things like,

"I'm so sick & tired of…… I'm so depressed… I feel terrible… I look horrible today…" When discouraged, pressured or angry, we may say, *"I just can't do this… I don't know what to do. I can't handle this anymore… nothing ever works out for me…I never get a good break… I just can't win!"*

By these words we are prophesying evil and condemning ourselves.

I was in the dollar store one day and a little old lady was looking in her purse for something and couldn't find it. She said, *"Oh I must be going blind!"* I wanted to run over to her and say, **"Don't say that!!"** We use expressions like, *"I could just die for that"* or *"I'd give my right arm for…"* Our subconscious mind registers everything we say literally and can't take a joke!

We are told to speak TO the mountain and it will move, not speak ABOUT the mountain and how badly we feel about it. We can declare and decree the truth of the Word of God instead of speaking forth the lies that the enemy puts in our mind. We need to speak by faith; and not by sight.

What are we saying? God hears every word we say. Do we realize this? God is listening to the words we speak and responding to them. When the Israelites journeyed through the wilderness, they spoke negative words, prophesying evil and so God basically said, *"Okay… you said it… you shall have it."*

We Are All Well Able

When the spies returned from spying out the Land of Canaan with a report of giants in the Land, and declarations that they are 'not able to overcome', the people's hearts melted with fear. They listened to the evil report of the ten spies instead of the faith-filled exhortation of Joshua and Caleb who said, **"Let us go up at once for we are well able!"** (Numbers 13:30)

Whose words are we listening to? The voices of fear or faith? What kind of reports are we giving out to people over social media? Doom and gloom? The world is collapsing? We are going to be victims? Or do we encourage people with the knowledge of the truth that we are overcomers and that God is with us?

The people of Israel lost heart in the wilderness and feared they would die there. Instead of keeping their thoughts to themselves, they agreed with the ten spies' slanderous report of the Land, and they prophesied that they would become victims. They wanted to turn back instead of moving forward with God in faith.

They said, "**'Why has the Lord brought us to this land to fall by the sword, that our wives and children should become victims? Would it not be better for us to return to Egypt?' So they said to one another, 'Let us select a leader and return to Egypt.'**" (Numbers 14:3-4)

Fear always seeks to shrink back, but faith boldly walks forward expecting God to part the sea and make a way where there is no way.

The Israelites' words grieved God's heart and angered Him. He said to Moses and Aaron: **"How long will this wicked community grumble against me? <u>I have heard the complaints of these grumbling Israelites. So tell them, 'As surely as I live,'</u> declares the Lord, '<u>I will do to you the very thing I heard you say</u>...**

'As I live,' says the Lord, 'just as you have spoken in My hearing, so I will do to you: the carcasses of you who have complained against Me shall fall in this wilderness.'" (Numbers 14:26-29)

Complaining words prophesy evil, keep us stuck, and draw more of that which we don't want into our lives, but praise lifts us up out of our circumstances; as has been said, *"Praise & be raised or complain & remain."*

The Israelites were on their way to a 'good land'; they had a destination and a vision – but they became discouraged along the way and began using their words in a wrong way. Complaining gives the enemy access into our lives to steal, kill and destroy.

"Then they journeyed from Mount Hor by the Way of the Red Sea, to go around the land of Edom; and the soul of the people became very discouraged on the way. And the people spoke against God and against Moses:

'Why have you brought us up out of Egypt to die in the wilderness? For there is no food and no water, and our soul loathes this worthless bread.' So the Lord sent fiery serpents among the people, and they bit the people; and many of the people of Israel died." (Numbers 21:4-6)

Instead of complaining we need to continually speak words of blessing and praise as the Psalmist wrote, ***"I will bless the Lord at all times; His praise shall continually be in my mouth."*** (Psalm 34:1)

We may very well be in a challenging, limiting situation that is testing our faith to the utmost. We may desperately want to find a way of escape; but complaining about the situation only keeps us there longer. What was meant to be an 11 day journey turned into a 40 year futile walkabout ending in death – for all except the two men (Joshua & Calev) who had faith.

When my youngest son, Avi, entered into the IDF, he qualified for an elite special forces combat unit that he may have been physically fit enough to enter; but the training was incredibly brutal and it soon became obvious that it was not the place for him. He is a kind, compassionate young man who cares about people; not the kind of hardened, fighting machines needed to stop terrorists.

Avi went through many serious hardships in the army and I was understandably concerned. He sprained his ankle on a long hike but was forced to continue walking on it; suffered sickness and food poisoning, often going without enough sleep, food or even water; risked hypothermia by having to sleep out in the open in winter without shelter, or even a blanket. Worse than all these physical trials, however, was the emotional abuse and bullying he suffered from his commander and fellow soldiers.

Although we did our share of complaining, which probably didn't help matters, we also prayed and praised God for His faithfulness. We thanked Him in advance for making a way of escape for my son. We blessed the Lord for all His goodness and mercy in our lives. It didn't happen immediately, but in time, as we continued to praise God for His power and might, He sent an angel in the form of a woman named Hila, who took up Avi's cause and advocated for him until Avi received an official letter of release.

Words of praise and thanksgiving along with united prayer brings victory; whereas bitter words, grumbling and complaining only seem to delay the answer and make the problem worse. We have seen this over and over again…

Seeds not Weeds

Our words are like seeds that we plant in the garden of our life. Seeds grow after their own kind. If we plant an apple seed it will grow an apple tree, not a lemon tree. What kind of seeds are we planting? The wrong words we speak are like weed seeds that we sow into our garden. If we don't deal with the weeds in our garden they will take over! We need to pull them out by the roots through repentance.

It is not enough, however, to just pull out the weeds (stop saying wrong things), we also need to intentionally plant new good seeds – ones that we would want to see bloom and blossom in our garden – by speaking forth those things which are not as though they are. ***"The kingdom of heaven is like a man who sowed good seed in his field."*** (Matthew 13:24)

What kinds of flowers do we want to grow in our gardens? If we want beautiful flowers, then we need to plant good seeds, not weeds. Here are some examples of faith-filled declarations we can speak over ourselves and others (just to get you started). These can be written or better yet, spoken aloud:

Examples of Faith-Filled Affirmations:

I am strong in the Lord and in the power of His might. The joy of the Lord is my strength.

I am strong and of good courage, for the Lord my God is with me.

I hope in the Lord and He renews my strength.

I will run and not grow weary; walk and not faint.

I am a blessed child of God; I am a new creation. I am free, forgiven and redeemed.

I am bold as a lion. If God is for me, who can be against me?

I will see the goodness of the Lord in the Land of the Living.

God's goodness and mercy follows me every day of my life.

I am flourishing and fruitful for my Father's glory.

I am prospering and in good health even as my soul prospers.

God is restoring health unto me; and by His stripes I am healed.

I am well able. I can do all things through Messiah who strengthens me.

With God all things are possible; nothing is too hard for Him.

God is my helper. I am surrounded with favor as a shield.

My God supplies ALL of my needs according to His riches in Messiah Yeshua.

I am beloved and accepted and nothing can separate me from the Love of God.

I am filled with the Spirit of God who leads and guides me in the way I should go.
God guides me with His Spirit and makes me know wisdom in my inner being.

I meditate on the word of God day and night; so I shall be prosperous and succeed.

No Man can Tame the Tongue

We have a problem, however, in trying to grow beautiful gardens in our life – no man, in their own strength, can tame the tongue. When Isaiah had a vision of the Lord he was immediately grieved about his 'unclean lips'. He could have been convicted of any sin in God's presence but it was specifically about his mouth (words).

"Woe is me, for I am ruined, because I am a man of unclean lips dwelling among a people of unclean lips; for my eyes have seen the King, the LORD of Hosts."
(Isaiah 6:5)

Arson Terrorism

Here in Israel, we often experience arson terrorism where the enemy sends out fiery balloons to set our fields on fire. These little fires can cause terrible destruction of agriculture, land, trees, forests and the animals who inhabit these areas.

A fire was set in the moshav (village) where my eldest daughter and five children (my grandchildren) live. It was a terrifying ordeal as we received messages that both exits to the village were blocked by fire and they had no way out! We got down on our knees and prayed for a miracle – and God shifted the wind enough that all the people could escape. Halleluyah! Praise Adonai!

We thank God that all lives were spared; but several horses perished when their owner couldn't reach their corral to free them; a harp studio was completely burned to the ground; and whenever we drive by this area that was once a lush, mountainous region, all we see are the blackened stumps of the burned trees.

The Tongue is Like a Fire!

The Bible says our tongue is like a little fire that can set everything on fire and leave terrible destruction in its wake.[5] We can all likely remember something that some cruel or unthinking person said to us that left a dark path of destruction in our heart and soul.

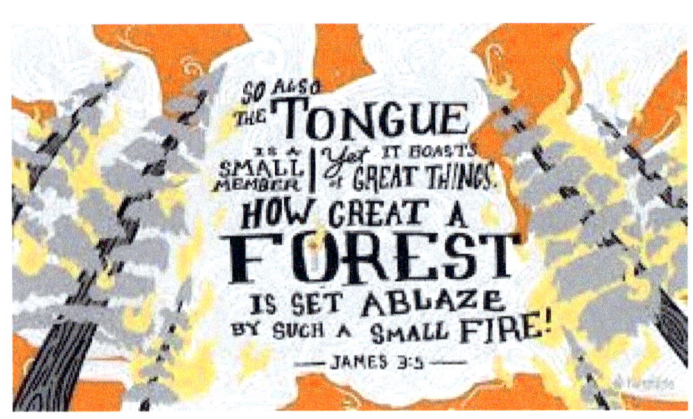

Our tongue is also compared to the rudder on a ship – it is very small but actually determines the direction or course of the ship. Similarly, our tongue can steer our lives in the direction of our words – and if we are not careful, it can steer us in a direction we may not want to go!

Only the Holy Spirit can control our tongue. We need to ask daily for God's help to guard our speech like the Psalmist prayed, ***"Set a guard, O LORD, over my mouth; keep watch over the door of my lips."*** (Psalm 141:3)

Guarding our mouth and being careful with our words can protect us; but careless speech can actually bring ruin into our life. ***"He who guards his mouth protects his life, but the one who opens his lips invites his own ruin."*** (Proverbs 13:3)

"A fool's lips cause strife, and his mouth invites a beating. A fool's mouth is his destruction, and his lips are the snare of his soul." (Proverbs 18:7)

None of us want to invite a beating; and no one wants to be a fool. The Bible is full of wisdom about guarding our words. If we want to have a good, long, blessed life, we need to watch our words:

"Who is the man who desires life, and loves many days, that he may see good? Keep your tongue from evil, and your lips from speaking deceit." (Psalm 34:12-13)

---

[5] James 3:5-6

Guard Your Heart

This is not really so much a mouth issue as it is a heart issue because whatever we speak is actually coming from our heart:

"A good man out of the good treasure of his heart brings forth good; and an evil man out of the evil treasure of his heart brings forth evil. For out of the abundance of the heart his mouth speaks."
(Luke 6:45)

We need to guard our hearts from bitterness, unforgiveness and all malice. If we have unhealed areas in our heart – pockets of resentment and bitterness – it is going to come out of our mouth at some point. Self pity, fear, hatred, or jealousy hidden in our heart: these will all eventually be expressed in our words.

No one is perfect in this; we are all on a journey. But we can become more aware, and strive to be more mindful of the words we speak about ourselves and others. Keeping control over our tongue is vital to our spiritual life.

"If anyone considers himself religious and yet does not bridle his tongue, he deceives his heart and his religion is worthless." (James 1:26)

Verbal Terrorism

What about the words others speak over us?? They also have power for good or evil. True confessions here. I was once so angry with someone that in a fit of rage I shouted, "You are such a **pain in the butt!**" (Yes, I did – chief of sinners…). Can you believe that this man actually developed such a bad case of hemorrhoids that he had to use a pillow to sit down for a week!! It's true. As I said, the subconscious mind can't take a joke!

The saying, *"Sticks & stones will break my bones but words will never hurt me" is NOT TRUE!* Words are powerful and can have a devastating effect on us. Oftentimes these negative words, especially when spoken by an authority figure like a parent or teacher, can pierce the heart and soul of an impressionable child and become false labels believed to be true: stupid, incorrigible, ugly, bad, lazy, selfish or unlovable.

Even as adults we can speak horribly cruel words to or about others. These comments can stick like poisonous darts in our mind and heart, causing a festering wound that never truly heals. It keeps coming to our remembrance – that mean statement that our ex-spouse said about us, or a so-called 'friend'.

The Bible tells us that our 'reckless or careless words' can be used as a sword to pierce and wound; but we can also use our words to bring healing. **"The words of the reckless pierce like swords, but the tongue of the wise brings healing."** (Proverbs 12:18)

The enemy will use unaware people to speak destructive words over us to help bring his evil plan into our lives instead of God's good plan.

We must always keep in mind that our struggle is not really with this person (flesh & blood), but with the principalities and powers of wickedness in high places that are gaining access through their mouth.[6]

The good news is that God's blessing overrides a curse and the blood of Yeshua is more powerful than any force of evil. We can and must pray for God's protection from the wicked words of the evil one; and to break off any negative word that has been spoken over us.

---

[6] Ephesians 6:12

"Hide me from the secret plots of the wicked, from the rebellion of the workers of iniquity, who sharpen their tongue like a sword, and bend their bows to shoot their arrows – <u>bitter words</u>." (Psalm 64:2-3)

We must keep up our shield of faith to protect us from all the fiery darts of the evil one. If we know our identity in Messiah, these words will have less of an impact – like water off a duck's back – they will slide right off and not enter our hearts.

Faith-filled, life-giving words can release blessing, comfort, grace, inspiration, edification, motivation and encouragement. But corrupt words can release damage and destruction over us. Evil words tear down, belittle, accuse, lie, slander, gossip, criticize and demean. We can ask God to deliver us from their poisonous words.

"Deliver me, O Lord, from evil men; preserve me from violent men, who plan evil things in their hearts; they continually gather together for war. <u>They sharpen their tongues like a serpent; the poison of asps is under their lips</u>."
(Psalm 140:1-3)

The Bible compares this evil speech to **murderous ambush, scorching fire, being stabbed with a sword, or being shot at with arrows…..verbal assassination**. We may even call this *"verbal terrorism"!*

We can be living under the effects of a word curse spoken behind closed doors for years and not even know it. Evil spirits can become attached to these word curses to release demonic assignments against us. King Balak of Moab hired the sorcerer Balaam on an assignment to speak a curse over the people of Israel; but he could not directly curse those whom God had blessed.[7]

And yet there was still a demonic assignment against them and the enemy used their weakness for women to destroy the Israelites. God protects us from curses; but the enemy looks for a weak spot in our armor to bring on curse. No undeserved curse will come to rest upon us; it needs a legal entry point – willful unrepentant sin or disobedience.

a

"Like a fluttering sparrow or a darting swallow, an undeserved curse does not come to rest." (Proverbs 26:2)

---

[7] Numbers 23:8

We need to watch for open doors that allow the enemy to bring curses upon us: robbing God (disobedience in tithing); ignoring the cries of the poor; dishonoring parents (rebellion against authority); idolatry; dabbling in occult; sexual sin; anti-semitism – these are all sins that open the door for curses to rest upon us.

The good news is that we can break off word curses that others may have placed upon us (or that we placed upon ourselves).

"'No weapon formed against you shall prosper, and every tongue which rises against you in judgment you shall condemn. This is the heritage of the servants of the Lord, and their righteousness is from Me', Says the Lord." (Isaiah 54:17)

Steps to Freedom

1. Forgive the person who spoke wrong things about you or over you. Guard your heart from any bitterness or unforgiveness against them.

2. Renounce the words in the name of Yeshua. Cancel them. Break their power. Declare them null and void and command these words to be uprooted from your soul, the arrows removed and the wounds healed.

3. Command any unclean spirit attached to these words to come out and leave you. Break off any demonic assignment that was against you.

4. Replace the lies with truth from the Word of God and blessing. Speak the opposite of what they said. Let God's love fill your heart and bring healing.

It was the Israelites' words (from wrong attitudes) that kept them out of the Promised Land. If we want to cross over into our 'Promised Land', then we need to speak faith-filled words,to praise and not complain. We can truly frame a new reality for our lives with our words.

"I will SAY of Adonai, 'He is my refuge and my fortress; my God, in Him I will trust.'" (Psalm 91:2)

Prayer: *Dear God, please forgive all my careless and slanderous words, both against myself and against others. Help me to be aware of the words I speak and to always be in remembrance that as I speak I am creating my reality.*

Thank you Holy Spirit for giving me the power to guard my tongue and to keep my soul from troubles. Grant me the grace to pull out the weeds I have allowed to grow in my garden; and to plant new seeds that will bear much good fruit for Your glory.

Break off any negative words or curses that have been spoken over me, either in my past or even in my present. I praise You and thank You for freedom and power to create an abundant, joyful, fulfilling life.

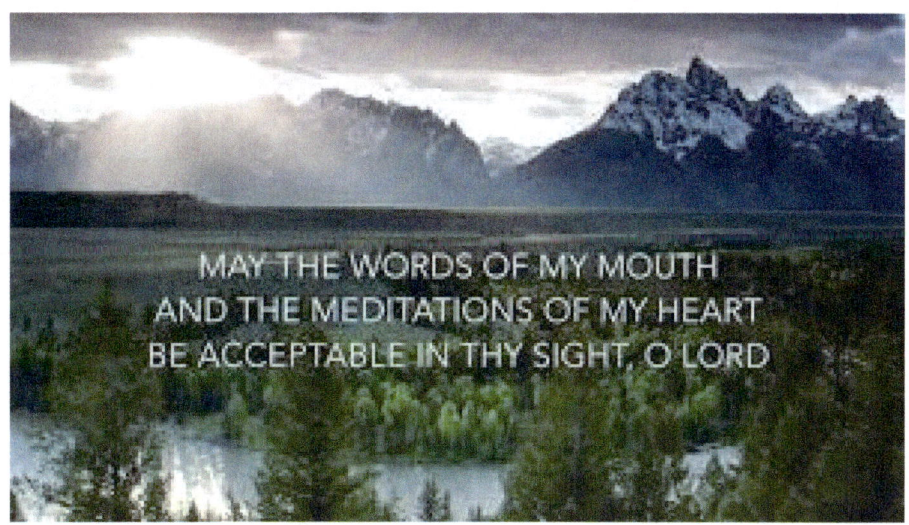

"May the words of my mouth and the mediation of my heart be pleasing unto You." (Psalm 19:14)

The Valley of Achor עָכוֹר - Turning Trouble into Hope

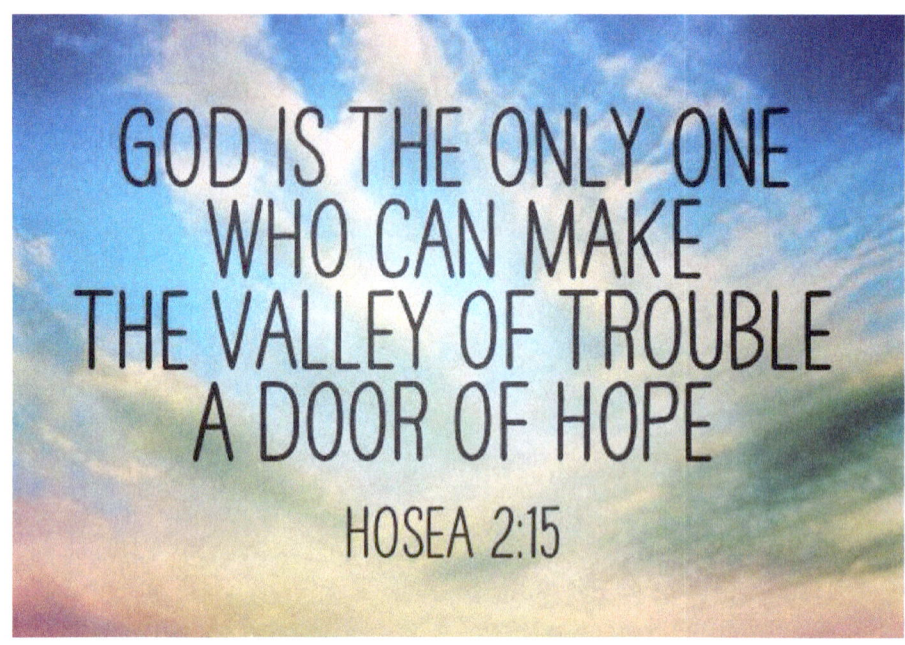

"So I will lead her into the desert and speak words of comfort to her. I will give her vineyards there, and make the Valley of Achor a door of hope." (Hosea 2:14-15)

In Hebrew, the Valley of Achor is called 'Emek Achor' עֵמֶק עָכוֹר which means a Valley of Trouble. Life sometimes feels like walking through an endless valley of trouble, doesn't it? At times it feels like it's one thing after another. Even Job, the man of God we admire for his patience in trials said, **"Yet man is born to trouble, as the sparks fly upward."** (Job 5:7)

Yeshua also warned us that in this life we would have trouble… but we are still to be of good cheer for He has overcome the world.[1] Yes, trouble is a fact of life in this world outside the Garden of Eden, but this Hebrew word, Achor, עָכוֹר can also mean 'gloomy'.

Enough trouble in our life can make us gloomy, negative and pessimistic – always expecting the worst – assuming that things will likely go wrong instead of right.

---

[1] John 16:33

It's like living with a dark cloud hanging over our heads, following us everywhere we go. Instead of looking for the goodness of God, we brace ourselves for the next disaster which, if not already upon us, is surely soon to come.

Other related meanings of this word, Achor, are: <u>muddy, murky, or foul</u>. When we find ourselves in the Valley of Achor, it's as if the pure, clean, living waters have become defiled and we can no longer clearly see through the muddied waters to the things of the Spirit. We lose our sense of spiritual discernment.

So what do we do when we find ourselves walking through this Valley of Achor? Perhaps if we explore the Hebrew Scriptures, we may discover some answers.

According to Hebraic tradition, we need to search for the first time the word or concept is used in the Scriptures for insight and revelation. For this purpose, we turn to the seventh chapter of the Book of Joshua for the account of *Achan* and the transgression of the 'accursed things'.

Here we find Joshua on his face before God, asking why Israel has been defeated by their enemies. **"Why have You brought us over the Jordan only to be delivered into the hand of the Amorites to destroy us?"** (Joshua 7:7)

This defeat followed right on the heels of their stunning victory in Jericho. Just after the mighty walls of Jericho came crashing down with the blasts of their shofarot,[2] Israel ended up being chased, tails between their legs, by the weak, insignificant army of Ai.

"Therefore the hearts of the people melted and became like water." (Joshua 7:5)

Don't we sometimes feel discouraged like this when walking through our own valley of troubles? We may ask, *"Why God? Why have you saved us just to let us be defeated by these small troubles, destroyed by even the weakest of enemies? If I can't even get victory over this insignificant issue, how can I expect to deal with the really serious trouble in my life?"*

What was God's answer to Joshua? **"Get up! Israel has sinned. They have taken some of <u>the accursed things</u> and put it amongst their own stuff."** (Joshua 7:10-11)

God revealed the reason He was no longer giving Israel victory – it was because of the accursed things. In Hebrew, the word used is **Herem.** חֶרֶם

---

[2] Plural for shofar, ram's horn, used in spiritual and physical battle

Until these accursed things were removed from their midst and destroyed, Israel would not be able to stand before their enemies. They were doomed to destruction!

God's presence would not be with them anymore until they got rid of all the 'herem'.[3]

"Neither will I be with you anymore, unless you destroy the accursed from among you." (Joshua 7:12)

God had warned Israel not to take anything from the spoils of Jericho lest they bring a curse upon it and 'trouble' it.
"And you, by all means abstain from the accursed things (herem), lest you become accursed when you take of the accursed things, and make the camp of Israel accursed, <u>and trouble it</u>." (Joshua 6:18)

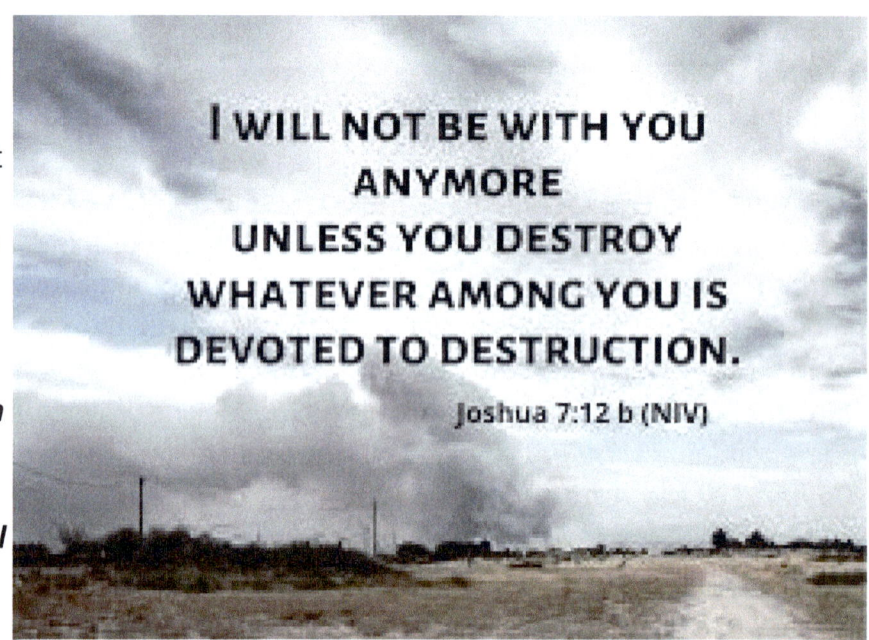

The Hebrew word used here is v'achartem וַעֲכַרְתֶּם from the same root for trouble – achar עכר. Normally the victors would help themselves to the spoils of their enemies; so why did God forbid Israel from taking any of the spoils of Jericho?

It is because the city of Jericho was the 'first-fruits' of their possession of the Promised Land. And the firstfruits always belong to God – they are 'holy unto the Lord' and not for our own personal use.

Oye vi voy (woe) to anyone who takes the firstfruits for themselves. This is why keeping the tithe, the firstfruits of our income, is such a grave sin. We are to bring the firstfruits of all of our increase into the house of God; and then we will be filled with abundance.

---

[3] Joshua 7:12

"Honor the Lord with your possessions, and with the firstfruits of all your increase; so your barns will be filled with plenty, and your vats will overflow with new wine." (Proverbs 3:9-10)

Even Israel itself is considered the 'firstfruits' and therefore holy unto the Lord. Woe to the one who tries to harm the apple of God's eye: *"'Israel was holiness to the LORD, The firstfruits of His increase. All that devour him will offend; disaster will come upon them,' says the LORD."* (Jeremiah 2:3)

God made His word very clear to Israel – not to take any of the spoils of Jericho. He called it 'cherem' – devoted to destruction. Those who took it would be doomed to destruction along with the cherem they took.

Who could have brought this trouble upon Israel? A man whose very name actually means trouble – Achar. *"The son of Carmi was Achar עָכָר, the <u>troubler of Israel</u> (ocher Yisrael) עוֹכֵר יִשְׂרָאֵל, who transgressed in the accursed thing (herem)."* (1 Chronicles 2:7)

In his greed, Achan had taken a beautiful Babylonian garment, as well as some gold and silver, and hidden it under his tent, thinking no one would ever discover it – which automatically reveals his unbelief in God who is all-seeing and all-knowing. This transgression in the accursed things brought trouble and defeat upon all of Israel.

"But the children of Israel committed a trespass in the accursed thing (herem) חֵרֶם: for Achan, the son of Carmi, the son of Zabdi, the son of Zerah, of the tribe of Judah, took of the accursed thing (herem) חֵרֶם: and the anger of the LORD was kindled against the children of Israel." (Joshua 7:1)

Destruction of the Herem!

What was God's remedy for Israel's defeat? Complete destruction of the Herem! When the accursed things were found under Achan's tent, evidence of his sin of covetousness and disobedience, everything was carried away to the Valley of Achor (Emek Achor): Achan, his sons, his daughters, his donkeys, sheep, oxen, the accursed things, his tent and all that belonged to him were carried away to the Valley of Achor.

Similarly, in our own lives, when we try to hide something that is not rightfully ours; or cover up some defiling sin, we bring trouble not just upon ourselves – but upon all that belongs to us!

Joshua said, *"Why have you troubled us? The Lord will trouble you this day."* (Joshua 7:25)

So all of Israel stoned them to death, burned them with fire and covered it all with a heap of stones. And to this day, that place has been called the 'Valley of Achor עֵמֶק עָכוֹר'.[4]

Achan's sin had a profound negative impact on the whole community of Israel, just as our sin today affects not only ourselves but our family as well as the entire body of the Messiah.

---

[4] Joshua 7:26

If we already know Yeshua as our Messiah and yet feel as if we are always walking in the Valley of Achor, in defeat, despair (hopelessness) and destruction, perhaps we need to also examine our lives for evidence of herem – accursed things – in our homes.

When the people of Israel came into the Promised Land, God warned them, ***"Do not bring an abomination תוֹעֲבַת יְהוָה (to'avat) into your house, lest you be doomed to destruction like it. You shall utterly detest it and utterly abhor it, for it is an accursed thing חֵרֶם (herem)."*** (Deuteronomy 7:26)

Could there exist something in our possession, even unknowingly, that God calls an abomination bringing destruction into our lives? What is an accursed thing (herem)?

Accursed things (abominations) include anything associated with foreign gods, idols, idolatry, or the occult. Any object from a witchdoctor, spiritualist, sign reader, fortune-teller, magician, or sorcerer; any New Age or Freemason paraphernalia, or anything associated with the Kingdom of Darkness is considered 'herem'.

Accursed things could include violent or demonic video games, immoral movies, or pornographic materials. It may be a demonic statue, piece of jewelry, home decoration, picture or image on clothing or even a children's toy.

I have visited very few homes of Believers where I did not see evidence of some kind of witchcraft, idolatry, or occult. It may take some spiritually discerning 'snooping' to cleanse our homes from this herem, praying and asking God to reveal anything in our possession that may be causing us to walk in defeat.

A friend of mine, a young mother, recently related an incident when one day, her baby would not stop crying. The mother became more and more irritated with her child to the point where she felt enraged. Thankfully, she was spiritually discerning enough to realize that the enemy was at work and she noticed a small toy that a homeless person had given to her child.

Looking closely at this toy figure, she could see the rage and demonic expression on its face. She immediately took it outside, her husband smashing it under his heavy work boots, and shortly, the crying and the rage completely disappeared. Halleluyah!

How many of us are living with the presence of the enemy in our homes because of herem – items devoted to destruction? We must be willing to give up and even destroy anything the Holy Spirit shows us that is not pleasing to Him. A return of God's favor and presence is well worth the sacrifice of whatever material possession that may be.

My Own Personal Valley of Achor

A sukkah at our temporary home in Arad

I recently experienced the frustrating consequence of 'herem' in a very personal way. We had been subletting someone's house in the Negev for over two years while they were traveling and touring in the United States. It was a lovely spacious home and had absolutely everything we needed – from furniture to bedding to all the kitchen supplies.

We were very comfortable there, which is why what was meant to be a place to quarantine for 14 days during Covid when we returned to Israel from Canada, turned into a couple of years.

We became quite comfortable in this place and it started to feel like home. Eventually, we got our own few belongings out of storage (to save the costs) and used them as well. Somehow, without even realizing it, our stuff got mixed in with their stuff; and when it came time to move out, it was a big balagan (confused mess) to try and sort out whose was whose.

Was this water bottle ours? Or theirs? What about these tools? Did the hammer come from our tool box or theirs?? Oye vey! We did our best, but once we moved into our new place, we kept finding things popping up that we were pretty sure belonged to the other house.

We also noticed bad things starting to happen once we moved out:

- My son began to get sick in the IDF and suffer anxiety. His asthma attacks and panic attacks meant repeated trips to the ER which meant a great deal of time and money were spent on these, not to mention the emotional stress which became exhausting!

- He eventually failed to complete his army service and got discharged.

- My daughter and her husband, who had just married and moved to Israel, were forced out of their beautiful apartment that they had just moved into a few months prior, due to the spraying of toxic chemicals in their building which they were reacting to.

- They could not find a new place to live no matter how hard they tried and wherever they searched and how fervently we all prayed – and so they were essentially homeless.

- Orders were sent to the wrong address.

- Money that should have come to me was blocked.

- All my family members received a generous inheritance from a relative who passed away – except me – I was cut out of the will because of my faith in Yeshua.

- All kinds of illness, sickness, pain, and weakness began showing up in our family – physically and mentally.

- A pervading sense of hopelessness and depression led me to feel totally defeated. Keep in mind that all this time I was tithing and praying… to no avail.

I felt like Joshua on my face before God; and all I kept hearing was the word 'herem'. God showed me that we had (inadvertently) taken things that did not belong to us and had put it among our own stuff – which is basically theft. So we began a thorough 'witch hunt' for anything that could possibly have belonged to the other house.

It was only a book here, a spoon there, a shoot of a plant taken from their garden… but we gathered it all up and brought it all back to the house. If we had any doubt whatsoever if it was ours or theirs, we just gave it back. We were actually shocked to find that everything we had accidentally taken was actually a car full!

Some things were, to be honest, tough to give back – because they were so small but they were American items hard or impossible to obtain in Israel. I wanted to hold onto one small eyeliner; and the Lord spoke to me asking if an eyeliner is worth our defeat? It wasn't just me being affected, but my entire family! So back it all went.

I thought we had collected it all and that we would be okay now; but such was not the case. Have you ever felt like you were just banging your head against the wall? That whatever you tried to do was blocked or doomed to failure? It was like that. Little things… but they added up to a big sense of utter defeat, and it was even causing me to doubt God.

Sitting out on my balcony one day, I again heard the word, 'herem'. WHAT??? How could there possibly be any herem left, Lord? I asked. And then my attention was drawn to a corner of the balcony where sat a kitty litter box. Yes. Actually it was one of those black, square, plastic bins that we used as a cheap litter box. But where did it come from?? Yup – from the garden of the other house! We had used it for so long that it just never occurred to me that it was 'stolen'.

Immediately, I got rid of it! And as hard as it may seem to believe, everything started to turn around after this last act of removing all the 'herem' from our home. The avalanche of trouble stopped. Favor and mercy started to flow back into our lives. My son started to feel better; my daughter and husband found a car and a place to live. I felt a renewed sense of hope and started detecting breakthroughs.

This experience has left me with a deep conviction that God means what He says He means; and that we need to be obedient if we are to walk in victory! As it is written, the fear of the Lord is the beginning of wisdom.

If you have been experiencing one troublesome thing after another, and no amount of prayer or giving or effort brings deliverance, I encourage you to prayerfully consider whether or not you have, even inadvertently, brought any 'herem' into your house.[5]

The balance to this is that however diligently we try to cleanse our lives and homes of things that displease God, some measure of trouble is part and parcel of real life in this fallen world amongst imperfect people. Not all trouble in life is evidence that we have hidden 'herem'. The reality is that we do have an adversary – an enemy of our souls – who seeks to kill, steal and destroy and can definitely 'trouble' us.

The good news is that God is a very present help in times of trouble.[6] He is our hiding place, and in the day of trouble, He promises to hide us in His tabernacle. In Hebrew, the word used is 'sukkah'. God has a huge sukkah where He will hide us in the evil day.

"For in the time of trouble He shall hide me in His pavilion (Sukkah) בְּסֻכֹּה;

In the secret place (Seter) סֵתֶר *of His tent He shall hide me; He shall set me high upon a rock."* (Psalm 27:5)

---

[5] See Podcast on Getting Rid of the Accursed Things (herem)
[6] Psalm 46:1

Spiritual Herem

Sometimes our 'herem', which continually brings trouble into our life, is spiritual, emotional or mental rather than physical. We may have wrong attitudes, wrong thought patterns or wrong habits that need to be destroyed.

Perhaps the fiery coal of an angel needs to touch our unclean lips and change the way we speak. The Word warns us that a root of bitterness will not only cause trouble in our own lives, but will also defile the lives of many people we come into contact with.[7]

We could be in a close relationship with someone who is bringing chaos, drama and trouble into our life. Those in the boat with Jonah were in danger of being destroyed along with him, even though it was Jonah who was disobedient and running from God. It took throwing Jonah overboard to calm the stormy tempest and restore peace (shalom).

An intimate relationship with one who is running away from God and in unrepentant disobedience may cause our destruction. We are warned not to keep company with an idolatrous, covetous person, even if he or she does claim to be a 'Believer' – not to even eat with such a person! (1 Corinthians 5:11)

Shun Evil

While ministering recently at a women's shelter in Israel, I discovered another meaning to the word Achor from a native Hebrew speaker. She told me that the word 'herem' in modern day Hebrew usage, means to 'shun'. It is used when, for example at school, when a certain child is completely ostracized or 'shunned' by his or her fellow students.

When it comes to 'herem', we are not to compromise with it or tolerate it in our lives; but to totally 'shun' it – having nothing to do with accursed things or abominations that God hates.

"The wise fear the LORD and shun evil, but a fool is hotheaded and yet feels secure." (Proverbs 14:16)

So the question remains, *"How may we eradicate 'herem' from our midst and walk out of the Valley of Achor (trouble) into a blessed place of peace (shalom), love and joy?*

---

[7] Hebrews 12:15

Discovering a Door of Hope

For answers, we must continue to follow the trail of the valley of Achor to the book of Hosea. Here, we read about a woman of harlotry named Gomer with whom I could well identify in the past.[8] Her name, Gomer, גֹּמֶר, means 'finished'. Without the grace of God we would all be finished!

She decked herself out in flashy earrings and jewelry, and chased after her lovers (thinking that they were her source of all goodness); without a thought to the One who is her true Beloved. This is so sad; and God's heart is broken. ***"'She decked herself with her earrings and jewelry, and went after her lovers; but Me she forgot,' says the Lord."*** (Hosea 2:13)

But God has His ways. In His incredible kindness and mercy, He absorbed all the rejection and wooed her back unto Himself. Hedging her way with thorns, and walling her in so that she could no longer catch her lovers, causing all her 'mirth' and immoral partying to cease, He then allured her, bringing her into the desert (midbar) and speaking comfort to her there.

The midbar (wilderness or desert) is a place where God speaks. Midbar מִדְבָּר comes from the root Daber דָּבָר which means 'speak' or 'word'. It was here that He spoke to Moses in the burning bush. It was in the desert where He spoke to the adulterous woman, Gomer. It is in the dry and parched places of our lives where God often speaks a word to us as well.

God actually promised to turn the Valley of Achor (Emek Achor) עֵמֶק עָכוֹר into a door of hope! How can the valley of our troubles be turned into a place of hope? How is the curse of Achor turned into a blessing? What (or should I say who) is the door?

Yeshua said, ***"I am the way, the truth and the life."*** [9] He is the way from trouble to hope.

---
[8] See Hannah's personal testimony: <u>Grafted in Again</u>
<u>Grafted in Again ebook</u>
[9] John 14:6

In English we usually read this translated as 'a door of hope' but this is a mistranslation. The Hebrew word for door is <u>delet</u> דלת but this is not the word used here; rather it is <u>petach</u> פתח, which means '<u>an opening</u>'. There is an opening through trouble to hope.

In the New Testament, Yeshua uses a metaphor well known to the people of Israel – a shepherd with his sheep.

He says, *"I am the door (sha'ar = gate) of the sheep."* (John 10:7).

"I am the sha'ar (gate). If anyone enters by Me, he will be saved, and will go in and out and find pasture." (John 10:9)

Yeshua is the opening through which we may enter into life. He is the good shepherd (Ro'eh Hatov) who leads His sheep to lie down in green pastures.

The enemy comes to steal, kill and destroy, but Yeshua said He has come to give us life and life more abundantly. He laid down His life for us. No one took it from Him but He laid it down of Himself; of His own accord.

Yeshua is the One who has turned the curse of Achor into the blessing of hope (tikvah).[10] The Messiah redeemed us from the curse:

"Messiah has redeemed us from the curse of the Torah, having become a curse for us." (Galatians 3:13)

Because of the curse of sin, we were doomed to destruction, just as were the Israelites under the curse of Achor. But Yeshua took the sin upon Himself so that we may have hope and walk in righteousness. ***"He who knew no sin became sin for us that we might become the righteousness of God in Him."*** (2 Corinthians 5:21)

---

[10] See chapter, "Hoping upon the Lord"

The blood of bulls and goats in the Old Testament sacrificial system could never truly remove or destroy our sins. The sacrifice had to be repeated over and over again, and even then the sin was only temporarily covered, not destroyed. But Yeshua entered the Holiest place with His own blood, thereby completely eradicating our sin. (Heb 9:12)

Our sin has been destroyed as surely as was Achan and all that belonged to him in ancient Israel. Because of the accursed things we hold unto our bosom, our 'herem', those things devoted to destruction that we refuse to relinquish, we are doomed to sure defeat, even from the most insignificant opposition such as the feeble army of Ai, but in Messiah, we may walk in victory.

Thanks be to God, who gives us the victory through our Lord, Adoneinu, Yeshua Hamashiach.[11] He always leads us in triumph.

We are more than conquerors through Him who loved us.[12] Our 'herem', our sin, dooms us to eternal separation from God. But through Yeshua we may be forgiven and have eternal life in God's presence. He is Immanu-El (God with us).[13] Death is swallowed up in victory. Halleluyah![14] Though our sins are as scarlet they will be whiter than snow.[15]

In the book of Hosea, the Lord promised a wayward, weak, sinful woman that He would give her an <u>opening of hope (Petach Tikvah)</u> פֶּתַח תִּקְוָה instead of the misery of a perpetual walk of condemnation through the Valley of Achor. But first, God had to hedge her way with thorns to keep her from chasing after her lovers.

"Therefore, behold, I will hedge up your way with thorns, and wall her in, so that she cannot find her paths. She will chase her lovers, but not overtake them; yes, she will seek them, but not find them." (Hosea 2:6-7)

He then promised Gomer an eternal covenantal relationship; and that she would then sing again in His presence as she had in her youth. ***"I will give her vineyards from there, and the Valley of Achor as a door of hope; she shall sing there as in the days of her youth…"*** (Hosea 2:15)

This is not only a beautiful story of Gomer's personal redemption and her husband's unconditional love for her; but also an allegory of God's everlasting love for His wayward people, Israel.

---

[11] Our Lord, Jesus the Messiah 1 Corinthians 15:57
[12] Romans 8:37
[13] Isaiah 7:14
[14] Isaiah 25:8, 1 Cor. 15:54
[15] Isaiah 1:18

As a young Jewish girl, I used to lead the singing of prayers and worship in our children's congregational Sabbath services. But as I grew older, I forgot my God and rejected my faith; choosing instead to walk in the ways of the world, looking for love in all the wrong places.

When God hedged my way in with thorns, causing my lovers to abandon me, and my mirth to cease, I thought I would never sing again. It felt like my life was over; my hope had been cut off. But then God performed a miracle in my life – He revealed Himself to me as a God of covenant, betrothing me to Himself forever in righteousness, lovingkindness, mercy and faithfulness through the Jewish Messiah, Yeshua.

He said, *"I will never leave you nor forsake you"*.

My first request was to sing for Him again; and He gave me that desire of my heart. The Valley of Achor has been turned into a door of hope and I sing to Him again as in the days of my youth.

Why are so many who have, by faith, walked through the sha'ar, the gate – this Petah Tikvah – opening of hope – still walking in hopelessness, despair and defeat? It is because of our stubborn refusal to take hold of everything that Yeshua died to give us.

He came to give us life and life more abundantly. He came to give us an inheritance of peace, love, joy and righteousness in the Holy Spirit. But we can be like prisoners, sitting in the gloom of our cells, depressed and discouraged, while the doors stand wide open, the brightness and warmth of sunshine and the musical sounds of birds singing beckoning us to freedom.

We are accepting a heavy covering of guilt and condemnation instead of the garments of praise and righteousness. **"Therefore there is <u>now no condemnation</u> for those who are in Messiah Yeshua, who live and walk not after the dictates of the flesh, but after the dictates of the Spirit."** (Romans 8:1)

God is good, merciful, and kind. He is longing to be gracious to us. He has a plan for our life – to give us hope and a future. When our relationship with the Lord is restored, then the murky waters of the Valley of Achor are cleansed and we can begin to see clearly again that there actually is hope for our future. The troubles of the past can be replaced with blessings:

"I will praise Your name, O Lord, for it is good. For He has delivered me out of all my trouble." (Psalm 54:6-7) Halleluyah!

Prayer: *God of Abraham, Isaac, and Jacob (Israel), thank You for revealing to us the sin of Achan and providing the remedy for the Valley of Achor through Yeshua, the door of hope (Petach Tikvah). Thank You, Yeshua, that You are the gate by which we may enter into eternal life by faith. Please reveal to us any 'herem' in our lives that may be causing us to continue wandering in the Valley of Achor, in perpetual trouble.*

Show us what we are holding onto or hiding that should rather be devoted to destruction. Burn it all away; for You, God, are a consuming fire. Forgive us and cleanse us. Help us to walk in the freedom that You died to give us. Teach us to walk in the peace, joy and righteousness that is our inheritance in You. Bring us through to victory, Lord, for Your namesake and to You be all the glory. Amen.

"Sharon will become a pasture for flocks, and the Valley of Achor a resting place for herds, for my people who seek Me." (Isaiah 65:10)

The Maternal Nature of God - El Shaddai אֵל שַׁדַּי

"*I appeared to Abraham, to Isaac, and to Jacob, as El Shaddai, but by My name YHVH* יְהוָה *I was not known to them.*" (Exodus 6:3)

El Shaddai is an interesting name for God which is usually translated in most English Bibles as 'God Almighty' or 'Almighty God'. We generally consider God as Father, calling Him Abba Father and praying, "*Our Father who art in Heaven….*"

I have heard some people even pray to God as 'Papa' or 'Daddy God'; but nevertheless we usually think of God in the masculine gender. This may prove to be problematic for those who suffered with an abusive, absent, or even an emotionally distant father.

No matter what kind of fathering we experienced as a child, good, bad or indifferent, we often tend to project the qualities of our imperfect earthly fathers onto our Heavenly Father – and this can create real problems in our relationship.

If we delve into the Hebrew meaning of the name, El Shaddai, however, we will discover quite a different, if hidden, dimension to the nature of God. El Shaddai אל שַׁדַּי actually relates to the Hebrew word, shad, שד which means **a woman's breast**. 'Shaddayim' שדיים is the Hebrew word for breasts.

El Shaddai therefore, reveals a maternal side to God's character: one of nurturer, comforter, and sustainer of life-giving nourishment.

Rather than a powerful 'Almighty God', El Shaddai more accurately portrays the image of a gentle, kind, nursing mother.

"Can a woman forget her nursing child, and not have compassion on the son of her womb? Surely they may forget, yet I will not forget you. See, I have inscribed you on the palms of My hands; your walls are continually before Me."
(Isaiah 49:15-16)

We must not forget that this scripture applies first and foremost to Zion (Israel). This is something that the Church often ignores in their spiritualization of scriptures relating to Israel. But I believe we may also take this promise of God for us personally. He created us. He loves us with the fierce and unconditional love of a mother for her nursing infant.

Several years ago, after giving birth, I gazed upon my newborn as he nursed and such love for him welled up within my heart. I thought, *"How I love you; I would do anything for you."* And I heard a little voice in my spirit whisper, *"I would do anything for you, too, Hannah."*

I realized that, in fact, Yeshua had done all that He could in sacrificing His life for me. Just as my little one hadn't done anything to deserve this great and tender love I have for him, so too does our God love us unconditionally; His love is totally unrelated to anything we may have done to try to earn or deserve it. His love for us is an even greater love than our limited and often fickle human capacity.

But can God be both mother and father? This is not some kind of feminist rhetoric; it is a biblical revelation that can bring healing to our relationship with God. If we look into the first book of the Bible, Genesis (Breisheet), we can see that when God created humankind in His own image, He created us male and female. Therefore, a clearer picture of God reveals both feminine and masculine qualities and characteristics.

"God created man in His own image, in the image of God He created him; <u>male and female</u> He created them." (Genesis 1:27)

The nation of Israel, in its infancy, had only known God as El Shaddai, the maternal nature of God – just as an infant is at first more closely bonded with its mother due to the intimacy of breastfeeding. The baby bonds with his mother through gazing into her eyes while suckling at her breast and receiving the life-giving nourishment he or she needs to survive.

When God sent Moses to deliver the children of Israel from bondage in Egypt, however, God revealed a new name: YHVH יְהוָה. Up until this point in Israel's relationship with God, they had only known Him as a mother who had cared for them, comforted them and nurtured this fledgling nation which had just been formed from the twelve sons of Jacob (Israel).

In order to bring forth new life, however, both a male and a female are required – both mother and father. When God brought His people out of Egypt, He was, in effect, birthing a new nation of holy people – a Royal Priesthood. Therefore, at this time, He revealed Himself to Moses and to the children of Israel as a Father. He revealed to them His name of power – protector, provider, deliverer, and redeemer.

Abba Father!

It was not going to take the sweet gentleness of a mother to deliver Israel out of Egypt – it was going to take the mighty hand and powerful, outstreched arm of the Father to set them free!

"So the LORD brought us out of Egypt with a mighty hand and with an outstretched arm, with great terror and with signs and wonders."
(Deuteronomy 26:8)

I dearly loved my sweet, gentle mother (may she rest in peace); but if I needed something done that was tough or difficult, or requiring physical strength, I would more likely call upon my father. Who do the kids call to get the stubborn lid off the jar? If possible, they usually call for Dad, Abba!

I remember a few days after my youngest son's circumcision (brit milah), the mo'el (the one who performs the circumcision) said we needed to change the bandages. Unfortunately, they had become stuck to the wound. Ouch!! My friend, Jennifer, who had come to help me with the birth, tried to remove the bandages, but even after soaking, they remained firmly stuck. Oye vey!

Brit Millah (Circumcision ceremony) with father holding the baby

Every time we tried to remove the bandages, the baby cried out in pain and our soft, maternal natures simply could not bear to cause him further suffering. So we had no other choice – the father had to be called in to do the dastardly deed – and he did.

God also wants to father us – not as our earthly fathers have perhaps, in their imperfect humanity, failed or disappointed us in some ways – but as our perfect Heavenly Father, who will never leave us or forsake us. He is good and all He does is for our good.

It took a powerful and mighty God to overcome Pharaoh and deliver the children of Israel from Egypt; and for some situations in our lives; we need this powerful, strong, incredibly awesome God's intervention as well. He is called 'El Gibor' (Mighty God). God wants us to know Him as a Father and feel comfortable in crying out to Him, Abba! (Daddy).

As important as a father is to provide, protect, train and discipline; the mother is equally important to raise a healthy, well-adjusted man or woman; and we need to know God as El Shaddai as well as El Gibor. It is the mother who provides the initial nourishment of breastmilk that is perfect for her infant.

True Nourishment

Soon after my youngest son, Avi-ad was born, we had a rough night. Every parent of a newborn experiences these at times. Avi just wouldn't or couldn't settle down to sleep for some reason. So we gave him a bottle of juice. When it came time for the next feeding, he fussed around and didn't want to nurse. So he got another bottle of juice just so we could get some sleep.

By the morning, he absolutely refused to nurse, screaming at the top of his lungs for another bottle of juice. Finally, with a great deal of patience and encouragement, Avi resigned himself to nursing even though it took more effort than the bottle and perhaps didn't taste as sweet.

The Lord showed me that His children are sometimes like this. God is not only our Father, but also like a mother who longs to nourish us with her breasts – the root word of 'Shaddai'. In our rebelliousness and stubbornness, we often seek for those things that appeal and promise quick gratification, but can never provide the true nourishment we need for life.

The Lord says, **"I have nourished and brought up children, and they have rebelled against Me."** (Isaiah 1:2)

Yeshua proclaimed Himself to be the fountain of living water. The Jewish people were shocked when He stood up on the last day of Sukkot (Feast of Tabernacles) and invited people to come and drink from the fountain: **"If anyone is thirsty, let him come to Me and drink."** (John 7:37)

Only El Shaddai can provide the real nourishment we need to sustain spiritual life. But instead of drinking from the fountain of living waters, we may instead turn to other sources of 'sustenance': relationships, work, possessions, entertainment and various addictions. But these 'quick fixes" can never truly satisfy the thirsting of our soul. Our flesh may crave these – but in actuality, they are broken cisterns that cannot hold water.

"For My people have committed two evils: they have forsaken Me, the fountain of living waters, and hewn themselves cisterns – broken cisterns that can hold no water." (Jeremiah 2:13) Let us surrender to His love and give Him the time to 'nurse' us, instead of running through life, hollering for a juice bottle.

Guardian of the Doors of Israel

The name, Shaddai, is often written on a Mezuzah, מְזוּזָה which is attached to the doorposts of every observant Jewish home to fulfill the biblical commandment to *"write the words of God on the gates and doorposts of your house."* (Deuteronomy 6:9)

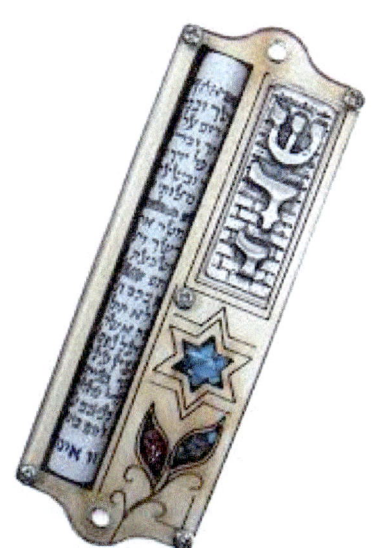

The mezuzah contains a piece of parchment, known as a 'klaf' upon which are written specific Hebrew verses (Deuteronomy 6:4–9, 11:13–21; Numbers 15:37–41) These verses contain the Jewish prayer, Sh'ma Yisrael, which begins with the phrase, *"Hear, O Israel, the Lord (is) our God, the Lord is One."*

Some Jewish people affix a mezuzah to their door simply as a means of affirming their Jewish identity or as a particular 'housewarming' ceremony.

A beautiful Jewish custom is that, whenever passing through a doorway, the person will touch a finger to the mezuzah as a way of showing respect to God. Many people also kiss their finger after touching it to the mezuzah. This is a way of saying, *"God I love you as I go in; and I love you as I go out"*. It is 'acknowledging God in all of our ways'.

But why is this specific name of God used to adorn the outside of a mezuzah? It is because the Hebrew letters *shin, dalet* and *yud* stand for *Shaddai* which is also an acronym for the words: <u>Shomer D'latot Yisrael</u> (Guardian of the Doors of Israel).

The mezuzah is not to be used as a kind of magical amulet which is forbidden in Scripture; but as a reminder that it is the Word of God which guards and keeps us. By affixing a mezuzah to the doorposts of the rooms of our home, we dedicate our dwelling place to Adonai and ask for His presence to dwell with us.

In the Shadow of Shaddai

There is a special kind of shelter we find only in the arms of our mother – a safe place of refuge from the dangers and perils of this world. It is a place of quietness, rest and peace. The Psalmist speaks of calming and quieting his soul – like a weaned child with its mother.

"Surely I have calmed and quieted my soul, like a weaned child with his mother; Like a weaned child is my soul within me." (Psalm 131:2)

The Hebrew name, Shaddai, describes this place of refuge: *"He who dwells in the secret place of Elyon* עֶלְיוֹן *shall abide under the shadow of Shaddai* שַׁדַּי*. I will say of the Lord, 'He is my refuge and my fortress, My God in Him I will trust.'"* (Psalm 91:1-2)

יֹשֵׁב, בְּסֵתֶר עֶלְיוֹן; בְּצֵל שַׁדַּי, יִתְלוֹנָן

God's maternal name, El Shaddai, is used in Psalm 91 in reference to abiding in the shadow (Betzel) of El Shaddai. The first artisan in the Bible was named Betzalel בְּצַלְאֵל, which means 'In the shadow (or shade) בְּצֵל of God

(El) אֵל.' Anyone serving the Lord in any kind of capacity needs to be hidden in the shadow of El Shaddai.

It is this maternal, protective quality that wants to hide our children under the shadow of our wings and keep them safe from every threat and danger.

Yeshua demonstrated this maternal, protective quality when he wept over Jerusalem, knowing the calamity that was about to befall them because they failed to listen to the warnings of the prophets who were sent to them.

"O Jerusalem, Jerusalem,…How often I wanted to gather your children together, as a hen gathers her chicks under her wings, but you were not willing!" (Matthew 23:37)

Abiding in the shade (tzel) or shadow of the Lord is such a secret, special place where we can find refuge.

"Be merciful to me, O God, be merciful to me! For my soul trusts in You; and in the shadow of Your wings I will make my refuge, until these calamities have passed by." (Psalm 57:1)

God, like a protective mother, wants to shield us from the harshness of this world – and it is often to our mother that we would run to get a hug and a bandaid after falling off our bikes and skinning our knees; or after a tough day at school being teased by bullies.

God wants to guard and protect us as well as comfort us when we are hurting. One of the names of the Holy Spirit is that of comforter.

"But the Comforter, which is the Holy Spirit, whom the Father will send in My name, He shall teach you all things, and bring all things to your remembrance, whatsoever I have said unto you." (John 14:26)

A hidden secret in the Hebrew is that the gender of the Holy Spirit (Ruach Hakodesh) is actually feminine! Yes, it is the female voice of intuition, her guidance, comfort and help that is the Holy Spirit – yet another expression of God's maternal nature.

There are times when we need a mother's comforting embrace. That is when Shaddai wraps her loving arms around us; and offers us a soft shoulder to cry on.[1]

"As a mother comforts her child, so I will comfort you, and you will be comforted in Jerusalem." (Isaiah 66:13)

The Lord literally fulfilled this promise to me when, after the agonizing death of my firstborn son in Canada, I returned to Israel and attended a women's conference in Jerusalem. Here, the Holy Spirit comforted me in my grief and loss as only a compassionate mother is able.

Shaddai the Peacemaker

Shaddai שדי is usually translated 'Almighty' in English from a Hebrew root שדד that means 'to overpower'; but many Bible scholars believe that this is a mistranslation. Interestingly enough, this root also can mean a demonic entity or power of darkness (shed שד). Therefore, El Shaddai means that God overpowers or prevails against all demonic powers. Once we are free of demonic oppression, we can enjoy inner peace and tranquility.

'Shaddai' can also mean *'to reconcile persons at enmity with one another'*. This expresses the oftentimes feminine ability to bring peace between two opposing and often hostile parties.

"He Himself (Yeshua) is our peace who has destroyed the enmity (hostility) between Jews and Gentiles by breaking down in His own flesh the dividing wall (machitzah) between us!" (Ephesians 2:14-16)

Yeshua Hamashiach, the Messiah, is the perfect representation of Shaddai – the compassionate, forgiving, nurturing, protective, gentle, maternal nature of God. Whenever we are in need of a mother's comforting embrace, may we find solace and healing in the gentle arms of El Shaddai.

---

[1] See chapter 20 The Comforter

Prayer: *Dear God, I have come to think of you as my Heavenly Father, and I give thanks that I can call you Abba Father. I know that You are a mighty God with all power to save, protect, provide and deliver. But I also want to know You as El Shaddai – a soft, gentle, compassionate mother who gives so sacrificially and loves so fiercely.*

Help me to see your soft, gentle, maternal side.

I need your comfort, nurturing care and the rich nourishment for my thirsty soul that only You can provide. Amen v'amen.

> **El Shaddai**
>
> **EL** – ALMIGHTY GOD
>
> **SHADDAI** is derived from the Hebrew word **SHAD** – meaning breast.
>
> **SHADDAI** means all-bountiful, all-sufficient, the breasty one who nourishes and supplies with more than enough

Trusting in the Lord - B'tach בְּטַח

"Trust in the Lord בְּטַח אֶל־יְהוָה *(b'tach el Yehovah) with all your heart and lean not on your own understanding; in all your ways acknowledge Him, and He will make your paths straight."* (Proverbs 3:5-6)

We are to trust in the Lord with all of our heart – even more so than in our own understanding of the situation from a natural point of view. Because our perspective is limited; but God sees the whole picture. He knows the end from the beginning.

If we trust in Him in this radical way; then we are promised supernatural guidance to walk in the right paths.

How often could we be spared immeasurable pain, heartache, trouble, and financial loss if we would simply trust in the Lord and submit to Him instead of following what we see, think and feel. But what exactly is trust from a Biblical Hebrew concept?

The Hebrew word for trust is b'tach בְּטַח; but there are several other words that are derived from this root word. In studying these, we can gain a deeper understanding of the concept of trusting in the Lord.

Definition of 'Trust'

Gesenius' Hebrew Lexicon defines 'trust' as: *"to set one's hope and confidence upon; to be secure fearing nothing"*, and it is many times translated as 'confidence', 'security', and 'hope'. We can see all these in the Hebrew word b'tach בטח.

Of course בטח

The word, **'betach'**, is an expression meaning, "of course!"; for example, if I was to ask my kids if they would like to go out for pizza, they would probably answer, "Betach!" It means: *"certainly, surely, sure, undoubtedly, of course."*

This is how we need to trust the Lord. Does He love us? Betach! Is He faithful? Betach! Is He good? Betach! Will He come through for us again? Betach! Will He provide for our needs? Betach! Is He fighting our battles for us? Betach!

Sure בטוח

Closely related to the word 'betach' is 'batuach' בטוח, which means 'sure', 'surely', assuredly, certain, or certainly. For example, it is this word used in the Hebrew song 'Ani Batuach':

"For I am certain (sure) (Ani Batuach) בטוח that neither death nor life, nor angels nor principalities nor powers, nor things present nor things to come, nor height nor depth, nor any other created thing, shall be able to separate us from the love of God which is in Messiah Yeshua our Lord." (Romans 8:38-39)

There are truths we must be so assured of that we can say, "Ani Batuach": that God is good; that nothing can separate us from His love; and that He will never leave or forsake us. Ani Batuach. I am so sure (certain) of these things that I know them as fact.

Confidence & Security ביטחון

Another related word is 'bitachon', which means confidence or security. Because we trust in God with all of our hearts; and being assured of the truth of His goodness and loving kindness, we can live with confidence and security.

We are living in a world that is ever increasingly unstable – where everything that can be shaken is shaking. In the natural, our future feels uncertain at best; and insecurity is running rampant with most people. But those who trust in the Lord are like Mount Zion which cannot be shaken. We are confident and secure – not in the state of the world, the economy or the government – but confident and secure in our God.

Insurance ביטוח

The Hebrew word for insurance is 'Bituach', ביטוח which is also closely related to batuach בטוח. Many people take out insurance policies – and for good reason!

Responsible people usually have a life insurance policy in place so that when they pass into eternity, their families are taken care of financially. At the very least, the deceased's debts will be paid off and funeral costs covered. Thank God my eldest son who passed away in 2017 had a life insurance policy through his work so that it paid for his estate expenses; and even left something for his two daughters.

I have, for some reason, a disability insurance policy that I've maintained for years. It seemed useless; but when my son broke his arm, that policy paid him a few thousand dollars.

Not having insurance can be problematic, as many people have found out when their homes were burned, bombed, broken into or flooded.

When my daughter and her new husband, Liat & Yanai, came to Israel, Liat automatically had health insurance as an Israeli citizen; but Yanai did not have any kind of health insurance. When he became sick; they had to pay for all the medical tests and expenses out of their own pocket. Yes, he should have taken out health insurance for tourists prior; but as my Dad always said, "Hindsight is 20/20".

Yes, insurance is important. Because the driver who rammed into my car from behind leaving it completely totaled had no auto insurance, I had to cover all the costs through my own insurance. Driving without car insurance is super risky.

My 19 year old son had been driving my car for months to go visit his girlfriend every weekend from the Negev to Tel Aviv. To my shock, I discovered that since his Canadian drivers license was no longer valid in Israel (you can only drive on a foreign license for one year), if any kind of accident had happened (God forbid), my insurance would not have covered him. And if he had injured someone else, he could have been sued for life! Oye vey!

That was the end of his driving until he finally got his Israeli drivers license. We dare not go through life without insurance (sounds like I should be an insurance salesman). :) Similarly, we can't make it through life safely and securely without our eternal life insurance policy – our Heavenly bitachon.

Yeshua has given us the assurance that if we believe in Him, even if we die, we will still live eternally. *Yeshua said*, ***"I am the resurrection and the life. He who believes in Me, though he may die, he shall live."*** (John 11:25)

This is the assurance we can have in God through Yeshua – we shall not perish but have eternal life.

"For God so loved the world that He gave His one and only Son, that everyone who believes in Him shall not perish but have eternal life." (John 3:16)

There is no security or trust outside of Yeshua; but in Him, there is nothing to fear.

Promise הַבטָחָה

There is one other related Hebrew word, and that is Havtachah, which means 'promise'. God's promises are sure – they are yes and amen; but we need to trust in Him to see them come to pass.

"For all the promises of God in Him are Yes, and in Him Amen, to the glory of God through us."
(2 Corinthians 1:20)

Let's be honest – there are things we go through in life that make it really tough to believe in God's promises. Loss, pain, sorrow, and all manner of trouble afflict us all; and yet through it all we need to trust in God and say, like Job, *"Though You slay me, yet will I trust in You."* [1] (Job 13:15)

We are not promised a trouble free life. In fact, Yeshua warned us of the opposite, saying, *"I've told you all this so that trusting Me, you will be unshakable and assured, deeply at peace. In this godless world you will continue to experience difficulties. But take heart! I've conquered the world."* (John 16:33)

That's a promise we don't like to say yes and amen to, but it is still true. So how do we trust when all of our circumstances are screaming at us to doubt and shrink back in fear? Like Paul, who probably experienced more tribulations than most in his lifetime of serving the Lord, we may declare that we are…

"…hard-pressed on every side, yet not crushed; perplexed, but not in despair; persecuted, but not forsaken; struck down, but not destroyed…"
(2 Corinthians 4:8-9)

And in the end, if we choose to continue trusting God, we will find ourselves in a beautiful place – the New Jerusalem – where God promises to *"wipe away every tear from our eyes"* and, *"there shall be no more death, nor sorrow, nor crying. There shall be no more pain, for the former things have passed away."* (Revelation 21:4)

---

[1] https://www.voiceforisrael.net/product-page/though-he-slay-me

The Hebrew letters in 'betach' בטח are 'bet' ב, 'tet' ט, and, a 'chet' ח.

Bet: Bayit בַּיִת

The first letter of the Hebrew word 'betach' בטח is 'Bet'. It represents a 'bayit' בַּיִת – a house – a place where we can abide and rest inside. We are told to trust 'in' . . . **"we have trusted *in* His holy name."** (Psalm 33:21)

Feeling like an outsider is painful. Life is full of rejection; but when we are 'in' covenant with God through His Son Yeshua, we become part of the family of God. Those who were once far away have been brought to a place 'inside' the house of God.[2]

There is such a sense of security in finding a home – a place to 'nest' and raise our young. ***"Yes, even the sparrow has found a home, and the swallow a nest for herself, where she may lay her young, even your altars, O LORD of hosts, my King, and my God."*** (Psalm 84:3)

---

[2] Ephesians 2:13

When we came back to Israel, God blessed us with a beautiful house to live in while its occupants were traveling in the United States. It was so peaceful in this quiet Negev town; it felt like a place of refuge as I sat in the garden, surrounded by flowers, watching the hummingbirds flit about and listening to the doves cooing.

"My people will dwell in a peaceful habitation, in secure dwellings, and in quiet resting places." (Isaiah 32:18)

When it became time to move, my sense of security evaporated; only to be restored once the Holy Spirit led me to my new home. Being homeless is not fun (been there, done that….). Several years ago, as new immigrants to Israel, we simply could not find a home at first; so we had to sleep wherever a kind soul would temporarily take us in – a humbling experience to say the least.

When my daughter married a nice, Messianic Canadian guy, and they came together to live in Israel, their first major challenge was to find a home. What a joy when they signed the lease on a beautiful apartment and received the keys to their first home in the Land. A home (bayit) is associated with safety, security, trust, and rest.

In the Beginning

The entire Bible begins with the letter bet. "In the beginning" (Genesis) is the word 'Breisheet' בְּרֵאשִׁית in Hebrew.

This shows us that even in the very beginning of time, God's desire for humanity is to have a peaceful, safe, secure home and family. In the beginning God created a beautiful garden of Eden in which mankind was intended to dwell.

The Bible also ends with a beautiful picture of perfect restoration, as God makes His home (dwelling place) with mankind again:

"Behold, the tabernacle of God is with men, and He will dwell with them, and they shall be His people. God Himself will be with them and be their God. And God will wipe away every tear from their eyes; there shall be no more death, nor sorrow, nor crying. There shall be no more pain, for the former things have passed away."
(Revelation 21:3-4)

Tet: Wrapped

The letter 'tet' is the second letter of the Hebrew word for trust, 'betach' בטח. This letter is a picture of something being wrapped or enveloped – like a mother holding a baby with her arm. Babies love to be wrapped or swaddled, as it causes them to feel safe and secure like they were in their mother's womb. Oftentimes, a mother will soothe a fussy baby by swaddling them tightly in a soft, cotton blanket. Even Yeshua was found wrapped in swaddling cloths in the manger.

To be unwrapped (or unswaddled), with limbs flailing about in the air, can feel like abandonment to an infant.

"As for your nativity, on the day you were born your navel cord was not cut, nor were you washed in water to cleanse you; you were not rubbed with salt nor wrapped in swaddling cloths." (Ezekiel 16:4)

God is our safe place of refuge. He wants to wrap us in His everlasting arms; to swaddle us in His soft blanket of love where we will find soothing comfort from the harshness and rejection of this world.

"The eternal God is your refuge (place of trust), and underneath are the everlasting arms." (Deuteronomy 33:27)

The letter 'tet' is also the first letter of the Hebrew word 'tov' טוב which means 'good'. Trust means knowing without a shadow of a doubt that God is good; and His mercy is everlasting.

"Oh, taste and see that the LORD is good; Blessed is the man who trusts in Him!" (Psalm 34:8)

Chet: Boundaries

The third letter in the word b'tach בטח is 'Chet' ח, which can look somewhat like a fence or wall. It is the first letter of the word 'chet' חטא, which means 'sin' and

also chaim חי"ם, which means life. While the letter bet is open on the side to indicate God's inclusive nature – willing to take anyone into His family who repents and turns to Him – chet speaks more of boundaries.

God is a boundary setting God; He sets limits for our own good. As His people, we tend to break these boundaries continually through sin. The wages of sin is death; but the gift of God is eternal life through Messiah Yeshua (Romans 6:23).

God sets before us a choice – life or death, blessing or cursing – but it is up to us to choose. ***"See, I set before you today life and prosperity, death and destruction. For I command you today to love the Lord your God, to walk in obedience to Him, and to keep His commands, decrees and laws; then you will live and increase, and the Lord your God will bless you in the land you are entering to possess."*** (Deuteronomy 30:15-16)

To trust God is to remain within the limits of the boundaries He sets up for us in every area of our life: our relationships, our finances, our work and rest patterns – even our food! If we will trust that God's way is best, then we will enjoy His protection and provision.

God is not under any obligation to protect us when we willfully step outside those fences He has built for our own good. Just like when the little Lion cub ventured into the Valley of the Dry Elephant Bones[3] and encountered the scavenging hyenas; so too do we put ourselves in the realm of the Kingdom of darkness and the domain of demons when we refuse to keep the commands of our Heavenly Father, the Lion of Judah.

---

[3] Movie Lion King

The promise of God's protection in His house is not for the disobedient and rebellious; but for the faithful, believing, and obedient.

"Blessed are those who do His commandments, that they may have the right to the tree of life, and may enter through the gates into the city. But outside are dogs and sorcerers and sexually immoral and murderers and idolaters, and whoever loves and practices a lie." (Revelation 22:14-15)

It is because of God's mercies, however, that we are not consumed in our sins; His compassions never fail; they are new every morning. Great is His faithfulness.[4] The word chesed חסד, meaning grace, mercy, and compassion, also starts with the letter chet ח. When we trust in the Lord, His 'chessed' surrounds us.[5]

"Many sorrows shall be to the wicked; but he who trusts in the LORD, mercy (chesed) shall surround him." (Psalm 32:10)

If we put these three letters together then: trust (b'tach) means resting in the Lord and abiding in His house; being secure in the knowledge of His goodness, wrapped in His everlasting arms of compassion, protected by the infinite wisdom of the boundaries He sets up for us; and embraced by His covenant love, compassion and favor. When we trust in God, we cling to Him like a fruit clings to the vine. A fruit that clings to the vine is the watermelon – called an 'avatiach'

אבטיח in Hebrew – it also contains the word for trust

בטח. Yeshua said, ***"I am the vine; you are the branches. If you remain in Me and I in you, you will bear much fruit; apart from Me you can do nothing."*** (John 15:5)

---
[4] Lamentations 3:22-23
[5] See chapter, "Favor, Grace and Mercy - Chen v' Chesed v' Rahamim"

.Some Trust In…

"Some trust in chariots, and some in horses; but we will remember the name of the LORD our God." (Psalm 20:7)

    The real question is, *"Who (or what) do you trust in?"*

People trust in all sorts of things: some trust in their relationships; some in their charisma or intellect; others trust in their career or bank balance. But trusting in these things is like standing on shifting sand instead of solid rock. It will never hold us up when the storms come.

"Everyone who hears these words of Mine, and doesn't do them will be like a foolish man, who built his house on the sand. The rain came down, the floods came, and the winds blew, and beat on that house; and it fell – and great was its fall." (Matthew 7:26-27)

God's word says not to trust in uncertain riches, for they can quickly fly away; but to trust in God who supplies richly all things needed for life and godliness.

"Command those who are rich in this present age not to be haughty, nor to trust in uncertain riches but in the living God, who gives us richly all things to enjoy." (1 Timothy 6:17)

In this uncertain world, the only sure place to put our trust is in God: *"Trust in the LORD בְּטַח בַּיהוָה, and do good; dwell in the land, and feed on His faithfulness."* (Psalm 37:3)

Trusting When We Don't Understand

Trusting in God is not always easy. If we are honest, we would admit that He is not completely predictable; His ways are not our ways. He doesn't always do what we want or give us what we ask for. God is not like a slot machine that we can just put in our $5 and get the exact drink we pushed the button for.

There are times when God doesn't seem to answer our prayers – how do we trust Him then? When my eldest son was suffering from a terrible wasting disease and addicted to doctor-prescribed painkillers, I begged and pleaded with God for his healing. But in December 2017 he was found dead in his apartment.

Photo by Lisa Swenson

For the longest time, I wrestled with my faith. How can I trust in a God who didn't heal my son? When I questioned God, I received no immediate answers, but (in true Jewish form) He answered my question with a question of His own, *"Hannah, will you still trust me even when you don't understand?"*

It took me a while; but finally I could say, *"Yes, Lord, I choose to trust You. Even though I don't understand."* After all, where else could I go? It was like Yeshua's disciples, who didn't understand His words when He said to drink His blood and eat His body. Many walked away from Him; but there were those who said, **"Where else would we go? You have the words of eternal life… and we have come to believe that You are the Messiah, the Son of the living God."** (John 6:68-69)

I don't know what may be standing between you and fully trusting in the Lord; but I hope to encourage you to trust Him anyways. He is faithful; and even when we don't understand, He will, somehow, in some way, at some time cause all things to work together for good. So… trust in the Lord with all of your heart. He is worthy of our wholehearted trust.

"The LORD is my strength and my shield; my heart trusted (batach) in Him, and I am helped; therefore my heart greatly rejoices, and with my song I will praise Him." (Psalm 28:7)

Prayer: *Dear God, thank You that no matter what happens in our lives, even if we don't understand, we can always trust in You, because You are absolutely faithful. There is so much in this life that we cannot trust in – we can't trust in our own abilities, strength or resources, our own understanding, or even at times in other people – but You are the One who is worthy of our trust. You are our confidence, our sure foundation, our help and our shield, and our hearts trust in You.*

Walking in the Wilderness - Midbar מִדְבָּר

"And the Lord spoke to Moses in the wilderness (B'midbar) of Sinai, in the tent of meeting, on the first day of the second month, in the second year after they had come out of the land of Egypt." (Numbers 1:1)

The desert (midbar) is a land of stinging scorpions, venomous snakes and giant, hairy spiders! It is a dry and thirsty land of endless sand; where water is scarce; and the scorching sun beats down mercilessly upon all its inhabitants.

The Psalmist, David, experienced this when he was in the Desert of Judah:

"You, God, are my God, earnestly I seek you; I thirst for you, my whole being longs for you, in a dry and parched land where there is no water." (Psalm 63:1)

Although the desert seems (on the surface) to be a place that is hostile to life, where we are dry and thirsty; the Hebrew contains a hidden secret, showing us that a wilderness experience can actually be both valuable and necessary for our spiritual growth.

Word of God Speak!

The Hebrew word for desert (or wilderness) '**midbar**' מדבר contains the exact same letters as the word for speak which is '**m'daber**' מדבר.

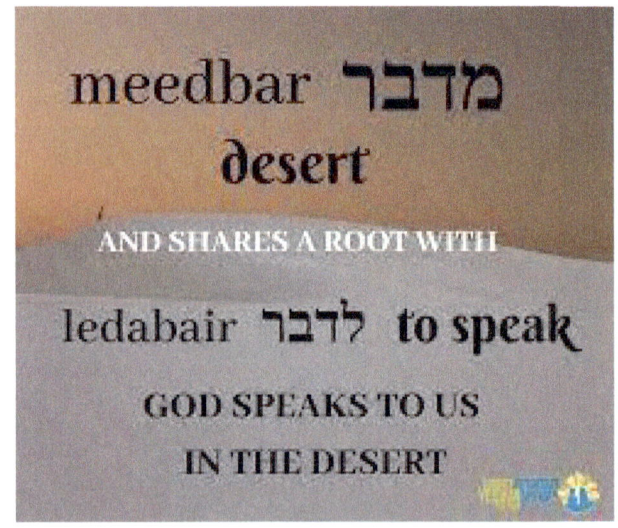

It is in the silence and isolation of the wilderness times of our lives that God can speak a 'word in due season' to our hearts. Many times in Scripture we see people receiving a significant word from the Lord in the wilderness.

Sometimes we find ourselves in the wilderness because we are running away from our problems. Sarah's maid was fleeing from her mistress when an angel found Hagar in the wilderness and gave her clear direction for her life. *"The angel of the Lord found her by a spring of water in the wilderness... The angel of the Lord said to her, 'Return to your mistress and submit to her.'"* (Genesis 16:7-9)

When we are running away from our problems and find ourselves in the wilderness; God might just tell us to go back and face them in submission and humility. Hagar also received a prophetic word that her unborn son would be called Ishmael (whose name means 'God hears') because God had heard her affliction and wanted to help her.

So she called God El Roi אֵל רֳאִי – God who sees. He hears our cries and He sees our troubles, even when we find ourselves lost in the wilderness of life.

It is in the very midst of the 'midbar' that God may speak a special word to our heart, and we may come to know Him as the God who sees everything we are going through;

who cares deeply about all the pain and suffering we endure. In all our afflictions He is afflicted.[1] He is a man of sorrows and well acquainted with grief.

Prepared in the Wilderness

The 'Word of the Lord' also came to John the Baptist (Yochanan the Immerser) in the silence and solitude of the wilderness.

"...the word of God came to John the son of Zacharias in the wilderness."
(Luke 3:2)

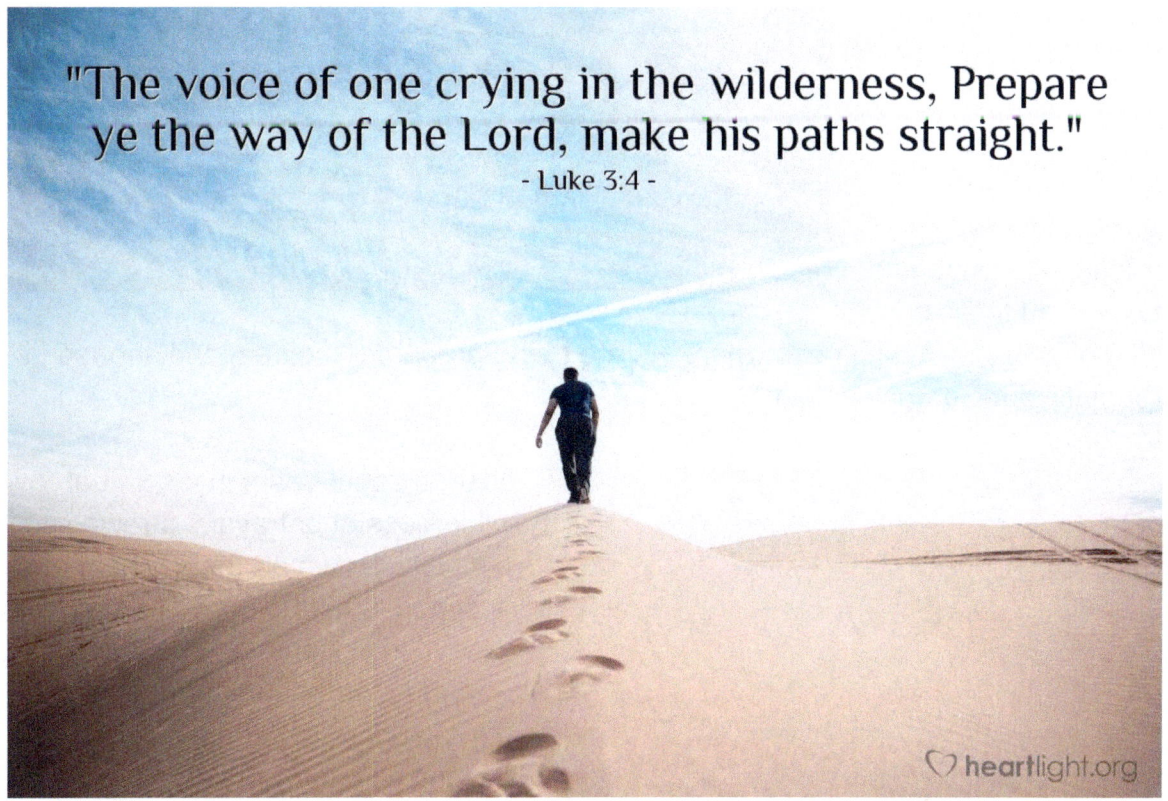

It was here in the 'midbar' that John became a *'voice crying out in the wilderness'* to prepare the way of the Lord. ***"I am the voice of one crying out in the wilderness, 'Make straight the way of the Lord', as the prophet Isaiah said."*** (John 1:23)

Moses also spent many lonely years in the wilderness simply tending his father-in-law's sheep after running away from Egypt. It seems like a complete waste of forty good years of his life; but during this time, he was being prepared for his destiny as a deliverer of His people Israel.

---
[1] Isaiah 63:9, Isaiah 53:3

It was on '*the far side of the wilderness*' that God spoke to Moses from the midst of a burning bush, sending him on a mission to deliver the children of Israel from slavery in Egypt.

"God called to him from within the bush, 'Moshe! Moshe!' And Moses said, 'Here I am (Hineini).'" (Exodus 3:4)

When God speaks will we answer, "Hineini (Here I am)"?

We need to understand that our seasons of wandering in the wilderness, far from being simply '*wasted time*', can be times of great spiritual growth where we are being prepared, molded, and shaped in order to fulfill our God-given destiny.

Joseph spent years in a spiritual wilderness of betrayal – thrown into a pit by his own brothers. The man destined to lead a nation served as a slave in Potipher's house, and was then forgotten in an Egyptian dungeon for a crime he did not commit.

And yet in one day, when God knew he was ready, he went from the prison to the palace!

Do you ever feel like you are in a **PIT**? Don't lose heart – you are simply a **P**rophet **I**n **T**raining!

Joseph was not running away from his problems, like Hagar or Moses or even David; but rather was pushed into a wilderness season by those who hated him.

David also was destined to be the King of Israel; and yet Saul forced him to flee to the wilderness caves of Ein Gedi and live like a fugitive!

We may sense that God has a special destiny upon our lives; and yet there are times when circumstances seem to force us into a wilderness season. At other times, it is the Holy Spirit who leads a person into the wilderness. Yeshua Himself was led into the wilderness by the Ruach Hakodesh (Holy Spirit) to be tested by the devil.

"Then Yeshua was led by the Spirit into the wilderness to be tempted by the devil." (Matthew 4:1)

This came immediately after God had placed his seal of approval upon Yeshua by announcing, **"This is my beloved son, in whom I am well pleased"** at His Jordan River baptism.[2]

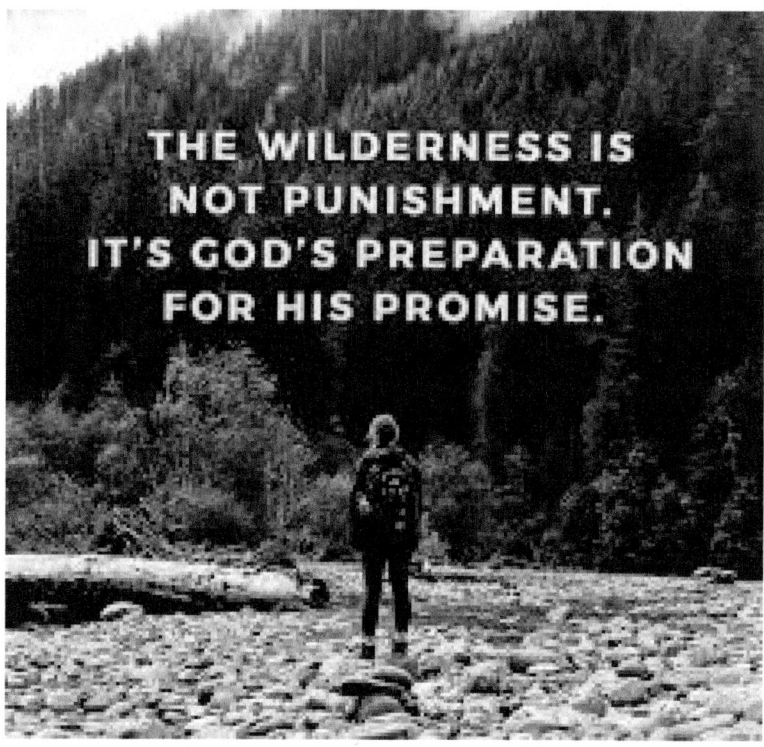

Being led into the wilderness was not a punishment from God; but rather a necessary stage of Yeshua's spiritual journey. God may take us directly from the waters of acceptance to the wilderness of testing where we must pass through many trials.

---

[2] Matthew 3:17

Broken, Humbled and Tested in the Wilderness

Whether we are running away from our problems, pushed in by our sin or the sin of others; or even following the leading of the Holy Spirit, the wilderness (midbar) is a tough place. It is a season of being broken, humbled, and tested by God to see what is in our hearts – whether we will obey His commandments or not:

"And you shall remember the whole way that the Lord your God has led you these forty years in the wilderness, that He might humble you, testing you to know what was in your heart, whether you would keep His commandments or not." (Deuteronomy 8:2)

It is in the 'midbar' that we learn to depend upon God for His faithful guidance and supernatural provision. We are refined of selfish ambition, pride, and the illusion of self sufficiency.

"And He humbled you and let you hunger and fed you with manna, which you did not know, nor did your fathers know, that He might make you know that man does not live by bread alone, but man lives by every word that comes from the mouth of the Lord." (Deuteronomy 8:3)

Where's my GPS When I Need it?

One of the worst things about the wilderness is feeling lost. I don't know if anyone has come up with a word for it yet, but I have a phobia of being lost. As soon as I start to feel like I don't know where I'm going or can't find my way, I start to panic! Sometimes I actually freak out!

Okay, I googled it. **Mazeophobia**, the scientific name for the fear of being lost, is caused by the emotional unsettling of being in an uncomfortable or unknown place.

In the age of GPS, we forget how easy it can be to get disorientated. I thank God for whoever invented the GPS, or in Israel a more commonly used app called WAZE. I think they should get the Nobel Peace prize. I honestly don't know how anyone found their way anywhere without it. I once tried to navigate from Tiberius back to my home in the Judean Hills without my GPS. It had become broken in a recent car accident (don't ask…).

It seemed very simple – just follow the road signs – never a good idea in Israel. My ex-husband was a professional driver; he had a crazy good sense of direction – but the road signs in Israel drove him nuts! What following them only does, is to keep you running around (or driving around) in perpetual circles.

At one point, I just pulled off the highway and had a breakdown, wailing loudly about being lost, much to the distress of my two young children in the back seat who didn't understand why their normally calm, normal mother was acting like a maniac.

Thankfully I had the good sense to call my daughter, who put her husband on the phone, who guided me onto the right highway to get me home. After a good cry, some coffee and way too many greasy fries from a gas station restaurant, I had the fortitude to make it safely home. Thank God.

I can imagine the despair of the children of Israel who wandered around and around the same mountain for forty years in the wilderness until they died.

Yes, the wilderness can actually be fatal – but it doesn't have to be.

The one thing we need to make it out of the wilderness alive is – simple, child-like, FAITH! It was unbelief that kept the Israelites out of their Promised Land. We must believe that God's plans for us are for good – to give us a hope and a future – and that He is guiding us through this dry and weary wilderness to a good land, flowing with milk and honey.

"For we walk by faith, not by sight." (2 Corinthians 5:7)

When we feel that we have lost our way, God still knows where we are and how to bring our feet back onto the right path. There is nowhere we can go that we are too lost or too far for God to find us.

"Where can I go from Your Spirit?
Or where can I flee from Your presence?

If I ascend into heaven, You are there;
If I make my bed in hell, behold, You are there.

If I take the wings of the morning, and dwell in the uttermost parts of the sea,

Even there Your hand shall lead me, and Your right hand shall hold me."
(Psalm 139:7-10)

Desert Dwellers

Hannah and her family standing in front of their home in the Negev

Are you walking through a wilderness season? I can sympathize with you!

As someone who lived for several years in the Negev desert region of Israel, '*schvitzing*' (sweating) in the sweltering summer heat while six months pregnant with my youngest son, Avi-ad, I can honestly say, *"Been there; done that"*!

(And, may I add, *"…wouldn't want to do that again!"*)

It was in the Negev that I very nearly lost my life and that of my precious son. What was supposed to be a home birth turned into a life-threatening emergency. Hemorrhaging profusely, I was transported by ICU ambulance to a hospital in Beer sheva for an emergency Cesarean section surgery. No one expected either me or the baby to live.. But God….

It was also from the midbar (desert) that our family was evicted from the Land of Israel. My (then) husband was refused a Visa and was given fourteen days to leave the country.

Receiving the bad news - our eviction notice from Israel Dec 2002

Yes, I know from experience that the wilderness can be a very challenging place to live indeed – and yet we can take heart in knowing that God is faithful. He will never leave us or forsake us. God's Word promises that He will not give us more than we can bear; but will always provide a way of escape.

Intimacy with God in the Wilderness

God will often speak to us in our wilderness experiences. I will always remember when they were transferring me on a stretcher from the regular ambulance to the ICU ambulance (that had finally caught up with us en route to the hospital) that I felt a gentle rain on my face and felt complete peace. It was so beautiful; I knew it was God's sweet, gentle presence.

God, speaking through the Prophet Hosea, said that *He would bring His bride into the wilderness (the midbar) not to harm her; but rather to* **"speak tenderly to her in the midbar.. and turn the valley of Achor (trouble) into a door of hope (Petah Tikvah)."** (Hosea 2:14-15)

There are times when God must, just as He did with Hosea's unfaithful wife, hedge our way with thorns; cause all of our merriment and partying to cease; cause friends and lovers to flee from us; and bring us into a midbar (wilderness) season – a dry and weary land where water is scarce.

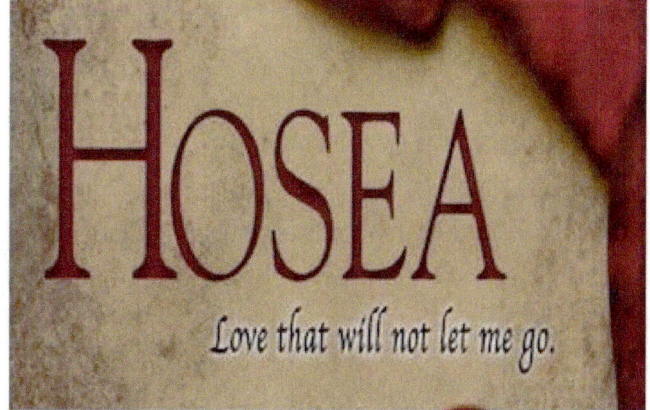

We can feel abandoned and lonely for a time. But do not lose heart, dear friends, because this is the place where God will speak tenderly to our heart and will allure us back to Himself.

"Therefore, behold, I will allure her, will bring her into the wilderness, and speak comfort to her." (Hosea 2:14)

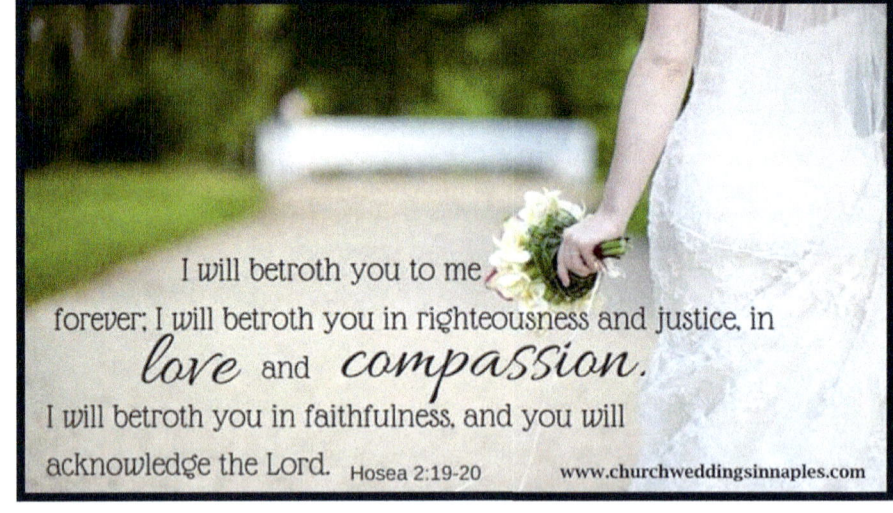

God's intention is not to punish us in the wilderness, but to woo us back into a close, intimate relationship with our Bridegroom who promises His beloved Bride, ***"I will betroth you unto Me forever"***, says the Lord. (Hosea 2:19)

Leaning on our Beloved

Once we are ledced out of our wilderness season, we have learned not to rely on our own strength or abilities, but to 'lean on our beloved'.

"Who is this coming up out of the wilderness leaning on her Beloved?" (Song of Solomon 8:5)

Journey to the Promised Land

The wilderness (desert, midbar) מדבר has so many beautiful lessons to teach us: intimacy with and dependency upon God; the value of silence and solitude; the necessity of rest; letting patience do its perfect work in us. We learn to endure, to persevere, to be faithful in the little things; and to forgive.

In the midbar we learn to trust and obey, for there truly is no other way to get through… Yes, the wilderness is a very important (if not essential) time in our lives, and yet God never intends to leave us there; He always points us to the 'better land' where He wants to take us – a land of beauty and abundance – flowing with milk and honey.

"For the Lord your God is bringing you into a good land, a land of brooks of water, of fountains and springs, flowing out in the valleys and hills, a land of wheat and barley, of vines and fig trees and pomegranates, a land of olive trees and honey, a land in which you will eat bread without scarcity, in which you will lack nothing." (Deuteronomy 8:7-9)

The only way to the Promised Land, however, is through the wilderness. Israel has done an amazing job of transforming her deserts into beautiful, blooming, flowering places that resemble the Garden of Eden, just as the ancient Hebrew prophets promised would one day happen. And this has taken place in our very generation! Selah….

"For the Lord will comfort Zion, He will comfort all her waste places; He will make her wilderness like Eden, and her desert like the garden of the Lord; joy and gladness will be found in it, thanksgiving and the voice of melody." (Isaiah 51:3)

The Prophet Ezekiel spoke of the day when, instead of lying desolate and barren, the land would become fertile again. ***"The desolate land shall be tilled instead of lying desolate in the sight of all who pass by."*** This would be so astonishing that people would marvel at the transformation and say, ***"This land that was desolate has become like the garden of Eden."*** (Ezekiel 36:34-35)

After the winter rains, entire regions of the wilderness are covered with pretty red poppies and we celebrate with a festival called **Darom Adom (Red South Festival).**

Red Anemone in Shokeda Forest during the blooming season (Mid- January to end of February), in northern Negev region of Israel.

Hannah at the Darom Adom (Red South) festival in the Negev Desert.

The deserts of Israel are now blooming and blossoming with beautiful flowering trees of every color that proclaim the glory and goodness of God!

"The wilderness (midbar) מִדְבָּר ***and the wasteland shall be glad for them, and the***

desert shall rejoice and blossom as the lily [3] *(havtzelet)* חֲבַצָּלֶת*; it shall blossom abundantly and rejoice, even with joy and singing."* (Isaiah 35:1-2)

"...for in the wilderness (midbar) מִדְבָּר *waters shall break out, and rivers in the desert."* (Isaiah 35:6)

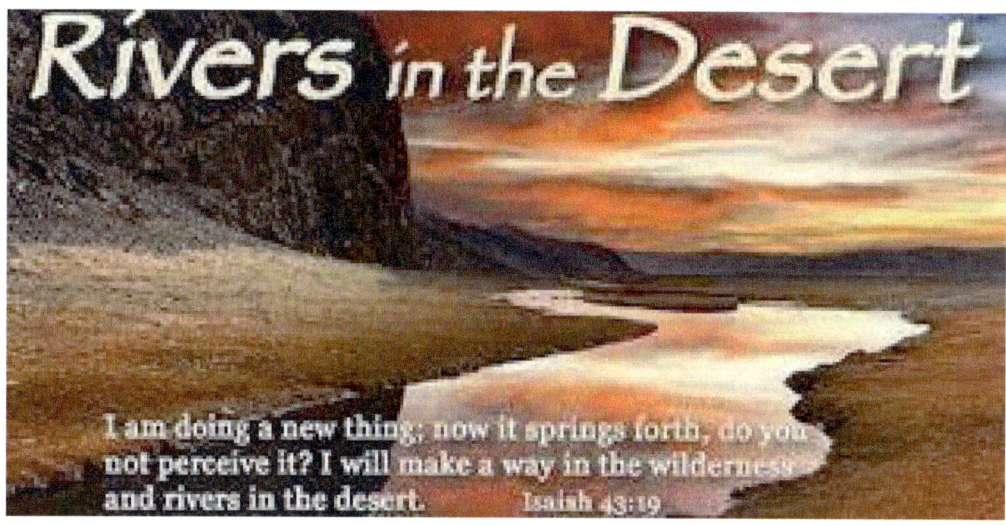

The Hebrew prophet Isaiah poetically called the desert "A highway for God" – a way of holiness that only those who have learned to walk in holiness will find.

"And a highway shall be there, and a way, דֶּרֶךְ *(derech) and it shall be called the way of holiness."* (Isaiah 35:8)

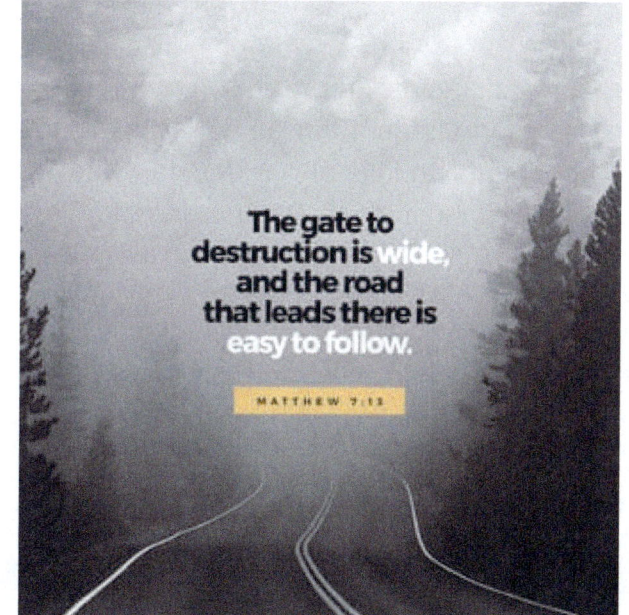

The unclean (defiled – tameh) shall not pass over it; but it will be for him who walks in purity and holiness.

Yeshua is **"the way, the truth and the life"**.[4] He is the 'derech' דֶּרֶךְ – the way to eternal life. But we must enter

---

[3] The Hebrew word used here, havtzelet, means the lily, not the rose as is commonly translated in English.
[4] John 14:6

through the narrow gate; for wide is the gate and broad is the way that leads to destruction – and many are walking along that path today –but narrow is the gate and difficult the way that leads to life, and few find it. (Matthew 7:13-14)

The Hebrew prophet, Isaiah, also spoke of a day to come when the sun-scorched land would become a pool of refreshment. *"And the parched land shall become a pool, and the thirsty ground springs of water."* (Isaiah 35:7)

Israel stands as a sign or beacon of hope for all peoples in all nations. If God can (and did) transform Israel's barren wilderness into a beautiful Garden of Eden, will He not also be faithful to take all the dry, desolate, barren areas of our life and transform them also into a flourishing, fruitful garden of glory?

"The righteous shall flourish like a palm tree…Those who are planted in the house of the LORD ***shall flourish in the courts of our God. They shall still bear fruit in old age; they shall be fresh and flourishing."*** (Psalm 92:12-14)

God wants to do a new thing in our lives – making a way in the wilderness and rivers of living water in the desert (midbar). If we will humble ourselves, stay in faith and be obedient, I believe we will hear His voice saying, **"This is the way, walk ye in it"**. [5]

Prayer: *Dear God, it feels, at times, like we are walking through an endless wilderness season, a dry and weary land, where it's just the same old, same old, day in and day out; and yet You are our source of Living Water. You can make the barren, empty places in our life fresh, fruitful and flourishing again. Come, Holy Spirit (Ruach Hakodesh) and revive our weary hearts with Your refreshing rain. Renew our vision, Lord, so we can see the 'good land' that lies beyond this wilderness, that we may not lose heart. Help us not to see this season as 'wasted time' or even a punishment; but rather Your way of preparing us for our destiny. May we come out of this wilderness in faith, leaning on our Beloved. In Yeshua's name. Amen v'amen.*

Blessings on your journey to the Promised Land!

---

[5] Isaiah 30:21
[6] Photos by Liat Whelan https://www.light-tothenations.com/

When Comfort Becomes a Handicap - Necheh נכה

We all like to be comfortable – at least I certainly do! My kids say I'm like one of those tropical fish that tolerate only a very narrow range of temperature variation. Anything outside their comfort zone, and they soon become sick or even die. As a former Canadian who somehow survived brutally long, cold winters, I really really don't like to be cold! But as an Israeli desert dweller, I can tell you that I also really really don't like to be too hot either!

Not too cold, not too hot – like Goldilocks in the story of the three bears, I like it 'just right'!

Yes, I'm a girl who likes her comfort – I generally refuse to wear anything that pinches, pokes, scratches, or squeezes – which means I'm perpetually in 'schlumpy wear' mode. No high heels for me! It's orthopedic sandals from the 'Comfort Store' all the way! They say there's a price to be fashionable; but if the price means giving up my comfort then I'm just not paying.

And since I tend to feel uncomfortable at social gatherings, I often try to find a cozy corner to hide out in rather than introducing myself to new people or striking up conversations with acquaintances.

My son, Avi, still calls this syndrome 'erev marak', meaning 'soup evening' from the disastrous social event in which all the parents from his school were to bring their favorite soup for everyone to sample – ie. meet one another. Needless to say, feeling woefully inadequate to converse in Hebrew, painfully shy as a single mother in the midst of all the two parent families, and completely unfamiliar with all the Israeli folk songs they were all jubilantly singing, Avi found me sipping my soup alone in the corner.

Ah... introverts – gotta love us!

Most of us, however, are creatures of comfort; not just in matters of temperature, clothing or relationships, but in almost every area of our lives. We park as close to the door of the mall as possible; we love our comfy recliners where we can put our feet up; and the idea of relaxing in a hammock on a beach somewhere under the shade of a palm tree seems utter bliss.

The Hebrew word for comfortable is 'noach' נוֹחַ from the root word 'nach' נַח which means 'rest' or quiet. It is the Hebrew name of Noah (as in Noah's ark), which can also mean comfort:

noah
{rest, comfort}

"And he called his name Noah, נֹחַ saying: 'This same shall comfort us יְנַחֲמֵנוּ in our work and in the toil of our hands, which comes from the ground which Adonai has cursed.'" (Genesis 5:29)

This is the same word used when God says, **"Comfort, comfort My people..."**

נַחֲמוּ נַחֲמוּ, עַמִּי

Nachamu nachamu ami

There is another related Hebrew word, ha'niach הֵנִיחַ, which means to **rest or lay** something upon something else. For example, when we lay our credit card on the machines that magically take the money out of our accounts, we use this word.

There are times when it's good to just lay something down, casting our cares upon the Lord and simply rest in Him. Our Good Shepherd will sometimes **"make us to lie down in green pastures"**[1] in order to restore our soul.

Yes, times of rest and quietness can definitely be a comfort to our body, mind, soul and spirit. God actually commands us to rest every seventh day on the Sabbath (Shabbat), in order that we may be refreshed, but there may be times when too much comfort can become a hindrance to our spiritual growth and development.

---

[1] Psalm 23:2

A Hebrew word that sounds the same but uses a different letter is necheh נכה which means 'handicapped'. It can also mean 'disabled', 'crippled' or invalid. There are times when too much comfort can actually cripple us or leave us handicapped in some aspect of our lives.

We all know the result of giving a child every creature comfort and indulging their every whim – like the spoiled little girl in 'Willy Wonka and the Chocolate Factory', she whines and cries, "*But I wanted a trained pony, Daddy!*"

Our flesh is never satisfied; and if given the opportunity, our carnal nature will seek out comfort at every opportunity. Soldiers, however, are trained and equipped not through comfort and ease; but rather through hardship – lying in the trenches, sleeping on the cold, hard ground; and trudging along on grueling, lengthy marches carrying heavy backpacks and the wounded on stretchers.

My son, Avi-ad, training with his IDF special forces unit on a 50 km march

We are all, as followers of Yeshua, in the army of the Lord; and He is training us to endure hardship as good soldiers.² He is training our hands for war and our fingers for battle.³

Because whether we like it or not, when we join the Kingdom of God, we find ourselves in a war zone – fighting against the Kingdom of Darkness.

"For our struggle is not against flesh and blood, but against the rulers, against the authorities, against the powers of this dark world and against the spiritual forces of evil in the heavenly realms." (Ephesians 6:12)

No JOBNIKS in the Army of the Lord

We sometimes moan and groan in our 'discomfort', *"Why does life have to be so hard?? Why couldn't it just come easy for a change?"* But God is training His soldiers for victory in the battle; and He selects His very best soldiers to go through especially tough training.

Within Israel's combat battalions are those selected for 'special forces units' such as commando, counter-terrorism, and hostage rescue. These highly trained soldiers are often given extremely dangerous missions and must go through grueling training.

My son, Avi-ad, qualified for a reconnaissance unit called Sayeret Matkal, and I know from his firsthand reports of the hardships they were required to endure: from long marches carrying 'wounded' soldiers on heavy stretchers through extreme heat in the desert wearing full military gear to suffering hypothermia in the cold northern regions of Israel without jackets, blankets or shelter. And this was just for a start….

In the IDF, those who choose not to join the combat forces are called 'jobniks' – the ones who technically serve in the military but have some kind of cushy, air-conditioned office job. They may be somewhat scoffed at by those who choose to endure the

---

² 2 Timothy 2:3
³ Psalm 144:1

rigorous training required for combat positions; those who put their lives on the line at the borders and who are sent out on dangerous missions.

But there are NO JOBNIKS in the army of the Lord. We are all engaged in mortal combat with spiritual forces of darkness who seek to steal, kill and destroy God's people. So how does God train and equip us for victory against the enemy?

It is not through comfort; but rather through the pressure of trials and tribulations which cause us to either 'do or die'.

What Doesn't Kill you Makes you Stronger

My Mom used to say, "*The troubles that don't kill you make you stronger.*" It is the first part of that saying that always concerned me! But God says He will never give us more than we can bear; but will always provide a way of escape.[4] He promises that His grace will always be sufficient for everything He allows to trouble us.[5]

We don't necessarily like these messages about how trials make us stronger. We just want to put our feet up in our recliner and watch netflix with a big bag of chips (or is it only me?). Have you ever pleaded with God, saying something like,

"Just leave me alone! I don't care about my character; I just want things to be easier!!"

Our human nature generally doesn't favor change; we like to stay in our little, comfortable (even if dull, boring and confining) comfort zones. We have our little boats and want to stay in them rather than walk on the water and risk drowning.

---

[4] 1 Corinthians 10:13
[5] 2 Corinthians 12:9

Life begins at the End of our Comfort Zone

The truth is, however, that life usually exists just outside our comfort zone! It is when we get out of our boat and step out on the water that we begin an adventure of faith that encounters Yeshua. And once we have even tried and failed to walk on water; we can never again return to our previously dreary existence in our so-called 'safe and secure' comfort zones.

When Yeshua called Peter out of the boat, He called him into a life of radical faith.[6] When we made aliyah[7] to Israel, we definitely stepped out of our comfort zone. We knew nothing about living in Israel – had no idea where we would go or what we would do to survive here – but God honored our crazy, perhaps foolish faith. He guided and provided every step of the way! And although we went through many hardships, I'm so glad that we dared to step out of our little boat.[8]

Why Should We Just Sit Here Till We Die?

The Bible tells us the story of four lepers who were safe and secure while under siege; but they were dying and they knew it. They said, **"Why should we just sit here until we die?"**[9] They got up, left their comfort zone; and God did a miracle! He made their footsteps sound like a mighty army to the enemy; and so they just walked straight into

---

[6] Matthew 14:29-30
[7] Aliyah - to immigrate to Israel
[8] https://www.voiceforisrael.net/product-page/journey-to-jerusalem-1
[9] 2 Kings 7:3

the enemy camp and gathered up all the spoils. Not only did they save themselves from sure death by starvation; but they saved all of Israel.

There are people spiritually starving out there, and we have the living bread they need – but we have to be willing to get out of our comfort zones and go out into all the world – making disciples of all nations.[10] If we stay in our 'safe and secure', meaningless, purposeless little lives, we will surely die of spiritual starvation.

Hineini - Here am I

We are called to the nations – but here's the catch – it's going to be uncomfortable; it's going to involve hardship, and maybe even persecutions. Are we still willing to say, **"Hineini – Here I am – send me!"** We need to count the cost, as Yeshua warned us, because the price of a life of adventure with God can require surrendering everything we have; and all we are.

And yet the cost of not heeding the call is so much more! We may be comfortable, but our soul will shrivel and die if we are not living with purpose and passion, fulfilling the calling and destiny that God has for us. If we are not willing to give up some of our comfort, then we may become spiritually handicapped, crippled or even an invalid – needing constant care from others in order to survive.

We know that the mother eagle makes the nest uncomfortable for her eaglets in order to persuade them to attempt flying. She starts pulling out the comfy bedding and throwing out the toys. Is our 'nest' becoming uncomfortable? Is it possible that we are being pushed to fly?

Perhaps as parents, we need to learn a lesson from Mama Eagle and not make our 'nest' so comfortable that our 'eaglets' never want to leave; unless we want to end up with our 30 something year old sons living in our basement playing video games.

Just saying….

---

[10] Matthew 28:19

And don't forget to flap like your life depends on it.

Another related word, Necheh נכא, with a letter aleph at the end, means 'smitten or afflicted'. It is related to necha'im נכאים, which means dejection or depression. If we are feeling depressed or dejected, perhaps we need to see if we have simply become too comfortable.

When we moved back to Canada for a season, I attempted to live a 'normal life': eating and drinking and shopping and running errands like every 'normal' person seems to do. I was definitely comfortable in my centrally heated house with instant hot water and wall to wall carpeting; but as the days, weeks and months dragged on, I grew more and more depressed and dejected.

A place to nest can be a blessing …until it isn't… When the cloud lifts and starts to move, we had better be ready and willing to pack up camp and move with the cloud or be left sitting there without the covering of the shechinah glory of God!

As I became more and more depressed and dejected in this nice, comfortable place, I kept asking myself (& God), *"Why can't I just settle down and live a 'normal life' like everyone else?"* Maybe it's because some of us are not called to live a so-called 'normal life'.

Perhaps we have instead been appointed, prepared and called as a Prophet to the Nations.[11] Prophets are never 'normal' and so maybe it's time to stop trying to fit in and

---

[11] Jeremiah 1:5

settle down. Maybe it's time to get out of the chicken coop and soar in clear, blue, open skies like the eagle we have been created to be.

As believers, we are not called to seek comfort; but to seek first the Kingdom of God and His righteousness and then all these other things we desire will be added unto us.

Lech Lecha!

God spoke to a man named Abram, saying, "Lech Lecha"! (Go ye!). He called him to leave his mother, father, land, home, possessions, people, and all that was comfortable and familiar to him in Ur of the Chaldees in order to embark on a great adventure to 'a place that God would show him'.[12]

He didn't even know where he was going, for goodness sake! But He knew the voice of the One calling him to go; and Abram obeyed.

"By faith Abraham obeyed when he was called to go out to the place which he would receive as an inheritance. And he went out, not knowing where he was going." (Hebrews 11:8)

Because of his obedience and radical faith, Abram became Abraham, the Father of our great, global family of faith today! What we sometimes forget, however, is that God first gave the call to another man – Terah – Abram's father. He set out for the Land of Canaan, but he never made it there because he 'settled' in Haran and died there.

"And Terah took his son Abram and his grandson Lot, the son of Haran, and his daughter-in-law Sarai, his son Abram's wife, and they went out with them from Ur of the Chaldeans to go to the land of Canaan; and they came to Haran and dwelt there. So the days of Terah were two hundred and five years, and Terah died in Haran." (Genesis 11:31-32)

Haran was the name of his son who had died;[13] and the name of the city where Terah settled and died. Haran represents death – spiritual if not physical as well. Once Terah came to Haran, he could go no further. He became stuck at the place of his deepest pain; and by settling in Haran, getting stuck in his 'comfort zone', he stopped short of reaching the fullness of his destiny.

---

[12] Genesis 12:1
[13] Genesis 11:28

Terah settled for so much less than God's best for him; and so the call was passed on to his son, Abram, who inherited a phenomenal blessing because of his faith and courage.

If we settle for less than God's best for us, we will end up wondering why someone else received the blessing that we so desired; when in reality, we had the opportunity but passed it up.

If we refuse the call, then God will find someone else who is willing and obedient to go all the way, to carry the torch of faith into an unknown future. If we are willing and obedient we will eat the good of the Land; but if we refuse and rebel, we will be devoured.[14]

Terah died in Haran instead of going all the way to the Land of Canaan. Maybe he just got tired; maybe he became ill; maybe he just lost heart and gave up. We don't know the reason, but we do know that he stopped short of his intended destination.

When we settle for less than God's best for our life, we may begin to die – maybe not physically; but spiritually, emotionally and mentally. Our hopes and dreams die; our vision dies; our passion and enthusiasm for life dies; and even our zeal for God Himself dies. If we get stuck in our pain like Terah in the place of Haran, the place of death, choosing comfort over obedience, then we will never experience the fullness of the life God has for us.

I know that God has so much more for us – for you and for me – if we refuse to give up and settle for less than God's best for our life. If we are willing to leave our comfort zone and fly into a life of adventure with God, it may be uncomfortable; it may be scary at times – even occasionally dangerous – but it will be so worth it!

I love the quote from the movie 'Secondhand Lions' when the man, still flying planes at over 90 years old, says to the young boy, *"Never fear death, my son; but fear the unlived life."*

When God calls us to come across the waters, let us step out with confidence and joy; keeping our eyes fixed on Yeshua, the author and finisher of our faith – the One who will never let us drown.

---

[14] Isaiah 1:19-21

Here's to leaving our comfort zones – and let the Kingdom Adventures begin!

"Those who do wickedly against the covenant he shall corrupt with flattery; but those who know their God shall be strong, and do great and mighty exploits."
(Daniel 11:32)

Prayer: *Thank you Lord that You have not chosen us to live a mediocre, limited life of defeat; but have called us to a life of adventure – doing great and mighty exploits for Your kingdom. Help us not to 'settle and die in Haran'; but to go all the way with You, to fulfill the destiny You have for us. Yes, why should we just sit here until we die? May we have the faith to step out of the boat – and if we perish, we perish… We trust You Adonai. Thy will be done, Thy Kingdom come... Help us to be strong and of good courage as worthy warriors in the army of the living God.*

In Yeshua's name. Amen.

As Iron Sharpens Iron - yachad יָחַד

*"As iron sharpens iron,
So a man sharpens the countenance of his friend (neighbor)."* (Proverbs 27:17)

בַּרְזֶל בְּבַרְזֶל יָחַד; וְאִישׁ יַחַד פְּנֵי־רֵעֵהוּ.

The Hebrew word used in this verse for 'sharpens' is yachad יָחַד from the word chad חַד which means 'sharp'. But the Hebrew contains a hidden powerful secret here; because this word, yachad, not only means to sharpen; but also means <u>'together in unity'</u>.

"Behold, how good and how pleasant it is for brethren to dwell together in unity! (yachad) יָחַד " (Psalm 133:1)

הִנֵּה מַה־טּוֹב וּמַה־נָּעִים - שֶׁבֶת אַחִים גַּם־יָחַד.

"For there the Lord commanded the blessing – Life forevermore." (Psalm 133:3)

There is such a power in unity – on being b'yachad (together in unity) with one another – for it is there (upon unity) that God commands His blessing!

Before He left this earth to go to the cross and then ascend to the Father, Yeshua prayed for all believers that we would be **one (echad),** just as He and His Father are one; and that we would come into complete unity with one another – that the world would know the same love of God that He has for Yeshua. Wow!

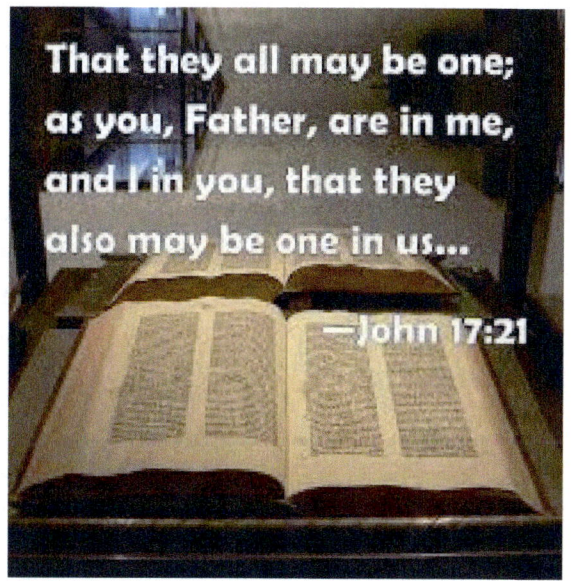

"I have given them the glory that you gave me, that they may be one as we are one— I in them and you in me—so that they may be brought to complete unity. Then the world will know that you sent me and have loved them even as you have loved me."
(John 17:22-23)

The Hebrew word for 'one', echad, אֶחָד is related to 'yachad' יַחַד. One of the most well known Old Testament Scriptures, and the foundation of the monotheistic Jewish faith is this, *"Hear O Israel, the Lord* יְהוָה *is our God; the Lord* יְהוָה *is one (echad)* אֶחָד*."* (Deuteronomy 6:4).

שְׁמַע יִשְׂרָאֵל, יְיָ אֱלֹהֵינוּ, יְיָ אֶחָד.

Shema Yisrael, Adonai Eloheinu, Adonai echad.

The 'oneness of God' is so crucial to our faith that it is the first prayer a Jewish child learns by heart. It is recited every morning and every night; and is likely the last prayer on the lips of a Jewish person on his or her deathbed.

These words would often be on the dying lips of Jewish martyrs who sacrificed their lives for their faith in the One True God.

Yeshua also affirmed the absolute oneness of God. When asked what is the greatest commandment in the Torah, He answered with this very scripture: *"Sh'ma Yisrael Adonai Eloheinu Adonai Echad."*

"Yeshua answered him, 'The first of all the commandments is: "Hear, O Israel, the Lord our God, the Lord is one (echad). And you shall love the Lord your God with all your heart, with all your soul, with all your mind, and with all your strength." This is the first commandment. And the second, like it, is this: "You shall love your neighbor as yourself." There is no other commandment greater than these.'" (Mark 12:29-31)

We know with absolute certainty that God is one; but this word 'echad' does not always mean only one (1). There are times when it is used for an intimate unity, such as the 'one flesh' relationship between a husband and wife.

"Therefore shall a man leave his father and his mother, and shall cleave unto his wife, and they shall be <u>one flesh</u>." (basar echad)

בָּשָׂר אֶחָד

Here are two people, a man and a woman, becoming one (echad) – joined together in complete unity. It has been said

that the coming together of a man and woman in a 'one flesh' marriage is a greater miracle that the parting of the Red Sea; since marriage requires the miracle of unity – while the parting of the Red Sea may have been miraculous but it was still division.

God loves unity in marriage; unity in families; and unity in the Body of Messiah; while the enemy always seeks to cause division.

One of the things that God hates is someone who causes division among brethren.

"These six things the Lord hates....And one who sows discord (strife & division) among brethren." (Proverbs 6:16-19)

There is so much strife and division in these last days. In Israel, division between extremist political viewpoints, as well as cultural, racial and religious differences threaten the nation's very survival. The Body of Messiah is scattered; families are splintering in these perplexing and challenging times.

We need to use discernment even in this area of unity, since not all unity is righteous or pleasing to the Lord. When we look at the construction of the ancient Tower of Babel, we see that they were together in perfect oneness of purpose and language.

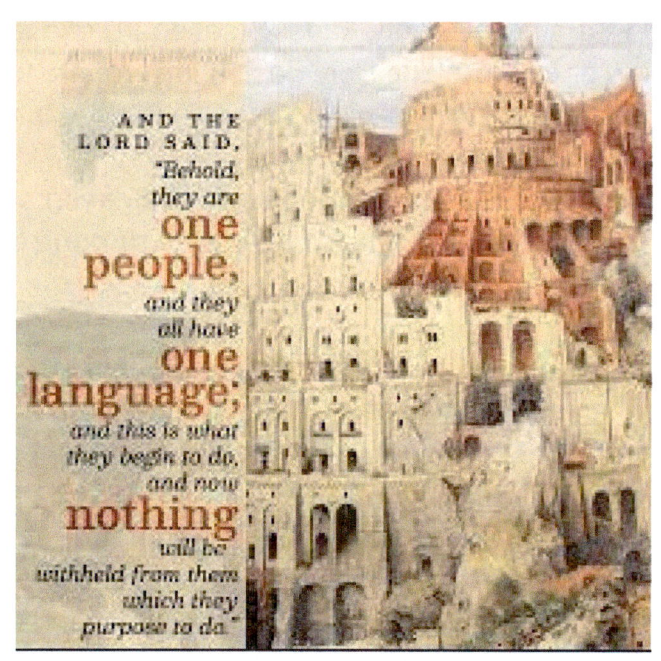

"And the Lord said, 'Indeed the people are one (echad)* אֶחָד *and they all have one language, and this is what they begin to do; now nothing that they propose to do will be withheld from them.'"
(Genesis 11:6)

This shows us the incredible <u>power of unity</u> – had they remained 'one' (echad), nothing would have been impossible for them! However since their motives were wrong, God needed to disrupt their unity and destroy their plans. Once He confused their languages, all building ceased; which is why in any relationship, business, ministry or endeavor, clear communication is essential to its growth!

We must examine the motives of who or what we are coming into unity with. Is it righteous and in line with God's holy purposes? Or is it self-serving (to make a name for ourselves); or to build the Kingdom of Babel instead of the Kingdom of God?

With the growing 'One World Order' that is so quickly making its global appearance across the earth, we need to understand its underlying agenda; and refuse to bow down or comply with it. This will of course create separation from those who are going along with their ungodly program; but there are times when separation is necessary.

God commands us to come out from among them and be separate from every unclean, corrupt and contaminating influence:

"Therefore, come out from among them and be separate, says the Lord. Do not touch what is unclean, and I will receive you. I will be a Father to you, and you will be My sons and daughters, says the Lord Almighty."
(2 Corinthians 6:17-18)

We are holy vessels, kadosh (set apart) for the sacred purposes of Adonai. We carry the anointing of the Holy Spirit and there are things and people that we must distance ourselves from, lest we become consumed in their plagues.

"Then I heard another voice from heaven say: 'Come out of her, My people, so that you will not share in her sins or contract any of her plagues.'"
(Revelation 18:4)

May we have the spiritual discernment of the Ruach Hakodesh (Holy Spirit) to know where to draw the line – what is a godly unity that we are to join ourselves with; and what are we to separate ourselves from in the fear and admonition of the Lord?

Once we have established that the foundation of the unity we are seeking is 'kadosh' (holy, sacred), then we are to endeavor to keep this unity in the Spirit by bearing with one another in love and walking in peace (shalom).

For there is only one body, one Spirit, one hope of our calling, one Lord, one faith, one immersion (baptism) and finally one God, the Father of us all! [1]

Hear O Israel, Adonai is our God; He is one (echad)!

God prophesied of a day when the Kingdom of Judah (the Southern tribes of Israel comprising the Jewish people of today) and the Kingdom of Israel (the Northern tribes, also called Joseph or Ephraim, that were exiled and 'lost' among the nations) would be one (echad) in His hand.

---

[1] Ephesians 4:2-6

*"**Thus says the Lord GOD: 'Behold, I will take the stick of Joseph, which is in the hand of Ephraim, and the tribes of Israel his companions; and I will put them unto him together with the stick of Judah, and make them one אֶחָד stick, and they shall be one אֶחָד in My hand.'"*** (Ezekiel 37:19)

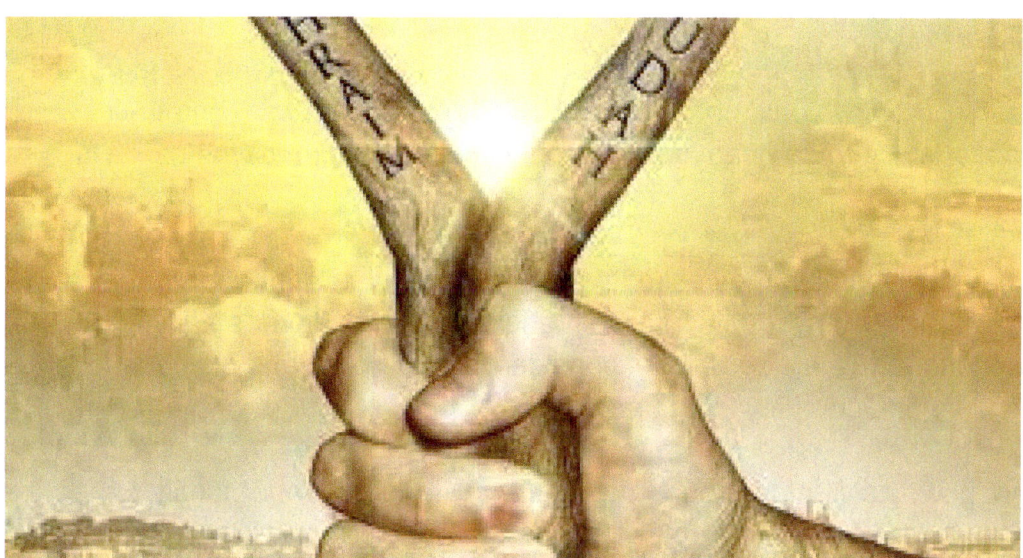

The 'lost tribes of Israel' may be lost to the world; but they are not lost to God. He knows who is His own. He knows each one by name; and He will also gather them and bring them back and cause us, Judah, to become one (echad) with them.

Hallelujah! What a glorious day that will be!

The truth is that we need one other! We need real and meaningful relationships with people who will encourage, comfort, and even correct us – people who will stick with us through life's hardships and sorrows. But our culture has placed such an emphasis on independence that many people are trying to do life on their own instead of as an integral part of an interdependent, interconnected community.

As the Body of Messiah, the eye is trying to function without ears; hands without feet; and it is becoming obvious that the way we are living is just not working. Social isolation and loneliness is increasing to epidemic proportions.

Despite the ease of digital connections, people seem to be more disconnected from real and meaningful relationships than ever before. Whereas families used to live together intergenerationally in tribal or community groups (and in some cultures continue to do so), most of us in modern, Western society exist in isolated nuclear families.

With the ease of mobility today, many families are separated by distance – living halfway across the world; and only able to visit occasionally. I vividly remember the time when my landlady, Tzipi, fell and broke her knee, requiring surgery and a long recovery period of bed rest in a full leg cast.

She needed help even to get to the bathroom and back, but her husband could not take any more time off work; they could not afford a home health care nurse, and their children lived too far away to be of any assistance – one in a distant city and one in America.

Since they had no family to help they asked if I would sit with her during the day until her husband came home from work. I believe it grieved them to have to ask me, a relative stranger, to tend to her needs; but I considered it an honor and privilege to demonstrate the love of God to my 'neighbor'.

I will never forget how she wept for hours, day after day, longing for her family to be near her during this painful trial. My heart broke for her, but also knowing that so many others weep in the darkness, feeling isolated and alone. Loneliness is becoming an epidemic in our society!

In Hebrew, the word, boded בּוֹדֵד can mean: lonely, alone, solitary, single or secluded.

It is God who has said, **"It is not good that man should be alone"**. God could see that something (someone) was still missing in Adam's life even though it was about as perfect as life can get here on earth. And so God said, **"I will make him a helper comparable to him."** [2]

God loves marriage and is the one who instituted it; in fact, God is a Bridegroom Himself and is betrothed to His beloved Bride. He says to Israel, **"'Return, O backsliding children,' says the Lord; 'for I am married to you.'"** (Jeremiah 3:14)

The entire book of Hosea is a picture of God's desire to be reconciled with His faithless wife. So He brings her into the wilderness, woos her back to Himself and turns the Valley of Achor (trouble) into a Petah Tikvah (Opening of Hope).[3]

---

[2] Genesis 2:18
[3] Hosea 2:14-15

God wants to be a husband, not a master to His beloved Bride.

"'And it shall be, in that day,' says the Lord, 'That you will call Me "<u>My Husband</u>", (Ishi) and no longer call Me "My Master", (Ba'ali)... I will betroth you to Me forever; Yes, I will betroth you to Me In righteousness and justice, in lovingkindness and mercy; I will betroth you to Me in faithfulness, and you shall know the Lord.'" (Hosea 2:16, 19-20)

A godly marriage can bring a wonderful balance, support and synergy that is simply not available as an individual. Even Solomon, the wisest man on earth, wrote that two are better than one.

*"Two are better than one,
Because they have a good reward for their labor.*

*For if they fall, one will lift up his companion.
But woe to him who is alone when he falls,
For he has no one to help him up.*

Again, if two lie down together, they will keep warm; but how can one be warm alone?

Though one may be overpowered by another, two can withstand him. And a threefold cord is not quickly broken." (Ecclesiastes 4:9-12)

This doesn't necessarily refer to being married; it could even mean teaming up with a good friend; but the truth is that we were never meant to live life alone.[4] This, "Just me and Jesus" attitude has got to go! We are hardwired by God for relationships; because God is a God of relationship.

Many people are feeling lost today, trying to 'find their tribe', asking "Where are my people?" Today's society highly regards independence and individualism; but the concept of communal life and interdependence is much closer to the ancient model of a Biblical community.[5]

I acknowledge that there are some individuals who are called by God to stay single; but God's will for most people is to marry (wisely) and raise godly families for His glory:

---

[4] https://www.jennieallen.com/find-your-people
[5] Acts 2:44-47

"Did not God make husbands and wives to become one body and one spirit for his purpose – so they would have godly offspring." (Malachi 2:15)

In the Book of Proverbs which contains such profound wisdom, it says that ***"whoever finds a good wife finds a good thing and obtains favor from the Lord."*** (Proverbs 18:22) [6]

The original Hebrew reads a little differently, however, indicating that whoever finds a good wife ***"fulfills the will of the Lord"***.

I see far too many single men and women not finding their 'besheret' (chosen one); and settling for a lifetime of singleness, childlessness and celibacy. I believe it is this wrongful (and destructive) *'singleness is holier'* attitude in the church that is causing believing singles to shrink back from pursuing a godly relationship; and hiding their desire for marriage.

Orthodox Jews have a whole network of people who help singles find suitable spouses. The whole community becomes involved in helping singles get married, with the belief that no one should be alone unless they truly want to be.

While out and about in Israel with my grown daughter, Liat, while she was still single (she recently married a godly young man from Canada) we would often encounter people trying to set her up with either one of their sons or the son of a friend. Once, an elderly man with a cane dragged us into a bakery, hollering for the young baker to come out from the back to meet this lovely young lady. Lol.

Even when visiting the local greenhouse to buy flowers, the owners suggested one of their employees would be perfect for her! The sad thing about this is that Messianic Israeli guys never asked her out or even showed any interest whatsoever. What is going on here in the believing singles community in Israel?

Have we become too embarrassed to admit that we desire a godly relationship? Do Messianic[7] men (in Israel and elsewhere) need to overcome their passivity and fear in order to actively pursue these beautiful, intelligent, godly women who sincerely desire a husband and children?

---

[6] https://www.youtube.com/watch?v=7RLYlEfYtVk&t=1s How to Find a Good Wife - Hannah Nesher // Voice for Israel Ministries

[7] Messianic is a term used to describe followers of Yeshua (Jesus)

Thank God, one Messianic young man finally had the boldness to pursue Liat (okay, I actually have to take some of the credit – I prayed that God would give him the boldness to ask her out). I had the joy of witnessing them join in holy matrimony under the chuppah, and pronouncing the Aaronic Benediction over them. As of this writing, they are approaching their 2 year anniversary – and more in love than ever! Hallelujah!

I am my beloved & my beloved is mine
SONG OF SONGS 6:3

Shadchanim (matchmakers) are well respected in Judaism; and it is considered a noble and high calling to find matches for people. So important is this role, that even our forefather Abraham made sure that before he died, he helped his son Isaac find a wife.[8]

I believe it's time that we encourage believing young people and singles to pursue a godly relationship leading to marriage, and even become involved in helping them find the right person to share their life with and raise godly offspring.

The Hebrew word for lonely (boded) is the same as one of the words used for 'single'. A single person doesn't necessarily have to be lonely, but singles are at a much higher risk for loneliness than those who are married with families. Loneliness is a huge

---

[8] Genesis 24

problem in our modern society, leading to depression and anxiety. It is a higher health risk than obesity, poor nutrition or even smoking.

The global situation with Covid seemed to have made things even worse. The Hebrew word for quarantine is '**bidud**' בידוד which is closely related to lonely (**boded**) בודד.

Researchers have found that people living in the 'Blue Zones'[9] – areas all over the world with populations that demonstrate an extraordinarily high level of health and longevity – all shared one common denominator: they experienced life as a vital part of an interdependent community and enjoyed the camaraderie of a close circle of friends and family with whom they had meaningful relationships. Selah (pause and think about that)....

What is the solution? We must intentionally engage with life and people; and refuse to become isolated, which the Bible says is not wise. **"A man who isolates himself seeks his own desires; he rages against all wise judgment."** (Proverbs 18:1)

May we return to a life of community like the early church, where we care for one another, and where no one has to be alone – whether married or single.

"God sets the solitary in families…" (Psalm 68:6)

Prayer: *Faithful Father, help me to be a strong friend to others, and lead me to those that You want to use to refine and sharpen my character. We know that it is not Your desire for us to live in 'bidud' (isolation) or as 'boded' (lonely). Would you show us the way to return to living as a loving, supportive, faith-filled community of people with whom we can be of one heart and one mind.*

Give us Holy Spirit discernment to know who we should not be in unity with; but grant us also the grace to accept people as less than perfect. You have created us to need social relationships and You have said that no good thing would You withhold from them that walk uprightly.[10]

Please bring the right people into our lives and cause the wrong ones to leave. Be the shadchan (matchmaker) for those who are seeking a godly spouse. Help us to live in unity with one another – to be one (echad) as You are one (echad); and command your blessing upon us. In Yeshua's name. Amen.

---

[9] https://www.bluezones.com/
[10] Psalm 84:11

"Behold how good and pleasant it is when brethren dwell together in unity."

"Hinei matov u'manaim shevet achim gam yachad." יַחַד (Psalm 133:1)

What is His name? (Mah Shmo) מַה-שְּׁמוֹ

"Then Moses said to God, 'Indeed, when I come to the children of Israel and say to them, "The God of your fathers has sent me to you," and they say to me, "What is His name?" what shall I say to them?'" (Exodus 3:13)

What is His Name? (Hint - it may not be what you think it is...)

When God called Moses from the midst of a burning bush, commanding him to deliver the people of Israel from bondage in Egypt, the first thing Moses asked God for was His name! What did God answer in Hebrew? What is the authentic name of God?

You may be surprised to find out that it is not, as is commonly believed in most Christian circles, *'I AM'*. The true name of God has been mistranslated and mispronounced for centuries. If we look into the original Hebrew Scriptures, we will discover the truth about the name of God.

Do you know the name of God? His Son's name? Tell me if you know....

"Who has ascended into heaven, or descended?
Who has gathered the wind in His fists?
Who has bound the waters in a garment?
Who has established all the ends of the earth?
What is His name, and what is His Son's name,
If you know?" (Proverbs 30:4)

God answered Moses' question with the Hebrew words: **_Eh'ye Asher Eh'ye_**

אֶהְיֶה אֲשֶׁר אֶהְיֶה

This name is not written in the present tense, '*I am that I am*', as most Christians believe; but due to the prefix of the letter aleph, א , this name indicates a future tense, more accurately translated as, **'*I will be what I will be'*.**

This is why I love studying the original Hebrew. We can determine for ourselves if we know the truth or if we only believe a falsehood that someone has passed down to us.

In calling Himself, 'I will be what I will be', God is saying, "I will be _____ to you. Whatever it is we need God to be (whether Deliverer, Redeemer, Savior, Healer, Provider, Counselor, Father, or even just a friend) God says, *"I will be this for you."*

God steps beyond time into our future to become whatever it is He knows we need. Whatever problems we are going to have in the future, He already has the solution.

This name, Ehye Asher Ehye is also shortened to simply 'Ehye' (I will be…..): אֶהְיֶה

"Thus you shall say unto the children of Israel: EH'YE אֶהְיֶה has sent me to you." (Exodus 3:14)

Moses knew that he could not go to the Israelites by his own commission, under his own authority, and in his own strength. He had learned this painful lesson from the past when he tried to deliver one of his fellow Israelites from being beaten by an Egyptian.

He ended up killing the Egyptian slave master and, after realizing that he had been discovered, running away from Egypt. In Midian, Moses spent the best part of forty years on the back side of nowhere, just tending his father in law's sheep.

This time, however, Moses knew that he must be sent by Divine authority in order to be successful in his mission and fulfill his destiny as a deliverer. Therefore, he asked God for His true name, to be able to proclaim in whose name he comes to deliver the Israelites.

In whose name are we doing what we do? Are we being sent by 'Ehye Asher Ehye'? Or are we just acting upon our own interests and desires? In order to truly make an impact for the Kingdom of God we must be 'sent' by Divine Authority.

Paul also desperately wanted to bring the good news of salvation and deliverance to his own people Israel. He said, **"Brethren, my heart's desire and prayer to God for Israel is that they may be saved."** (Romans 10:1)

But, Paul wrote, *"How then shall they call on Him in whom they have not believed? And how shall they believe in Him of whom they have not heard? And how shall they hear without a preacher? And how shall they preach <u>unless they are sent</u>?" That is why the Scriptures say, 'How beautiful are the feet of messengers who bring good news!'"* (Romans 10:14-15)

God assured Moses that He was, indeed, being sent; and that this time around, God would be *'with him'* in his rescue mission. One of the names given to the Messiah, born of a virgin, is Emanuel. This is not a 'Christian' name; but a Hebrew name consisting of two words, 'Immanu' עִמָּנוּ (with us) and El אֵל (God).

"Therefore the Lord Himself shall give you a sign: behold, the young woman shall conceive, and bear a son, and shall call his name Immanuel. עִמָּנוּ אֵל*"*
(Isaiah 7:14)

What is the only thing we need to fulfill God's calling on our lives? It is God's assurance that He will be with us: **"Certainly, I will be with thee."** (Exodus 3:12) To be used by God, we don't need supernatural abilities, only a willing response to His call, **"Hineini"** (Here am I).

There is only one difference between Moses' attempt to deliver the people of Israel forty years before and his second attempt. The second time, it was a 'God thing'. It was God who was initiating the action, God who chose the time, and God who was with Moses, rather than Moses trying to carry out a noble deed on his own.

Yeshua warned us that by ourselves we can do nothing! But with Him, all things are possible. Is God directing us to do something? Is God 'with us' in this action? Is it His timing? Or is it some good thing we are trying to do in our own strength (works of the flesh)? These are good questions to ask ourselves; and sometimes we only find out that God is not in it when we fall on our faces. God is love; and love never fails.

Calling upon the ancient lineage of Abraham, Isaac and Jacob, God revealed His sacred name. This was not some 'foreign god' that the people had not known; but the God of their fathers – the God of Avraham (Abraham), Yitzchak (Isaac), and Yaacov (Jacob/Israel).

"And God said to Moses: 'Thus shall you say unto the children of Israel: יְהֹוָה (Yehovah), the God of your fathers, the God of Abraham, the God of Isaac, and the God of Jacob, has sent me unto you; <u>this is My name for ever</u>, and this is <u>My memorial unto all generations</u>." (Exodus 3:15)

Moses could proclaim to the children of Israel that their God and the God of their Fathers (Avraham, Yitzchak, Yaacov) had sent him.

This was the God to which they had been crying out for so many years, "How long, O Lord?" It is by this name, יהוה that our God shall be remembered forever throughout all generations.

The sacred name of God is made up of four Hebrew letters: yud, hey, vav, hey יְהוָה (reading from right to left rather than left to right as is in English).

The pronunciation of the letters is according to the first letter of its name, therefore yood is a 'y' sound, hey, an 'h' sound, and vav, a 'v' sound.

The dots and dashes underneath and on top of the letters add the vowels; however these do not appear in the original Scriptures, making it very difficult to know the exact pronunciation of this name.

In Hebrew today, we could pronounce this name Yehovah[1]. Since there is no 'w' or 'j' sound in modern Hebrew, we do not say Yahweh or Jehovah. Any word containing the w or j sound is known to be a foreign import or intrusion into the language.

Sacred Name Cult

Recently, a 'Sacred Name' cultish type of movement has arisen among some Messianic or 'Hebrew Roots' believers. People who adhere to this community believe that they know, without a shadow of a doubt, how to pronounce the true name of God and have all kinds of unfamiliar and strange sounding pronunciations which they insist on using. They refuse to say God, Lord, or even Adonai (even though this is contained in Scripture).

This movement has caused a great deal of needless strife, contention and division within the Messianic community. We have friends who find it hard to fellowship with others because they can't find believers who pronounce the name of God exactly as they do.

Those who adhere to the sacred name movement usually argue over dates on the Biblical calendar, believing the traditional Jewish calendar to be in error. Some of this stems from a new kind of 'Hebrew roots' anti-semitism. Most 'Sacred Namers' also believe that the Sabbath (Shabbat) does not begin Friday evening at sundown as

---

[1] Since the vowels (nikkudot) are not written in the original Hebrew Scriptures, this name could also possibly be pronounced other ways such as Yaveh, however this is not a common pronunciation.

traditionally practiced, but instead observe it from morning until morning (instead of from evening to evening as the Bible dictates).

The Bible warns us not to argue over disputable matters such as these.[2] Assuredly, as a good Father, our God is happy when we call upon Him, even if our pronunciation of His name is not 100% perfect.

Hashem - The Name

This sacred name יְהוָה is considered so holy that Jewish people will not speak it, for fear of saying His name in vain. Instead, they refer to God as simply '*Hashem*'. A popular expression containing this phrase is 'Baruch Hashem', meaning 'Thank God' (literally Blessed be 'The Name'). Another is 'Be'ezrat Hashem' (With the help of God/The Name).

Orthodox Jewish people will not even write the word 'God' in English, but instead write G-d; such is the reverence that is held for the name of Adonai. If any Hebrew text contains the written name of God, it cannot be thrown away; but must receive a ceremonial burial befitting the holiness of God.

This name is derived from the root word 'to be'; and contains the past, present and future forms of this verb. Through His name, God proclaims His eternal nature: He is the God who was, who is, and who forever will be! Halleluyah!

This is the song the angels sing around His throne: *"Kadosh, kadosh, kadosh, יהוה T'sva'ot – Holy Holy, Holy is the Lord God of Hosts. Who was and is and is to come (Asher hayah v'hoveh v'yiheyeh."* (Revelation 4:8)

He is the God of our past, the God of our present and best of all, the God of our future. And He promises us that the future He has planned for us is a good one. Halleluyah!

"'For I know the plans I have for you,' declares the Lord, 'plans to prosper you and not to harm you, plans to give you hope and a future.'" (Jeremiah 29:11)

---

[2] Romans 14:1

The Way is Always Open

The name of God, when written, is often abbreviated to ה'. This, in itself, is a beautiful word picture hidden in the Hebrew. This letter, hei, looks like a door with a small opening on the top left hand side.

It means that the way back to God is always open to us through Yeshua, who declared,

"I am the way, the truth and the life and no one comes to the Father but through me." (John 14:6)

The small accent on the side of the opening ה' is like a hand beckoning all to come into the shelter of covenant with God.

Yeshua Himself is the doorway to eternal life. He said, *"I am the door of the sheep."* (John 10:7)

The Hebrew word for 'door' is delet דלת. This is also the name of the 4th letter in the Hebrew alphabet, dalet.

When this letter ד is inserted into the name of God, יהוה it becomes יהודה – Yehudah – which is the Hebrew word for Judah.[3]

This is an amazing message hidden in the Hebrew! It is God, in union with the Messiah Yeshua (the door) which creates the tribe of Judah – the Jewish people. <u>Yeshua is the Lion of the tribe of Judah</u>. The Jewish people, with God but without Yeshua, is as yet incomplete in their fullness of calling and destiny to be a light to the nations.

---

[3] Jewish people are called Yehudim in Hebrew

If we want to reach the Jewish people with the 'good news' that God has sent a deliverer even greater than Moses, then we need to come with the authentic name of God – the God of their fathers, the one they know, not some foreign god.

In order to go to the Jewish people with news of a mighty Deliverer, one cannot come in the name of a foreign God. Most Jewish people will not respond if you speak to them in the name of Jehovah or Yaweh, or even in the name of Jesus Christ.

Why? These names, in the minds of most Jewish people, are the names of foreign, unknown gods. They will not recognize them. 'Christ' is not Jesus' last name; He is not the son of Mr. & Mrs. Christ. It is a Greek translation of the Hebrew title, Mashiach (Messiah, or Anointed One). His first name is Yeshua, which means salvation, and is a word most Jewish people would recognize which is used throughout the Hebrew Scriptures.

So why do we need to use the Greek when our Messiah was not a Greek, but a Hebrew? The gospel is for the Jew first and also for the Gentile. Should we not then prefer to use the Hebrew terms? This is especially important when trying to reach the Messiah's own brethren, the Israelites, with the good news that God has sent a deliverer to free them from their oppression and bondage.

The Shelter of His Name

The sacred name of God, Yehovah, יְהֹוָה is used over 6000 times in the Bible; but most English translations use the generic term 'Lord' which waters down the meaning along with its power. Some believe this is an intentional strategy of the enemy to rob God's people of the knowledge and power of His name.

Knowing the authentic name of God, however, is so powerful. We can run to it and be kept safe.

"The name of the Lord is a strong tower; the righteous run into it and are safe." (Proverbs 18:10)

The name of the God of Jacob can also defend and protect us.

"May Yehovah יְהוָה answer you in the day of trouble; may the name of the God of Jacob defend you... Some trust in chariots, and some in horses; but we will remember the name of Yehovah יְהוָה our God." (Psalm 20:1,7)

There is salvation in the mighty name of Yehovah!

"And it shall come to pass, that whoever calls upon the name of Yehovah יְהוָה will be saved." (Joel 2:32)

God's will is that His people will know His name:

"Therefore My people shall know My name; therefore they shall know in that day that I am He who speaks: 'Here am I (Hineini).'" (Isaiah 52:6)

There are many other names of God – each one reveals another aspect of His multi-dimensional character.

Some of these are: Adonai (Lord), Elohim (Creator), El Elyon (God above all), El Shaddai (Almighty God), and Yehovah Tzeva'ot (Lord of Hosts). Some of these are covered in other chapters.

Here are some other names of God from Scripture

- *Adon Olam* — "Master of the Universe."
- *Avinu Malkeinu* — "Our Father, our King."
- *Elohei Avraham*, Elohei Yitzchak ve Elohei Ya`acov — "God of Abraham, God of Isaac, God of Jacob."
- *El ha-Gibbor* — "God the hero" or "God the mighty one."
- *El Emet* — "God of Truth."
- *Ro'eh Yisra'el* — "Shepherd of Israel."
- *Kadosh Yisra'el* — "Holy One of Israel."
- *Melech ha-Melachim* — "The King of Kings."
- *Magen Avraham* — "Shield of Abraham."

- *YHVH-Yireh* — "Yehovah will provide." (Genesis 22:13,14)
- *YHVH-Rapha* — "Yehovah the healer." (Exodus 15:26)
- *YHVH-Nissi* — "Yehovah my Banner." (Exodus 17:8-15)
- *YHVH-Shalom* — "God of Peace." (Judges 6:24)
- *YHVH-Roi* — "Yehovah is my Shepherd." (Psalms 23:1)
- *YHVH-Tsidkenu* — "Yehovah our Righteousness." (Jeremiah 23:6)
- *YHVH-Shammah* — "God is there." (Ezekiel 48:35)
- *Tzur Yisra'el* — "Rock of Israel."

The Blessing of His Name

Most people are familiar with the Aaronic Benediction (the Priestly Blessing), called Bircat Hacohanim in Hebrew.

"And the Lord spoke to Moses, saying: 'Speak to Aaron and his sons, saying, <u>"This is the way you shall bless the children of Israel</u>. Say to them..."'" (Numbers 6:22-26):

יְבָרֶכְךָ יְהוָה וְיִשְׁמְרֶךָ:

The LORD bless you, and keep you;

יָאֵר יְהוָה פָּנָיו אֵלֶיךָ וִיחֻנֶּךָ:

The LORD make His face shine on you, And be gracious to you;

יִשָּׂא יְהוָה פָּנָיו אֵלֶיךָ וְיָשֵׂם לְךָ שָׁלוֹם:

The LORD lift up His countenance on you, And give you peace.

But the second lesser known part of this special divine blessing is the name of God.

"So they shall put My name on the children of Israel, and I will bless them." (Numbers 6:27)

Praise - Yah!

Did you know that every time we shout Halleluyah we proclaim the name of God?

Hallel means Praise (n)	הַלֵּל
Hallelu means Praise (v) (plural)	הללו
Yah is a name of God	יה
So Hallelu - Yah means 'Praise Yah'	הללויה

"Sing unto God, sing praises to his name: extol him that rides upon the heavens by his name Yah יה*, and rejoice before him."* **(Psalms 68:4)**

As covenant people of the God of Abraham, we can reclaim God's authentic name and its accompanying power as part of our Divine inheritance.

"Therefore behold, I will this once cause them to know, I will cause them to know My hand and My might (G'vurati) and they shall know that My name is יהוה*."*
(Jeremiah 16:21)

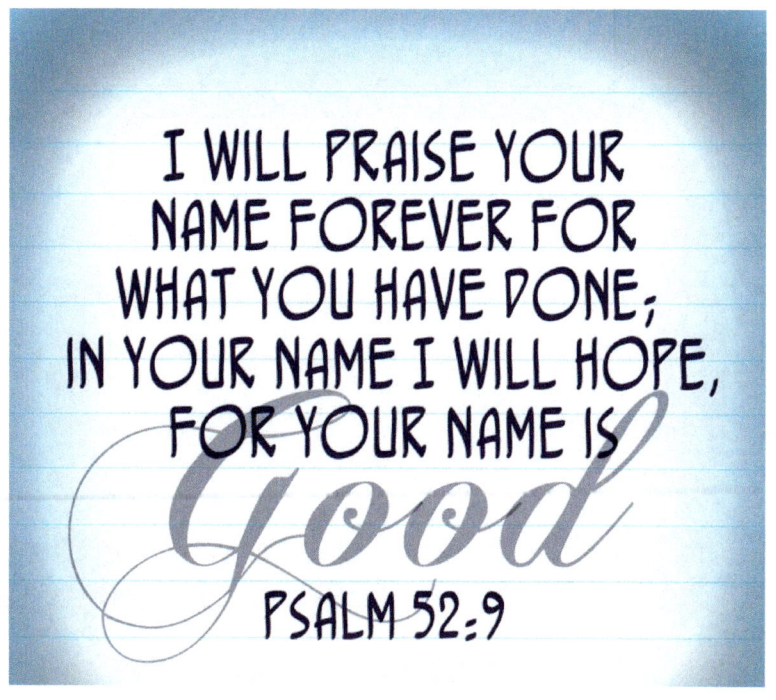

Prayer: We praise You, Yehovah God, for the power of Your name that can break every chain of bondage and tear down every stronghold in our life. Thank you that we may run to Your name at any time and be protected. You have promised that all those who call upon Your name, Yehovah, יהוה will be saved.

May we always remember Your holy name and call upon it to defend us whenever we are in trouble. Thank you for revealing Your awesome character to us through Your wonderful name. Hallelu-Yah! Hallelu-Yah! Amen.

Called by a New Name - Hephzibah חֶפְצִי-בָהּ

"You shall be called by a new name, which the mouth of the Lord will name."
(Isaiah 62:2)

What is your name? In our modern, North American culture, we may name someone after a relative, or even just pick out a favorite name from a '1001 Baby Names' book. In Hebrew, however, names often have a significant meaning; for instance, '*Eli-tzur*' means '*My God (Eli) is a rock (Tzur)*', and a change of name may affect a complete change of destiny.

I began to think about the spiritual significance of names while reading in the Bible that during a census, each male eligible to go to war found his position in his family by his father's house. I wondered about all the children growing up today without fathers. So many children today (including my own) have grown up in homes where the father is absent. Where would they be listed? What would be their place in the census?

Even today in the synagogue, when a man is called up to read from the Torah, he is always called by his father's name: _____ ben (son of) _____.

This is why, in the Hebraic culture in which Yeshua (Jesus) lived, they called out to him, "*Yeshua, ben David, t'rachem alai*!" "*Yeshua, son of David, have mercy on me!*"[1]

---
[1] Luke 18:38

By acknowledging Yeshua as a son of David, they declared him the Messiah who would sit on the throne of His father David according to the Word of the Prophets.[2]

If the father's identity of a Jewish man is not known, he will be called by his name _____ , ben Avraham, Yitzchak and Yaacov (son of Abraham, Isaac and Jacob); signifying that he is still a covenant child of God through our forefathers.

As His Name is, So is He

We see an example of the significance of a name in the story of Naval נָבָל and Avigail אֲבִגַיִל in the Bible (1 Samuel 25).

Avigail was a beautiful, intelligent woman; but her husband, Naval, was a fool, as is the meaning of his name. Now why someone would name their child 'fool' is beyond me… but there it is.

"And the woman was of good understanding (Avigail was intelligent), and of a beautiful form (gorgeous); but the man was churlish (harsh) and evil in his doings." (1 Samuel 25:3)

Here are some meanings of the name Naval: n. *A wicked, vile, ignoble, villainous person, scoundrel, fool, obscene; v. to disgrace or degrade.* Nice name, eh? Why a beautiful, intelligent woman would marry a guy like Naval is another mystery to me; but there have been whole books written on this phenomenon.

What did other people say about him? They described him in this way, ***"He is such a base fellow, that one cannot speak to him."*** (1 Samuel 25: 17)

We need discernment about people; and it is good to listen to what other people say about this individual. Avigail saved the day by pleading with King David not to slaughter all her husband's men just because of the arrogance, rudeness and foolishness of her husband:

"Please, let not my lord regard this scoundrel Naval. For as his name is, so is he: Naval is his name, נָבָל ***and foolishness (navlah*** נְבָלָה ***– wickedness, vileness, obscenity) is with him!"*** (1 Samuel 25:25)

---

[2] Isaiah 9:6-7

Naval's name revealed his negative character. This principle is also shown in the names of Naomi's sons who died in Moab.³ They were named Machlon מַחְלוֹן and chilyon כִּלְיוֹן which means 'sickness' and 'failure'. Again, why would a mother give these names to her children?? Go figure....

Perhaps, knowing the spiritual significance of a name, it may be worth more than a little consideration and prayer in choosing the names of our children.

My son, Timothy's lovely wife, Victoria, just gave birth to their firstborn son, a beautiful, healthy, baby boy – praise Adonai! According to Jewish tradition, they will officially announce his name in the synagogue on the 8th day at his Brit Milah (circumcision ceremony).

They called him Rei רֵעִי which is both a Japanese and a Hebrew given name.⁴ In Hebrew, it means 'my shepherd', 'my companion', 'my friend'. In the Bible, this was the name of the warrior who was loyal to King David (1 Kings 1:8).

In Japanese, depending on the kanji,⁵ it can mean 'beautiful in spirit', 'to be ready', 'encourage', or 'king'. What an awesome name for such a special little boy.

How are you Called?

In Hebrew, people don't ask your name. They ask, "How are you called" ? (Eikh korim lecha), (lach for a female)?

איך קוראים לך ?

To which we usually answer , "I am called (kor'im li) _____" (fill in the blank with your name).

_____ קוראים לי

---

³ Ruth 1:5
⁴ Timothy is Japanese on his father's side and Jewish on his mother's side
⁵ Kanji is a system of Japanese writing using Chinese characters.

Should be an easy answer right? Wrong. When people ask me that simple question, it stumps me. Seriously, I don't even know how to answer that question. As a Jewish child, I was given two different names – a legal English name; and also a Hebrew name at my dedication in the synagogue.

And then it becomes more complicated – mostly because of all the name changes that come with marriage, divorce and remarriage – and if that didn't cause enough confusion, my then husband legally changed our last name to a Hebrew one instead of his given Polish family name. After our divorce I went back to using my maiden name.

It took Israel seven years and a whole bureaucratic mess of red tape to get my divorce recognized – which meant that for years, I officially had two different identities with two different names on two different passports. Oye! My brother in law who worked for Israel's El-Al airlines said they likely would have arrested me at the airport when boarding a flight had he not pulled some strings.

Even after I finally had my name legally changed back to my maiden name, Israeli authorities spelled my first name in English as 'Chana' (how it is pronounced in Hebrew), rather than 'Hannah' as it is spelled on my Canadian passport – a slight variation which almost meant me not getting on my flight back home to Israel last time!

The whole thing makes me dizzy and I'm not even going to try to sort it out anymore so when someone asks me what I am called, I just look at them like a deer caught in someone's headlights and they usually politely walk away! :)

God Calls us by Name

Hopefully you don't have to deal with such a confusing dilemma, but seriously, what is your name? How are you called? How do people call you? How do you call yourself?

When my youngest daughter was about to be born in Israel, I prayed and sought God for her name. I attended a women's prayer group at the time; and these ladies prayed me through that pregnancy to the birth of a healthy baby girl, even though several pregnancies prior had ended in miscarriage.

With these ladies' help, we settled upon the name 'Liat' ליאת, which means 'You are Mine',[6] which is taken and feminized from a Scripture in Isaiah: *"I have called you by name, you are mine (Li - atah לִי־אָתָּה)."* (Isaiah 43:1)

Every time someone calls Liat by name, they are declaring that she belongs to the Almighty God who says to her, *"You are Mine"*. And she knows it!

I keep wondering, if God also calls me by name, what is it? The book of Revelation tells us that God is going to give those who overcome a new name, a secret name written on a white stone, which only those who receive it will know.

I can hardly wait to find out my new name spoken from the mouth of God. **"You shall be called by a new name, which the mouth of the Lord will name."** (Isaiah 62:2)

In the Scriptures, there was a young man who was called in Hebrew, Mephiboshet, מְפִיבֹשֶׁת. His name means, *'From the mouth of Shame'*: Mephi מְפִי means *'from my mouth'*; and *'boshet'* בֹשֶׁת means *'shame'* or disgrace.

It wasn't his fault that he carried such a handle; it was because his nurse accidentally dropped him, leaving him crippled for life!

We may have been 'dropped' at some point, either accidentally or on purpose, by someone who failed to care for us and protect us in the way they should have. This may have left us trying to limp our way through life, carrying a heavy load of shame, guilt and condemnation.

But here's the good news – God is going to give us a new name from His very own mouth. No longer *'from the mouth of shame'*; but instead we will be called a new name *'from the mouth of the Lord'*. God calls us His beloved son or daughter, chosen, holy (kadosh), a special treasure, forgiven, redeemed and accepted.

---

[6] See 'You are Mine' chapter in book Devotionals for the Animal Lover's Heart on Amazon or ebook: https://www.voiceforisrael.net/product-page/devotionals-animal-lovers-heart

2 Samuel 4:4

•Jonathan son of Saul had a son who was lame in both feet. He was five years old when the news about Saul and Jonathan came from Jezreel. His nurse picked him up and fled, but as she hurried to leave, he fell and became disabled. His name was Mephibosheth.

We may have received a negative name, but God wants to change our name to ones that describe the faith and hope He has for us. When Rachel lay dying in giving birth to her son, she named him, 'Ben Oni' בֶּן־אוֹנִי (Son of my sorrow) because of the pain and agony she was going through in birthing him into the world.[7]

The hurtful names people call us are likely no fault of our own; but only because of their own pain and brokenness. As has often been said, "*Hurting people hurt people*".

"Rachel died while giving birth to her son. Before dying, she named the boy Ben oni. But Jacob called him Benjamin." (Genesis 35:18)

This boy would have walked around his whole life being called Ben Oni, '*Son of Sorrow*', continually reminded of the pain and sorrow his birth had caused; but Jacob would have none of it! He changed his name to 'Ben Yamin' בְּנְיָמִין, which means '*Son at my Right Hand*'.

 As we journey through life's trenches (and sometimes its sewers) we may receive names for ourselves that are false, negative or destructive.

---

[7] Genesis 35:18

Perhaps as a child, you were taunted with a derogatory name by some cruel children and it stuck. Maybe something like: *"Fatty, fatty two by four – can't get through the kitchen door."* Oh yes…. :(

Other people may label us with words that pierce like a sword. In a brief but abusive marriage, my (then) husband said, *"I feel sorry for your children that they have you for their mother."* So I received the *'Bad Mother'* label. Besides the bad mother label, I also received (from a later marriage) *'bad cook, bad housekeeper, bad driver'*, and worst of all *'rebellious wife'*. Oye vey!

These labels are not always overcome so easily. During my rebellious teenage stage of life, my exasperated father said, *"For a girl who gets such good marks in school, you have absolutely no common sense!";* and so another label stuck to me that read, *'dumb, foolish, or idiot'* – and I lived up to that negative assessment by making one foolish choice after another.

What have people said to you or about you? In my mind, I see a person walking around as an adult – fearfully and wonderfully made by God – but with all these labels struck all over their body. These labels carry names like, *'Loser, failure, stupid, fat, ugly, bad, dirty, not good enough, unwanted, unloved, and unlovable'.*

These negative labels cover over the magnificence of who we were created to be. The good news is that these labels are not stuck to us with crazy glue; they are more like 'post-it-notes' which can just be pulled off and thrown away.

A Little Lower Than Elohim

The word of God says that He created us just a little lower than *'Elohim'* אֱלֹהִים (a name for God). Wow! (Psalm 8:5) Obviously most translators couldn't handle this powerful truth so they falsely translated it as *'angels'* instead of Elohim.

We were made in the image of the Almighty and have His nature as our true selves. But this beauty has been marred by all the false names we call ourselves.

What are the negative labels people have put on you (or you have put on yourself)? Are you called poor? Pathetic? Incapable? Sick? Weak? Foolish? Stupid? Not enough? Damaged? Let's take off those negative labels.

We can change how we are called by using new words to describe ourselves. Even if we feel weak and poor we can call ourselves strong and rich.

"And now let the weak say I am strong; let the poor say I am rich…" (Joel 3:10)

Even if we don't feel it is true, we can begin to say, *"I am blessed and highly favored. I am prospering and in good health. I am accepted, approved and valuable. I am talented. I am confident. I am wise. I am bold as a lion."*

Change of Name = Change of Destiny

We can find, hidden in the Hebrew, several other instances of name changes that affected that person's entire destiny. Joshua was Moses' chosen successor – destined to lead the children of Israel across the Jordan into the Promised Land. But to fulfill his destiny, he needed a name change.

Moses changed his name from Hoshea הוֹשֵׁעַ to Yehoshua,[8] יְהוֹשֻׁעַ which means 'Yehovah saves' by adding the letter 'yud', a representation of the hand (yad) of God.

yad

Father Abraham

God began our family of faith with a man named Av-ram אַבְרָם whose name means *'Exalted Father'* and a woman named Sarai, שָׂרַי whose name means *'My Prince'*.

Together, they carried a Divine destiny which they could not fulfill because they were barren. But once God added His own Divinity to their names, they bore the son of promise; and thereby began to fulfill their destiny.

---

[8] Numbers 13:16

The God Letter

God's name is often abbreviated as the Hebrew letter 'hey' ה. When God added His own Divine name, ה to both Avram and Sarai, they became 'Avraham' and 'Sarah'. Avram אַבְרָם was changed to Avraham אַבְרָהָם.

God said, *"No longer shall your name be called Avram, but your name shall be Avraham; for I have made you a father of many nations."* (Genesis 17:5)

Avraham literally translates as the '*father of a multitude of goyim (Gentiles)*'. Many little children in church today sing, "*Father Abraham has many sons, many sons has father Abraham. I am one of them and so are you….*"

All those who are of faith in Messiah now belong to our Father Abraham's house. By himself, Avram could do nothing; but Avraham (with God), became the father of a multitude of nations/Gentiles.[9]

God did not change Avram's name in order to make him a King or Monarch but to make him a father (Abba).

Adding the letter 'hey' הָ made all the difference! because ה represents the name of God. This letter looks like a door with an opening. It is telling us in pictorial form that the way to God is always open through repentance.

With God all things are possible; and by abiding in Him we are able to fulfill our destiny. But without Him we can do nothing.

"I am the vine, you are the branches. He who abides in Me, and I in him, bears much fruit; for without Me you can do nothing." (John 15:5)

---

[9] Galatians 3:7,29

God also changed the name of Avram's wife, Sarai שָׂרַי (my prince) to Sarah (princess) שָׂרָה.

Sarah

Then God said to Abraham, "As for Sarai your wife, you shall not call her name Sarai, but Sarah shall be her name. And I will bless her and also give you a son by her; then I will bless her, and she shall be a mother of nations; kings of peoples shall be from her."

Genesis 17:15

Again, adding the letter ה to her name caused Sarah to have the supernatural ability, even at an age well past childbearing years, to fulfill her destiny as a mother of nations. The very physical nature of Sarai changed after her name included God's Divine name.

In Hebrew, the letter hey ה with the vowel 'ah' also functions to feminize a word. When God added His feminine nature to Sarai (my prince), she became Sarah (princess). Her previously barren womb came to life and she became fruitful and bore a son, Isaac (Yitzchak), which means laughter. Those things which are birthed by God, in His perfect timing, bring great joy!

The letter hey ה at the end of a word is also like a silent exhalation. It represents the breath of spirit (ruach) of God. The Holy Spirit is also referred to in Hebrew in the feminine gender. Adding the letter hey to the end of Sarai's name not only restored her femininity; but God also breathed His life into her – His very essence!

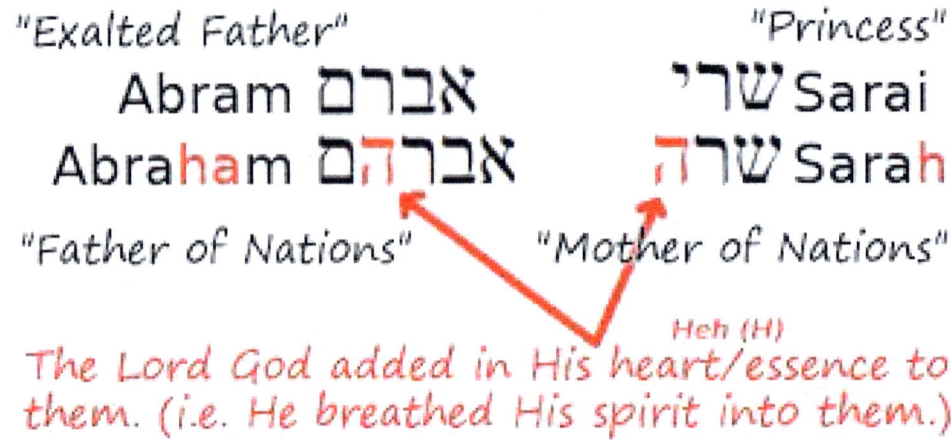

From Jacob to Israel

God also changed Jacob's name to make him a father. The change of name from Jacob to Israel, after wrestling with a Divine Being (a physical manifestation of God), brought Jacob into his divine destiny as the father of the twelve tribes of Israel.

Hidden within the Hebrew, we can see the deeper meaning behind this change of name. Jacob's name in Hebrew is Yaacov יַעֲקֹב meaning a 'twisted deceiver'.

It comes from the Hebrew word, 'ekev' עָקֵב – the heel of the foot. It also means *'to follow after'*; because Yaacov was born grasping onto Esau's heel, following after him. As Yaacov, Jacob always seemed to be behind, grasping ahead for the blessing and the inheritance.

But his new name, Yisrael יִשְׂרָאֵל means 'Prince of God'; and with this change of name, he became the head and not the tail – above and not beneath – a leader and not a follower.

"Then Jacob was left alone; and a Man wrestled with him until the breaking of day....And He said, 'Let Me go, for the day breaks'. But he said, 'I will not let You go unless You bless me!'" (Genesis 32:24,26)

"So He said to him, '<u>What is your name?</u>'

He said, 'Jacob.'" **Yaacov** יַעֲקֹב (Genesis 32:27)

This divine 'man' asked Jacob his name – a simple question. Something tells me he already knew, since God says He knows each one of us by name. So why did he ask?

Jacob had to admit who he was before he could be changed. His name was Yaacov יַעֲקֹב – deceiver, conniver, and manipulator. He confessed this ugly truth before the angel of the Lord, who then changed his name to Yisrael יִשְׂרָאֵל, *"because you have striven (Sarita)* שָׂרִיתָ *with God and with men, and have prevailed."* (Genesis 32:28)

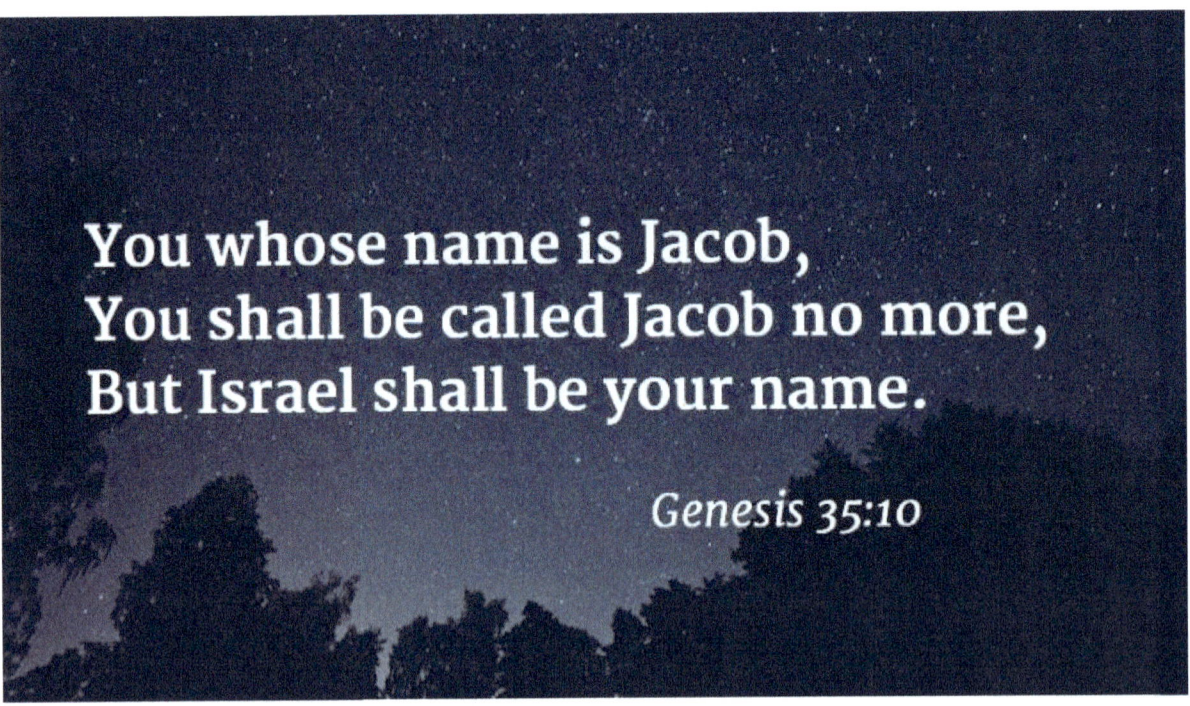

What is your name? Only by facing the truth can we be set free: **"And you shall know the truth and the truth shall set you free."** (John 8:32)

It is the truth that will set us free – not the truth about someone else – but the truth about ourselves. I love the story a woman minister tells about how she went to God complaining about all the things her husband did that bothered her. She then heard God say, *"Your husband is not the problem"*. So she asked, *"Well who is then?"* Lol.

The Holy Spirit revealed to her the truth of who she was at that time; and all the bitterness, anger and rebellion within her that had been causing problems in their marriage relationship. She tells of how she cried for days once she faced the truth; but it was only then that the process of true and lasting transformation was able to begin.

After his encounter with this 'man/angel'; Jacob's entire character was also transformed as evidenced by his new name – Yisrael יִשְׂרָאֵל.

El אֵל = God Yasar ישׂר = strive, wrestle Yashar ישׁר = straight, righteous, or honest Sar שׂר = prince	El אל means <u>God</u> and the word **yasar** ישׂר means to <u>strive</u>, <u>struggle</u> or <u>wrestle</u>. These same three Hebrew letters can also spell the word **yashar** ישׁר which can mean '<u>straight</u>', '<u>honest</u>' or '<u>righteous</u>'.

Jacob was not simply given a new name; he was given an entirely new nature! No longer Yaacov – the deceiver, liar, cheater – now Yisrael; honest, straight, righteous man with God.

No longer a 'taker' but a giver. When he met his brother Esau, he no longer grasped after his blessings; but instead sought to give him from all he had been blessed with.

And Jacob said (to Esau),

"No, please, if I have now found favor in your sight, then receive my present from my hand....

Please, take my blessing that is brought to you, because God has dealt graciously with me, and because I have enough." So he urged him, and he took it." (Genesis 33:10-11)

Jacob sees Esau, painting by James Tissot

Yaacov the grasper, taker, deceiver, became a giving, righteous man by the transforming power of the Holy Spirit (Ruach Hakodesh). We cannot force these profound changes in our character, but God is faithful; He will complete the good work that He has started in each and every one of us.[10]

God wants to do the same for us! He wants to give us – not just a new name to be called by – but a whole new identity!

Called by a New Name

"You shall no longer be called Forsaken (azuvah) עֲזוּבָה *(forsaken, abandoned, deserted), nor shall your land any more be termed Desolate (shmamah);* שְׁמָמָה *But you shall be called Hephzibah* חֶפְצִי־בָהּ*, and your land Beulah* בְּעוּלָה*; For the Lord delights in you, and your land shall be married."*
(Isaiah 62:4)

Yes, God calls us by a new name. When we come to Him in faith, we no longer need to be called forsaken, rejected, abandoned, deserted, or desolate. Our new names are 'God's delight' and 'married' – chosen and accepted.

---

[10] Philipians 1:6

Loved. Because Adonai our Maker is our husband and He delights in us, therefore we can rest in the assurance that we are loved and desired.

<u>What names does God call us</u>? He calls us **"A crown of glory and a royal diadem (precious jewel or gem) in His hand."** (Isaiah 62:3)

A Special Treasure

God calls us His special treasure. In Hebrew the word used is segulah סגולה, which comes from the word, sagol סגול, which means purple. He sees us clothed in purple, in the colors of royalty. He calls us a 'royal priesthood; a holy nation.' (Mamlechet cohanim v'goy kadosh.)

"Now therefore, if you will indeed obey My voice and keep My covenant, then you shall be a <u>special treasure (segulah)</u> to Me above all people; for all the earth is Mine." (Exodus 19:5)

God made this promise to Israel; but all those who are grafted into the olive tree, who have joined the commonwealth of Israel through the Jewish Messiah, are now also joint heirs and partakers in this same promise.

"But you are a chosen generation, a royal priesthood, a holy nation, His own special people, that you may proclaim the praises of Him who called you out of darkness into His marvelous light." (1 Peter 2:9)

We are not rejected, abandoned and without hope. We are a chosen generation, God's own special people with a special purpose – to proclaim His praises for calling us out of darkness into light.

We need to let go of our sad stories of the past in order to be about our Father's business in the now. We are not weak. God calls us 'Mighty oaks of righteousness'; 'more than conquerors'; 'armed with strength for every battle'.

We can do all things through the Messiah who strengthens us. We are called to rebuild the ruins of many generations.

We need to rise up and be who God has called us; not those sorry, pathetic names we call ourselves. Gideon called himself the least of the least; but the angel of the Lord called him a mighty man of valor (Judges 6:12)

David was also called the least, even by his own father, and not even worthy of calling out of the shepherd's fields; but God told the prophet Samuel to call him, 'KING OF ISRAEL'. Halleluyah!

"And they shall call them The Holy People, The Redeemed of the Lord; and you shall be called Sought Out, A City Not Forsaken." (Isaiah 62:12)

God wants us to call ourselves as He calls us. We need to start calling ourselves by our new names. When they say *"How are you called*?"

We can answer, "*Blessed and highly favored. Strong in the Lord and in the power of His might. A chosen beloved son or daughter of the King. Royalty. A special treasure. Holy, Redeemed, Sought out, Free and Forgiven!*" Halleluyah!

It doesn't matter what we have gone through in the past; because when we come to faith in Messiah Yeshua, we are a new creation! The old things have passed away; and all things have become new!

New Creation Butterfly Photo cards by Liat https://www.light-tothenations.com/

Calling God by a New Name

Finally – we see that <u>God also desires for us to call Him by a new name</u>. **"'And it shall be, in that day,' says the Lord, 'That you will call Me "My Husband" (ishi), אִישִׁי and no longer call Me "My Master" (ba'ali), בַּעְלִי'"** (Hosea 2:16).

We totally miss the word play here without seeing it in Hebrew. God says you will no longer call me 'ba'ali' בַּעְלִי which means '*my Lord & master, or owner*'. For instance, a *ba'al bayit* בעל בית in Hebrew is a landlord; also *ba'al* בעל is the name of a false god. God doesn't want us to serve him out of fear or obligation; but out of love.

God wants to be called 'ishi' אִישִׁי which means *'my man'* (term of endearment) but the word ishi also means 'PERSONAL'. Whether a man or a woman, God wants a personal relationship of intimacy with each one of us!

"I will betroth you to Me forever; yes, I will betroth you to Me In righteousness and justice, in lovingkindness and mercy; I will betroth you to Me in faithfulness, and you shall know the Lord." (Hosea 2:19-20)

Prayer: *Dear God, thank you that we are being transformed, like the transformation of a lowly caterpillar into a beautiful butterfly, by the renewing of our minds[11] with the truth of Your Word. Help us to pull off all the old negative labels others have placed upon us and believe the new names that You call us: chosen, delightful, holy, righteous, and beautiful. Help us to walk with our heads held high, wearing our crowns – secure in our new identity! In Yeshua's name. Amen v'amen.*

---

[11] Romans 12:2

Building with Wisdom & Understanding - Binah בינה

"Through wisdom (hochmah) חָכְמָה *a house is built, and by understanding (t'vunah)* תְבוּנָה *it is established; by knowledge the rooms are filled with all precious and pleasant riches."* (Proverbs 24:3-4)

The Scriptures tell us that it is through wisdom we build our house; and by understanding it is established. There is a secret connection hidden in the Hebrew between building, wisdom, understanding, and discernment.

The Hebrew word for wisdom is 'hochmah' חוכמה.
It also means, intelligence, knowledge, prudence and insight.

A word that often goes together with wisdom in Scripture is understanding, which is in Hebrew, 'havana' הֲבָנָה or binah בִּינָה.

The root of these words is 'boneh' בנה which means to '**build**'.

This clearly shows us that in order to build anything that will stand the storms of life – a secure home, family, business, ministry or marriage – we need wisdom and understanding.

The Bible tells us that, *"The wise woman builds her house; but a foolish one pulls it down with her own hands."* (Proverb 14:1)

But there is something else we need when trying to build and establish a solid foundation. To understand (v.) is the word 'mavin' מבין which contains the word 'beyn' בין which means 'between'. This word is also a derivative of the root word boneh (build).

In order to build our house with wisdom, we also need 'discernment' to know the difference *between* right and wrong; to discern *between* good and evil.

"Get wisdom (hochmah) חָכְמָה! Get understanding (binah) בִּינָה!
Do not forget, nor turn away from the words of my mouth.
Do not forsake her, and she will preserve you; love her, and she will keep you.
Wisdom is the principal thing; therefore get wisdom.
And in all your getting, get understanding." (Proverbs 4:5-7)

The Hebrew in these Scriptures for the word 'get' actually uses the word k'neh קְנֵה which means to 'buy or purchase'. We should be willing to sell all that we have to buy the pearl of great price – wisdom!

"...and upon finding one pearl of great value, he went and sold everything that he had and bought it." (Matthew 13:46)

The One Thing

What is the one thing that you most desire? If you were asked that simple question, what would you answer? Honestly.... What do you most desire? Good health? To meet the man/woman of your dreams and get married? To find your purpose in life? Lose 20 pounds? A home of your own? To take your family on a dream vacation? A better job? Or maybe all you want is for some semblance of peace in your heart and home?

These are all legitimate desires and there is nothing wrong with any of them; but the Word of God tells us, through the wisest man that ever lived, King Solomon, that wisdom is the primary thing – and there is nothing we desire that can even come close to the value of finding her.

"For wisdom is more precious than rubies, and nothing you desire compares with her." (Proverbs 8:11, 3:15)

The original Hebrew actually uses the word for **pearls,** פְּנִינִים (p'ninim), not rubies; which makes more sense in light of Yeshua's parable about the pearl of great price.[1] But never mind – the point is that wisdom is of immense value and according to Scripture, it should be our primary desire.

And yet how is it possible that wisdom should be our #1 desire when we have so many pressing and seemingly urgent needs?

A few years ago, when I was in constant pain and could only limp around a few steps with the help of a cane, all I wanted was to be able to walk freely and without pain. I couldn't even take my kids shopping at the mall like other mothers. I had to use an electric scooter just to get around the grocery store. It was agony just to get in and out of the car.

---
[1] Matthew 13:45-46

Plus, I was tired of feeling and looking so old and feeble! When I would see people walking and moving around normally, I would think, *"God, this is the one thing I want – just to walk. If You give me this one thing, I will never ask you for anything again in my life. I will always be thankful."*

Of course you know how long that lasted, right? After healing and recovering from two hip replacement surgeries, I can now walk freely without a cane. Halleluyah! All praises to the Most High God! But ... contrary to my foolish vow, I still have needs and desires that I go to God with on a daily basis. There are many things that I still need, want, desire, and petition God for. Wisdom, too often, is not at the top of the list where it should be.

The reality is, that even if God gives us what we ask for, if we don't have wisdom along with it, then we either won't be able to keep it, or it will end up being a curse instead of a blessing. God may supernaturally rescue us from our dumb decisions and their consequences; but if we don't get wisdom, then like a dog returns to its vomit,[2] we can end up repeating the same foolish mistakes over and over again.

We may receive healing; but we need wisdom on how to maintain good health. We may finally meet the man or woman of our dreams; but if we don't have wisdom on how to build a happy marriage it may just end in a heart-breaking divorce…. You get the picture…

A Listening Heart - Lev Shomeah

A young man named Solomon had just taken over the throne of Israel after the death of his father, the great King David. He apparently felt woefully inadequate to lead the nation of Israel; and so when God appeared to him in a dream one night offering Solomon anything his heart desired, he asked only for one thing – wisdom!

"So give your servant a discerning heart to govern your people and to distinguish between right and wrong. For who is able to govern this great people of yours?" (1 Kings 3:9)

Can you imagine if God actually appeared to you and said, *"Ask me for anything and I will give it to you!"* Wow! What would be the first thing out of your mouth? As for me, I honestly don't think I would have given the same answer as young Solomon's – would you have?

---

[2] Proverbs 26:11

In actuality, what Solomon asked for was not exactly 'wisdom' ; but rather something

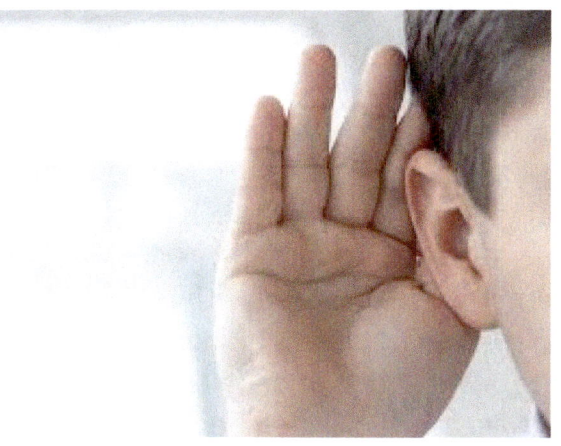

called in Hebrew a *'lev shomeah'*, לֵב שֹׁמֵעַ which literally means, *a 'listening heart'* or a 'heart that hears'.

My NKJV translation calls it a 'wise and discerning heart'.

If we are going to walk in wisdom, we need a heart that listens for and hears the voice of God.

Wisdom of the Heart

King Solomon asked for the ability to understand and to discern between right and wrong (good and evil) in order to judge the people of Israel rightly. He used these words 'l'havin' לְהָבִין (to understand) and 'bein' בֵּין (between). We also need understanding and discernment for every situation that we face in life.

So often, we make decisions out of our intellect – our human reasoning – but there is also an intuitive wisdom we may draw upon. If we are ever to know true wisdom that comes from above, heavenly wisdom, then we must develop a unique listening skill – the ability to listen from the heart.

Two women were brought to King Solomon with one baby. Each woman said that the live baby was hers and that the dead baby belonged to the other. There were no witnesses.

How could King Solomon judge this case with righteous judgment? If we listen only to the facts and judge only from the standpoint of justice, then all we hear is that a terrible criminal act has been committed:

one of these women has kidnapped the other woman's baby and has also committed the crime of perjury – lying in court under oath.

But if we listen from the heart – if we have a 'lev shomea' – then we can hear another voice. We hear the voice of loneliness and desperation. These two women are prostitutes. Men come and go, take what they came for, pay a few shekels, and leave. Most likely these two women experience little if any caring or true affection in their lives.

The woman says, **"we were together"** and **"there was no one else with us in the house"** and again, **"no one except the two of us in the house."** (1 Kings 3:18) Can we hear from our heart that these two women, except for one another, were alone in the world? No father to attend the birth; no midwife, no family member present to welcome these little ones into the world. How very different from the loving embrace of a family who welcomed my children and grandchildren into the world.

These women were alone, without hope, without love – except for this one tiny ray of light that had come into their lives through an infant – someone to cuddle, to nurse at their breast, to look into their eyes and smile with a smitten love reserved only for infants and mothers. Finally, there would be someone in their lives to give a pure love, untainted by lust and corruption – finally a bed companion that would not hurt or abandon.

But suddenly this spark of hope is snuffed out – smothered into oblivion – when one of the infants stops breathing. Can we understand when we listen with our hearts, the desperation of the woman who crept over and ever so quietly exchanged her dead baby for the living one?

King Solomon heard the case and proposed a just solution – cut the baby in half and give a half to each of the women. Here comes a man, not with love, but with brutality – much as these women, as harlots, have likely known in their experiences with men.

But Solomon is using this means to determine who is the real mother. He is not so much after who the biological mother is, but who is the 'real mother', for a real mother is the one who has compassion. All mothers carry their infants in their womb for nine months; but a real mother is one who carries the child all their lives with compassion.

The Hebrew word for mercy is rachamim רחמים – a word that stems from another word – 'rechem' רחם – the Hebrew word for 'womb'. Each biological mother carries a child in her 'rechem'; but a true mother has 'rachamin' for her child until the day she dies.

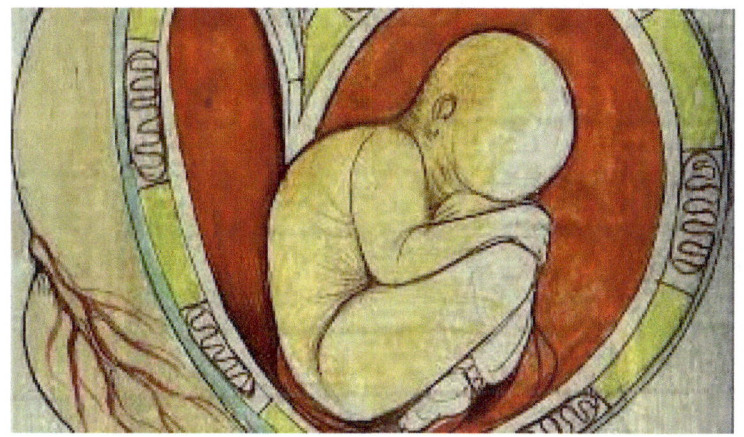

This is why abortion is such a grave sin – because the woman's womb (rechem) was created by God to be a place of mercy (rachamim) to her yet unborn child. And instead, through abortion, it becomes a brutal, dangerous place for a helpless, developing infant.

Hebrew4christians.com

We need both justice and mercy to walk in true wisdom; only God knows how to keep these and administer each in perfect balance. Often we fail by falling into the ditch on either side. But I believe that our sin nature tends to gravitate more easily towards justice; which is why Yeshua emphasized the need for mercy. He showed us the way of the cross; and as His followers we need to pick it up daily and follow Him, showing mercy to those who may not necessarily deserve it.

Law and justice came through Moses but mercy and grace through Yeshua Hamashiach (the Messiah), **"because while the Law was given through Moses, grace and truth came through Yeshua the Messiah."** (John 1:17)

May we each ask God and receive, not only 'hochmat Elohim' – wisdom to do justice, but also 'hochmat YHVH יהוה – wisdom to do mercy – by listening with our heart and not just our head.

Not only did Solomon receive God's wisdom; but he also applied it. Wisdom is not going to do us any good unless we apply the wisdom we have received.

God was, in fact, so pleased with Solomon's request for wisdom rather than long life, wealth, or vengeance on his enemies; that He gave him even what he didn't ask for: <u>honor and wealth</u> as well. [3]

"Riches and honor are with me (wisdom), enduring riches and righteousness."
(Proverbs 8:18)

Riches and honor and just some of the 'side benefits' of having wisdom:

"Length of days is in her right hand; in her left hand are riches and honor. Her ways are ways of pleasantness, and all her paths are peace. She is a tree of life (etz chayim) to them that lay hold upon her, and happy is every one that holds her fast." (Proverbs 3:16-18)

Wisdom is called a 'Tree of Life' (Etz Chayim) to those who take hold of her. These are some of the blessings of seeking wisdom – but it goes even deeper than just enjoying a blessed life.

We are living in perilous times; and if we want God's protection, then we need to heed the voice of wisdom.

"Fools despise wisdom and instruction …. But whoever listens to me (the voice of wisdom) will dwell safely, and will be secure, without fear of evil."
(Proverbs 1:7,33)

---

[3] 1 Kings 3:10-14

The Call of Wisdom

"Wisdom calls aloud outside; she raises her voice in the open squares. She cries out in the chief concourses, at the openings of the gates in the city."
(Proverbs 1:20-21)

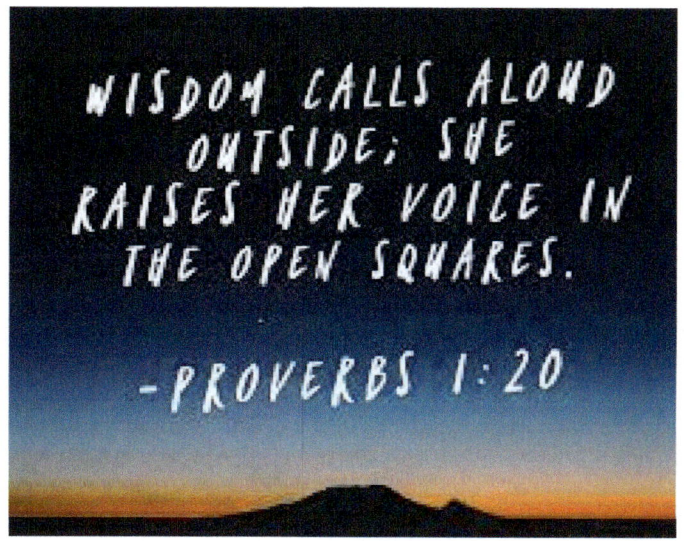

Wisdom calls aloud; she cries out for people to listen to her (yes, the Hebrew uses the feminine gender when referring to wisdom). So if wisdom is calling out to us, it should be an easy matter to hear her voice, right?

Actually, it's not so simple. Because there are counterfeit voices calling out to us also. In Proverbs chapter 9, there are two voices calling out an identical message: *"Come to me…. I have the answers you need…"*

The Way of Wisdom

"She (wisdom) cries out from the highest places of the city, "Whoever is simple, let him turn in here!...Forsake foolishness and live, and go in the way of understanding." (Proverbs 9:3-6)

This is the voice of the wise woman; but then there is also a foolish woman who knows nothing. And she is also calling out to anyone who passes by: **"Whoever is simple, let him turn in here…"** [4] but what she offers to those who turn in to her is not life, but death – a place in Sheol.[5]

Both voices may, on the surface, sound identical: *"Come here, and I will show you the way to go…"* but only one leads to life – the other to death. There are so many voices calling out to us today! With one click of a button on our cell phones, a whole world opens up to us with millions of voices saying, "Listen to me. I know the answer. I know the way…"

---

[4] Proverb 9:16
[5] Sheol is a Hebrew word for the place of the dead

The world promises answers; but Yeshua said, *"I am the way, the truth and the life; and no one comes to the Father but through me."* (John 14:6)

If we want to make sure we are listening to the right voices; then we need to tune out the voice of the foolish woman who entices with sin; and have a *'lev shomeah'* – a heart that listens for the voice of our Good Shepherd.[6]

Yeshua gives us a promise – that His sheep hear His voice and the voice of a stranger they will not follow. So my prayer is that we may have wisdom, understanding and discernment to judge between all the voices calling out to us today.

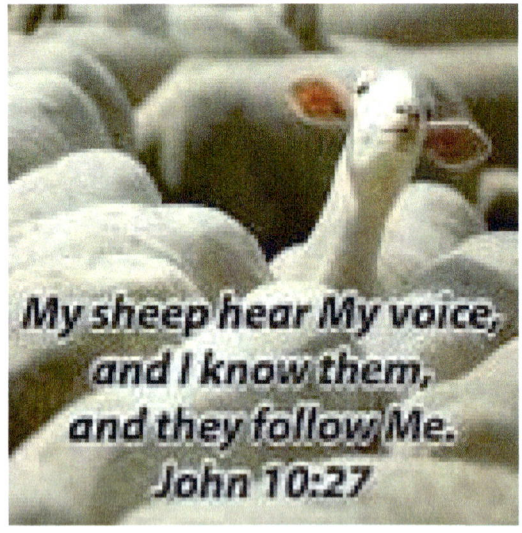

May we clearly hear the voice of Yeshua and follow Him with boldness, faith, courage and obedience; tuning out every voice that tries to entice us onto the broad path that so many walk on which leads to destruction.

In order to walk in the ways of wisdom, we might need to follow along the path less traveled. For the way that leads to life is narrow and few find it.

---

[6] John 10:4,5,27)

So let's assume that we have already established the primary importance of seeking after and finding wisdom. The question is, "How do we find her?"

One of the best known Scriptures in the Bible is a simple formula: *"Ask, and it will be given to you; seek, and you will find; knock, and it will be opened to you."* (Matthew 7:7)

1. ASK   *"Ask, and it will be given to you... "*

Wisdom may be found simply by 'asking'. God promises that those who ask Him for wisdom will receive it – liberally and without reproach![7]

God desires us to have wisdom; and He will gladly give it to us when we ask: *"Behold, You desire truth in the inward parts, and in the hidden part You will make me to know wisdom."* (Psalm 51:6)

Perhaps we simply have not because we ask not…

---

[7] James 1:5

2. SEEK *"...seek, and you will find..."*

If we want to receive wisdom and walk in her ways; the first thing we need to do is seek it. The Word of God promises that those who seek wisdom diligently will find it.

"I love those who love me, and those who seek me diligently will find me." (Proverbs 8:17)

3. KNOCK – on Heaven's Door *"...and it will be opened to you."*

To find wisdom, we need to knock on Heaven's door and spend time with our Heavenly Father. The way to hear from God is to ensure that we have enough quiet times of stillness and solitude with God in His word and in prayer.

Just like Yeshua we need to get away from the crowds and be alone with God. In all the noisiness of this world; we need to hear His still small voice. As Elijah found out, it is not always found in the dramas of life – the strong wind, the earthquake and the fire – but in a quiet place. Are we making room in our daily life for this sacred space of quietness and stillness to hear the inner voice of wisdom? The whisper of the Holy Spirit within our hearts?

Beware Evil Company - Find Wise Companions

If we want to be wise, then we need to walk with wise people and dissociate ourselves from foolish companions who will at best hold us back, or lead us astray; and at worst will completely destroy our life.

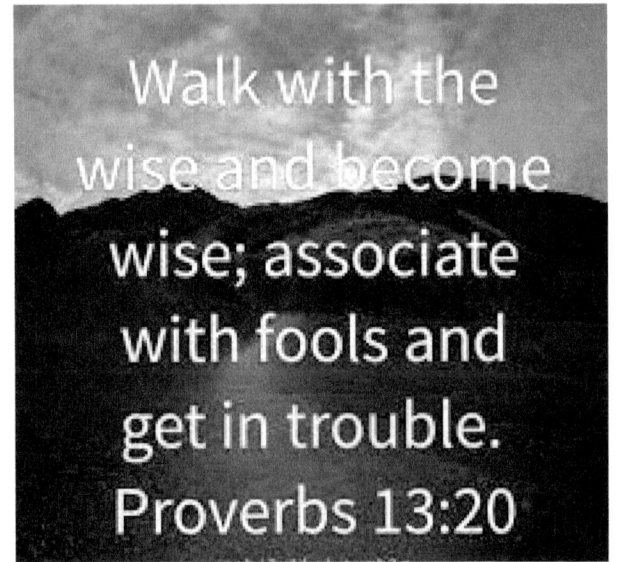

"He who walks with the wise will become wise, but the companion of fools will be destroyed." (Proverbs 13:20)

We desperately need to find wise people to help us in our search for wisdom. The Bible says that it is **by <u>wise counsel</u> that we wage our war**.[8]

---

[8] Proverb 24:6

King Rehoboam, the son of King Solomon, unfortunately listened to the advice of his peers instead of his elders' counsel; thereby sparking a rebellion against the House of David. This caused a civil war that divided the nation of Israel; and cost Rehoboam the entire Northern Kingdom (Ten Tribes of Israel).[9] It's important whose counsel we are listening to!

You may say, "I just don't even know any wise people!" I understand the familiar lament; but in this day of the internet we have no excuse. YouTube is filled with wise, godly mentors willing to give their nuggets of wisdom to anyone for free. We can receive wisdom simply by listening while driving in the car, peeling potatoes or even folding laundry.

We can also read inspirational, motivational and informative books – either on-line as ebooks or hardcopies. Libraries are filled with books written by believers sharing their wisdom. Our living rooms, laundry rooms, kitchens and cars can bestow upon us a Masters degree from the 'University of Wisdom'.

Receive Correction

There's no nice way of putting this – those who refuse to receive correction are just plain stupid. I didn't say it – the Bible did:

"Whoever loves discipline loves knowledge, but he who hates correction is stupid." (Proverbs 12:1).

If we want to walk in wisdom, then we need to get over our ego, our pride and our defensiveness in order to receive correction – especially from those who love us. My daughter was going out with a guy I didn't like. Not that I had anything against him personally, I could just plainly see that even as a PK (Pastor's Kid), he was a selfish, self-centered, prideful, vain young man who did not treat my daughter with the love she deserves.

And I told her so. Actually not just me, but almost everyone who knew and loved her told her so too. Thank God she listened to correction. She broke it off with him and is now married to a real prince who loves and cherishes her as the princess she is.

---

[9] 1 Kings 12

How can you tell a fool? When you try to correct them, they just hate you for it; and you only end up hurting yourself.

Balaam, the sorcerer, was walking in a way that was contrary to God's will. His donkey saw the angel in the road with a huge sword ready to kill him; and so the donkey stopped and refused to go any further.[10]

How did Balaam react? By kicking the donkey who was only trying to help. There are times when we are only going to get a kick in the pants from someone we are trying to help – because they are a fool. And if we want to be wise, then maybe just maybe we had better listen to the ass trying to correct us!

Live a Holy Life of Peace

We don't want wisdom from the world, however; we need wisdom from above, from the Holy Spirit (Ruach Hakodesh), who knows the end from the beginning and who will lead and guide us into all truth. ***"Real wisdom, God's wisdom, begins with a holy life and***

---

[10] Numbers 22

is characterized by getting along with others. It is gentle and reasonable, overflowing with mercy and blessings." (James 3:17 msg)

Wisdom begins with walking in the Fear of the Lord – in holiness – and understanding comes from truly knowing God.

"The fear of the Lord is the beginning of wisdom, and the knowledge of the Holy One is understanding." (Proverbs 9:10)

Keep God's Commandments

By keeping God's commandments and observing the laws in His Torah, all people should be able to see that we are a wise and discerning people because Yehovah יהוה is our God.

"Therefore be careful to observe them (God's laws and commandments); for this is your wisdom and your understanding in the sight of the peoples who will hear all these statutes, and say, 'Surely this great nation is a wise and understanding people.'" (Deuteronomy 4:6)

There is only one way of observing God's commandments; and that is to know what they are! And the only way I know of to do that is to read and study His Word. When I first came to faith, I had never read the Bible; and so I knew only the laws that my family kept as part of our Jewish tradition. As I read the Torah, I came to discover that many of the laws we were observing were not actually commanded by God at all – but were rather man-made rules and regulations decided upon by the rabbis.

Thus began my journey of sorting out which laws God had truly commanded; and which laws some rabbi had just decided to impose upon us. What a relief to find out that I really could rip the toilet paper or drink from the water fountain on the Sabbath (examples of some man-made rabbinic regulations).

I encourage you to read and study the Word of God for yourself. Read it all the way through – from Genesis to Revelation – and then read it again and again….

Word of God, Speak!

Because one of the ways that God gives us wisdom is through His written word. Yeshua is the Word of God that became flesh and dwelt amongst us.[11] He is the living Word; so the Scriptures are not simply ancient words written in an old book, but a supernatural way of communicating personally with us through the Holy Spirit (Ruach Hakodesh).

---

[11] John 1:14

We, as a family and as a ministry, are diligently seeking wisdom from God about the direction we should take in the near future. Every time I open my well worn, marked up, pages torn and taped back together, Hebrew-English Bible, I expect to receive a Word of Wisdom from God to my heart. I don't always understand it immediately; but in time, God makes it clear. It is so amazing, I know you are going to be astounded at the wisdom you will receive from the written Word of God.

Ask… seek… knock…

Prayer: *Dear God, we desperately need Your wisdom, guidance and direction. Without it, we are like lost sheep wandering in circles, taking dead ends, and venturing into traps set by the 'wolves'. Thank you for Your gracious promise that if we will but ask for wisdom, You will give it to us liberally and without reproach.*

You have promised to make us know wisdom in our inner being; and we need this wisdom to build our homes on the rock. We need wisdom to choose the right companions; to raise our children in a way that, when they get older, they will not depart from You; we need wisdom to have a marriage that honors You and stands the test of time; a family, ministry, or business, that brings glory to Your name.

Wisdom is the principal thing, and so we seek for a lev shomeah, a listening heart, to know the way in which we should go, that we may live securely, without any fear of evil. We seek for wisdom and expect, according to Your word, that we will find it.

"For whoever finds me (wisdom) finds life, and obtains favor from יהוה"
(Proverbs 8:35)

Amen v'Amen

Shabbat שבת An invitation to Rest

What is Shabbat? The Foundational Feast

Shabbat, the Sabbath, is the first of God's Appointed Times (Mo'adim in Hebrew), as described in the 23rd chapter of the book of Leviticus (Vayikrah). It is the foundational feast upon which all the others are built; and even though it is ignored and violated by a large majority of God's people, we all know what happens to a building that lacks a solid foundation.

In the beginning (Genesis/B'reisheet), God instituted Shabbat, a Sabbath day of rest for all humanity. It stands as a memorial of God's creation of the universe.

"Thus the heavens and the earth, and all the host of them, were finished. And on the seventh day God ended His work which He had done, and He rested on the seventh day from all His work which He had done. Then God blessed the seventh day and sanctified it, because in it He rested from all His work which God had created and made." (Genesis 2:1-3)

It is Finished

Does God really get tired and need to rest? Does He need afternoon naps like I sometimes do these days? In actuality, God never grows weary like we mortals do. He never comes home exhausted from a hard day at the office.

"Have you not known? Have you not heard? The everlasting God, the LORD, the Creator of the ends of the earth, neither faints nor is weary. His understanding is unsearchable." (Isaiah 40:28)

So why did God rest on the seventh day? God did not rest because he was exhausted from all His creative efforts. Even creating an entire universe is not hard for God; but God rested in a different sense – he stopped creating. We enter into His rest in a Sabbath sense, when we stop all our creative activity; and cease from interfering with our world.

God rested to set a boundary on His role as Creator of the Universe; and to model a pattern for humanity to follow. In keeping the Sabbath day holy, we are imitating God. After working, creating, and manipulating our universe, causing things to happen in our world for six days straight, we need to say, by faith, "It is finished, complete and done".

Thus, we are entering into the finished work of Yeshua who said to His Father, *"I have glorified You on the earth. I have finished the work which You have given Me to do."* (John 17:4)

When he made this proclamation, there were still people not healed, not saved, not delivered; and yet He knew He had completed His God-given assignment; and when He died on the cross He was able to say, *"It is finished."*

On the seventh day, we can cease from all our labors and rest just as God rested, trusting that what we have been able to accomplish in the six days God has given us to work is enough.

Dayeinu (It is Enough)!

Often, we need to rest by faith, since nothing around us seems to have been brought to completion. Unlike God, we are limited beings and sometimes don't seem to accomplish all we would like to in any designated week. But with all the piles of unfinished business, we can, in obedience to the model God showed us, say 'dayeinu' (it is enough) – I have worked enough now for a human being and I will now stop and rest – and be refreshed.

Sitting at the Feet of Yeshua

The Hebrew word, Shabbat, שַׁבָּת has several related meanings which give us added depth to our understanding of the Sabbath – and what it means to us. La'shevet לשבת means 'to sit'.

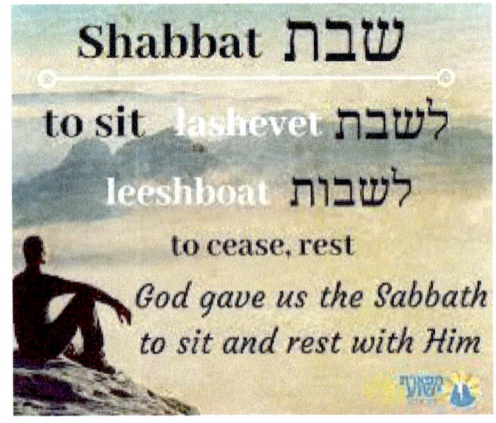

We are always running here and there; doing, doing, doing; but we are not human 'doings' – we are human 'beings'; and Shabbat is a time to just 'sit' and 'be'. It is a day when we just sit in our recliners or become a couch potato – resting without any guilt whatsoever, knowing that we are fulfilling the commandment of the Lord. We don't need to go anywhere or do anything.

Martha was so busy preparing the meal for Yeshua that she resented her sister, Mary, who was simply sitting at his feet listening to Him. But Yeshua said that Mary was doing what is better than serving; she was listening to the Son of God.[1]

We can become addicted to 'doing'; and for some 'go-getter' type of people, it may seem like torture to just sit and rest. But like Mary, we can take a break from all our striving; and just sit at the feet of Yeshua, soaking in His presence. This is not only a good idea, or an 'optional suggestion'; rather, it is one of the Ten Commandments, written on stone with the finger of God.

---

[1] Luke 10:38-42

Seated in Heavenly Places

It is such a blessing to just 'sit down', isn't it? When I've been on my feet for hours, preparing food for my family, I love to put it in the oven and then sit, even for a few minutes, with my feet up in my comfy recliner. Ah.... rest....

There was no seat in the temple for the cohen (priest) because his work was never done, so he could never sit down and rest in the fact that he was finished for good. He could never sit; he had to **"stand ministering daily and offering repeatedly the same sacrifices, which can never take away sins."** (Hebrews 10:11)

This is a picture of religion which attempts to be justified by works. We never know when our work is finished. By contrast, Yeshua, our **"High Priest (Cohen Hagadol) offered himself to God as a single sacrifice for sins, good for all time. Then he <u>sat down</u> in the place of honor at God's right hand."** (Hebrews 10:12)

Since we are saved by grace through faith, and not through our own works, we are invited to a seat at the table. God, in His infinite love and mercy, raised us up to **"<u>sit together</u> in the heavenly places in Messiah Yeshua..."** (Ephesian 2:6)

Can we rest in the finished work of the cross and invite others to 'pull up a comfy seat' and join us in our blessed Sabbath rest?

Ceasing from our Work לִשְׁבּוֹת

Another related Hebrew word to shabbat is 'lishbot' לִשְׁבּוֹת which means 'to cease'. It is this word used in the Scripture: *"… and He ceased on the seventh day from all His work which He had made."* (Genesis 2:2).

In my mind, I can still hear my father singing this exact line as he did for forty years while reciting the kiddush[2] over the wine every Friday evening to usher in the Sabbath.

In the New Testament, in the Book of Hebrews, it affirms this principle of ceasing from our work on the Sabbath day just as God ceased from His work on the seventh day.

"For whoever enters God's rest also ceases from his own work, just as God did from His." (Hebrews 4:10)

The ancient Hebrew Scriptures use a specific word for 'His work' and that is '<u>melachtoh</u>' מְלַאכְתּוֹ which carries more of the connotation of 'occupation, vocation, or employment'. We are not to do on the Sabbath what we do to make a living on the other six days of the week. For example, if we are a professional chef, we are not to cook on Shabbat.

No Longer Slaves שביתה

One more related word I find most interesting is 'shvitah' שביתה – which means <u>to go on strike</u>. This is one of the first new Hebrew words we learned when moving to Israel; because people seemed to go on strike so often. Every week, there was someone else on strike – the garbage men, the kindergarten teachers, or the bus drivers…. It was annoying to have piles of stinking garbage all over the streets of Jerusalem – but an effective strategy indeed.

---

[2] Kiddush is the blessing recited or chanted over the special wine on Friday evening before the Sabbath meal.

Keeping Shabbat is almost like going on strike. We can say, *"I am on strike from all the chores, responsibilities and duties of every other day of the week. I'm not doing dishes or laundry or even answering emails."*

Even our mind can go on strike from worrying about or talking about finances.

Keeping Shabbat is a sign of our freedom from slavery: **"Remember that you were slaves in Egypt and the Lord your God brought you out of there with a mighty hand and an outstretched arm. Therefore the Lord your God has commanded you to observe the Sabbath day."** (Deuteronomy 5:15)

Ceasing our work – going on strike – on the seventh day as God has commanded gives a powerful message that declares, *"God is my provider and my source of all good. I am no longer a slave to work or money; I will not serve two masters. I belong to God and He takes care of me."*

It All Starts With Rest

All of our activity must come out of a place of rest and peace. This concept goes all the way back to the Garden of Eden. God created the first man and woman on the sixth day and on the seventh day, He rested.

Adam's first day on earth after his creation was a day of rest! Doesn't it seem logical that in all of his excitement, Adam would want to explore this wonderful garden, set some short term and long term goals and then immediately get started on his ten point action plan? But no – being comes before doing. The commandment to rest on the seventh day is still one of the Ten Commandments; one that we disregard at our own peril.

God has given us a precious gift in the Sabbath; but people are, by our sin nature, boundary pushers if not outright boundary breakers. Like little children, we're always trying to push the limits of grace. But the fear of the Lord is the beginning of wisdom.

The One who created us knows best how we can keep a balance of work and rest in our lives. The Creator of our minds, souls, and bodies wrote an owner's manual, the Bible, and we would do well to heed its instructions. The command to keep Shabbat is not an optional suggestion, and in keeping God's commandments there is great reward.[3]

Many people these days are suffering from fatigue, stress and chronic pain in their bodies as well as an emptiness of soul and despair of spirit.

God has given us the remedy: ***"In returning and rest you shall be saved; in quietness and confidence/trust shall be your strength (might or courage)."*** (Isaiah 30:15)

But the Israelites refused God's counsel, saying, ***"No, for we will flee on horses."*** (Isaiah 30:16) I wonder how many precious, weary, worn out saints are riding fast horses while the Lord is patiently waiting for them to slow down so that He may reveal to them His grace?

Because our physical selves are so intricately connected to our emotional, spiritual and mental states, our healing can come once we learn to obey Him, not only in what He wants us to *do* for Him, but also in what He wants us to *not do*.

In my book, <u>Messiah Revealed in Shabbat</u>,[4] I write, "*In a tension-filled, competitive, hurry-up world, Shabbat is an island of time, a sanctuary to create for ourselves and our families. The sun will still rise if we stay away from the malls for a day and simply rest. It is necessary for the survival of our souls, especially in these end times, to isolate ourselves from all the pressures of life and rest in the arms of our heavenly Father.*"

Shabbat occurs every seven days, since our Creator knew that this pattern of work and rest would be necessary to ensure that work does not rule our lives.

Shabbat gives us time to reflect on the priorities in our lives, and to focus more on the spiritual than the physical. Shabbat ensures that we give sufficient love and attention to those in our families who need our undivided time.

---

[3] Psalm 19:11
[4] https://www.voiceforisrael.net/product-page/messiah-revealed-in-the-sabbath-1

God never intended for Shabbat to become a legalistic, joyless, dutiful conformity to a set of do's and don'ts (mostly don'ts) of man-made rabbinic rules such as I grew up with in an Orthodox Jewish home. Shabbat is God's gift to humanity, a gift that sets us free from the bondage of believing the lies that we have to do it all; and that the source of our value and worth is in our works. Can resting be holy? God's word says that it can be, when done His way.

Welcoming the Sabbath as a Bride

Here in Israel, each day is measured by its relationship to the Sabbath. As the week progresses, preparations are made to receive the Sabbath bride. On Yom Shishi (the sixth day), most women are busy finishing the housework, shopping for last minute provisions, preparing the traditional braided bread called challah, and cooking a special Sabbath meal. Candles are lit and the family gathers for a special meal, to praise God, to welcome this holy day, and to bless our children.

By the afternoon, men are off work, construction ceases, buses stop running, businesses close their doors after the frantic pre-Shabbat rush. Peace begins to descend upon the pale yellow stones of Jerusalem as the sun sets.

We wake up late on Shabbat (Saturday) morning to the quiet of streets with little traffic and a glorious day ahead of knowing that we need do nothing other than spend time with one another and with our God, reading and discussing His Word, and catching up on our rest. Often, we will attend a Shabbat service at a Messianic congregation.

What about Sunday?

Worshiping God is good and beautiful any day of the week, including Sunday, but even going to church on Sundays does not change the fact that God created the Sabbath to be on the seventh day of the week (Saturday).

Yeshua kept the seventh day Sabbath and did not change it. This was a man-made change when the Emperor Constantine, in an act of anti-semitism, required believers to worship on Sunday. Keeping the 7th day Sabbath became punishable by death!

Most Christians now worship and attend services on Sunday, to honor the day that Yeshua rose from the dead; however this does not nullify the Sabbath day.

The first day of the week symbolizes a new beginning; but the 7th and last day of the week represent completion, "It is finished."

> **SUNDAY SERVICES**
> Early believers kept Saturday as the Sabbath until March 7, 321 CE when Constantine passed a law requiring believers to worship on Sunday, the day the pagans worshipped the sun-god. Believers still kept Saturday as the Sabbath until another law was passed eleven years later. This law signed into decree by Constantine forbid believers to worship on the Sabbath *(Saturday)* and it was punishable by death by the Catholic Church. Many believers were burned to death by the Catholic Church for keeping the Sabbath. *(Saturday)*

Is Shabbat for Christians?

A question is often asked whether or not keeping Shabbat is valid for non-Jewish believers? Did God give the Sabbath only to the Jewish people? Many Christians, who accept the validity of the Ten Commandments, seem to forget that the law of the Sabbath is most comprehensively stated in the fourth of the Ten Commandments:

*"**Remember the Sabbath day, to keep it holy.** Six days you shall labor and do all your work, but the seventh day is the Sabbath of the Lord your God. In it you shall **do no work**: you, nor your son, nor your daughter, nor your male servant, nor your female servant, nor your cattle, nor your stranger who is within your gates. For in six days the Lord made the heavens and the earth, the sea, and all that is in them, and rested the seventh day. Therefore the Lord blessed the Sabbath day and hallowed it."* (Exodus 20:8-11)

Notice that even the cows and the slaves enjoyed a day of rest. It is a gift to everyone to enjoy, not just the Jewish people. Even our servants are to take this day off to rest and relax. Shabbat is a testimony to God's love for all people and His desire that all be treated humanely and fairly. It was not just the Jewish people who were to rest on Shabbat, but also the aliens and strangers, the servants and slaves. On this day, everyone stands equal before the Lord in deserving a day of rest – slave and free, Jew and Gentile, male and female, rich and poor.

Shabbat is a gift from God to us with a promise of great blessings to those of us who will receive. Even foreigners who bind themselves to the Lord to keep His Sabbaths and not desecrate the Sabbath will receive joy in the Lord's house of prayer on His holy mountain.

"Also the sons of the foreigner who join themselves to the Lord, to serve Him, and to love the name of the Lord, to be His servants – everyone who keeps from defiling the Sabbath, and holds fast My covenant – even them I will bring to My holy mountain, and make them joyful in My house of prayer. Their burnt offerings and their sacrifices will be accepted on My altar; for My house shall be called a house of prayer for all nations." (Isaiah 56:6-7)

We often quote the last line of these verses out of context in Churches; without connecting this promise to keeping the Sabbath holy. Many Christians use the seventh day, Saturday, as a busy day of shopping, house cleaning and errands.

Sunday can be stressful as well, with morning and evening church services, and numerous ministries that people are committed to and involved in. They really have no day designated as a day to simply rest!

What have we done with this fourth of the Ten Commandments? Do we chisel it out of the rock each week?

If even the animals and slaves are to be given this day to rest, how much more so must God desire to see His people receiving and accepting the gift He has given us to rest on Shabbat.

The Sabbath was made for all mankind: **"The Sabbath was made for man, not man for the Sabbath. So the Son of Man is Lord even of the Sabbath."** (Mark 2:27-28)

Contrary to what some people believe, the Sabbath is not just a day off work to do as we please; it is to be a holy day. And when we will keep these boundaries; then God will give us great joy!

"'If you keep your feet from breaking the Sabbath and from doing as you please on my holy day, if you call the Sabbath a delight and the Lord's holy day honorable, and if you honor it by not going your own way and not doing as you please or speaking idle words, then you will find your joy in the Lord, and I will cause you to ride on the heights of the land and to feast on the inheritance of your father Jacob.' The mouth of the Lord has spoken." (Isaiah 58:13-14)

What about the New Covenant?

Some believe that keeping the Sabbath day holy is no longer valid under the New Covenant. Yeshua, however, clearly stated that He did not come to abolish the Torah, but to fulfill it.[5] We are also told what happens to God's commandments under the New Covenant. They are not tossed into the trash; but rather they become internalized – in our mind and heart – and kept out of love for God, not fear of punishment.

"...I will put My law in their minds and write it on their hearts. I will be their God, and they will be My people." (Jeremiah 31:33)

We do not keep Shabbat to try and rack up brownie points from God in order to earn our way into Heaven; rather, because we know we are saved, we demonstrate our love for God by keeping His commandments.

"For this is the love of God, that we should keep His commandments; and His commandments are not burdensome." (1 John 5:3)

Fourth Commandment

And you, speak to the children of Yisra'ĕl, saying, 'My Sabbaths you are to guard, by all means, for it is a sign between Me and you throughout your generations, to know that I, יהוה, am setting you apart.
Exodus 31:13

SABBATH SIGN OF COVENANT

And I also gave them My Sabbaths, to be a sign between them and Me, to know that I am יהוה who sets them apart.
Ezekiel 20:12

Chloe

The Sabbath is not only the fourth of the Ten Commandments, but also a special sign (ot) אות between God and His covenant people to demonstrate that we are a set apart, holy (kadosh) people.

Therefore, we are to guard (shomer) שומר (keep watch over), protect and preserve the Sabbath to keep it holy. The question is, are we guarding what God has given us to protect and preserve?

---

[5] Matthew 5:17-19

Guarding the Gates

Why do we lock our homes at night or when we go out? Why do we lock our cars? Why do we watch over our children while they play at the playground?

Isn't it because these are precious to us or of great value that we guard them so carefully? What happens when the people assigned to guard something, someone or some place fail to do so? Disaster!

We once went out to a congregation in Jerusalem without checking that our house was securely locked and secure with the electric metal blinds pulled down over all the windows. That night, thieves broke into the house and we came home to find that all our worldly possessions had been stolen! What a shock!

Adam and Eve were charged with an assignment: to work (la'avdah) לְעָבְדָהּ and to 'guard' (shomerah) שָׁמְרָהּ the Garden of Eden.[6] Their failure to guard the garden from evil elements such as the lying serpent caused them – and all future generations of humanity – to be exiled from paradise and doomed to live in a world full of pain and sorrow (thorns and thistles).

Moses left his brother, Aaron, in charge of guarding the camp while he went up the mountain to receive the Ten Commandments.

What happened when Aaron failed to 'shomer' (guard) the Israelite camp and did not restrain the people? In Moses' absence, they created a golden calf (egel ha'zahav - a pagan cult image) and bowed down to it in worship, bringing upon themselves the wrath of God.

---

[6] Genesis 2:15

This resulted in not only the destruction of the original stone tablets when Moses threw them down in anger, but also the deaths of three thousand men who had committed the sin of idolatry.[7]

Nehemiah was a man of God who took his role as a guard (shomer) seriously. When Nehemiah saw the people of Israel breaking Shabbat by doing their business on the Sabbath day, he warned them:

"In those days I saw people in Judah treading wine presses on the Sabbath, and bringing in sheaves, and loading donkeys with wine, grapes, figs, and all kinds of burdens, which they brought into Jerusalem on the Sabbath day. And I warned them about the day on which they were selling provisions." (Nehemiah 13:15)

Nehemiah warned the people that they would bring disaster upon themselves by this evil thing that they were doing in profaning the Sabbath day:

"Then I contended with the nobles of Judah, and said to them, 'What evil thing is this that you do, by which you profane the Sabbath day? Did not your fathers do thus, and did not our God bring all this disaster on us and on this city? Yet you bring added wrath on Israel by profaning the Sabbath.'" (Nehemiah 13:17-18)

We lived for several years in a small village in Israel that held a spring market day (Shuk Aviv) every year. People would set up their booths and stalls to display their wares; and to sell them. There was music, laughter, food, and fun for the whole family. So what's the problem? It was held on the Sabbath. Really….

Every year we would protest; and every year they would ignore us and go ahead with their spring market on the Sabbath day. I find it no coincidence that this particular village was plagued with thefts.

For all the years that we lived there, a week would rarely go by that we would not see someone post in the local WhatsApp group that someone's house was broken into or someone's car had been stolen. God will not be mocked. We are not to do our business on Shabbat.

So Nehemiah posted guards (perhaps this is what we should have done) to guard the gates to keep the Sabbath holy.

---

[7] Exodus 32

"And I commanded the Levites that they should cleanse themselves, and that they should go and guard the gates, to sanctify the Sabbath day."
(Nehemiah 13:22)

Is it not perhaps time to cleanse ourselves and guard the gates to keep the Sabbath day holy once again? Later, we see the real reason that the Israelites had begun to so flagrantly break Shabbat – they had married pagan women.

Cleansing from Paganism

"In those days I also saw Jews who had married women of Ashdod, Ammon, and Moab." (Nehemiah 13:23)

They had become so adapted to the culture of their pagan wives, that half of their children no longer even spoke the language of Judah! Nehemiah cursed them, struck them and even pulled out their hair! Granted this seems extreme to us; but so radical was Nehemiah's zeal for the Lord! He reminded the people of Israel that marrying foreign women was King Solomon's downfall.

Is it possible that we have become so 'adapted' to the foreign, pagan culture in which we live that we no longer 'speak the language of Judah'? No longer keep the ways of the God of Israel? Do not even consider the commandment to keep the seventh day holy?

Nehemiah declares, *"Thus I cleansed them of everything pagan."* (Nehemiah 13:30)

We need to cleanse ourselves and make covenantal relationships with those who keep the ways of the Lord, not 'pagan women'. Let us return to a Biblical path – the narrow way that leads to life; and one of the most significant ways is through keeping Shabbat.

God warns us not to worship Him in a pagan way[8]. It is God who commanded us to keep the Sabbath on the seventh day; but pagans worship the sun god on the first day of the week – 'Sun-day'. Let us keep the ways of the God of Jacob, instead of worshiping God with pagan festivals and man-made traditions.

---

[8] Deuteronomy 12:4

Death Penalty for Sabbath Breakers

God takes the commandment to keep the Sabbath day holy and do no work on it very seriously. In fact, breaking the Sabbath carried the death penalty in Israel.

"For six days, work is to be done, but the seventh day shall be your holy day, a day of sabbath rest to the LORD. Whoever does any work on it is to be put to death." (Exodus 35:2)

Observing the Sabbath was an important sign of the covenant between God and His people; therefore, breaking this important symbol of the covenant was such a serious breach of the relationship that it was assigned the death penalty.

When a man was found gathering sticks on the Sabbath day, God ordered him to be stoned to death.[9] If God considered this day of rest to be so vitally important, should we not also take it seriously?

"There remains therefore a rest for the people of God." (Hebrews 4:9)

Prophetic Shabbat in the Messianic Era

One of the most beautiful things about Shabbat is that it points to the future state of perfect rest and peace that we will enjoy in the Messianic Age, under the righteous reign of the Messiah Yeshua.

This is called the day when all will be Shabbat. There will be no more strife or protests, no racial riots, no genocide and no more wars:

"They shall beat their swords into plowshares and their spears into pruning hooks; nation will not lift sword against nation and they will no longer study warfare." (Isaiah 2:4)

The Messianic Era as a time when there will be no hunger, lack, violence, jealousy or rivalry (even among the animals), and all people will know God, as it is written:

"The wolf will live with the lamb, the leopard will lie down with the goat, the calf and the lion and the yearling together; and a little child will lead them.

---

[9] Numbers 15:32-36

The cow will feed with the bear, their young will lie down together, and the lion will eat straw like the ox.

The infant will play near the hole of the cobra, and the young child will put his hand into the viper's nest.

They will neither harm nor destroy on all my holy mountain, for the earth will be full of the knowledge of the Lord as the waters cover the sea." (Isaiah 11:6-9)

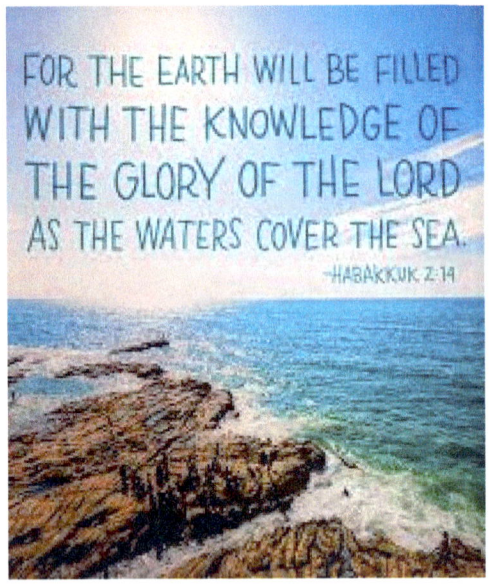

Let us, therefore, call the Sabbath day a delight; celebrating our freedom from slavery to the world system; proclaiming God as our provider; demonstrating our love for God; and enjoying a foretaste of 'Heaven on Earth' – each and every seventh day.

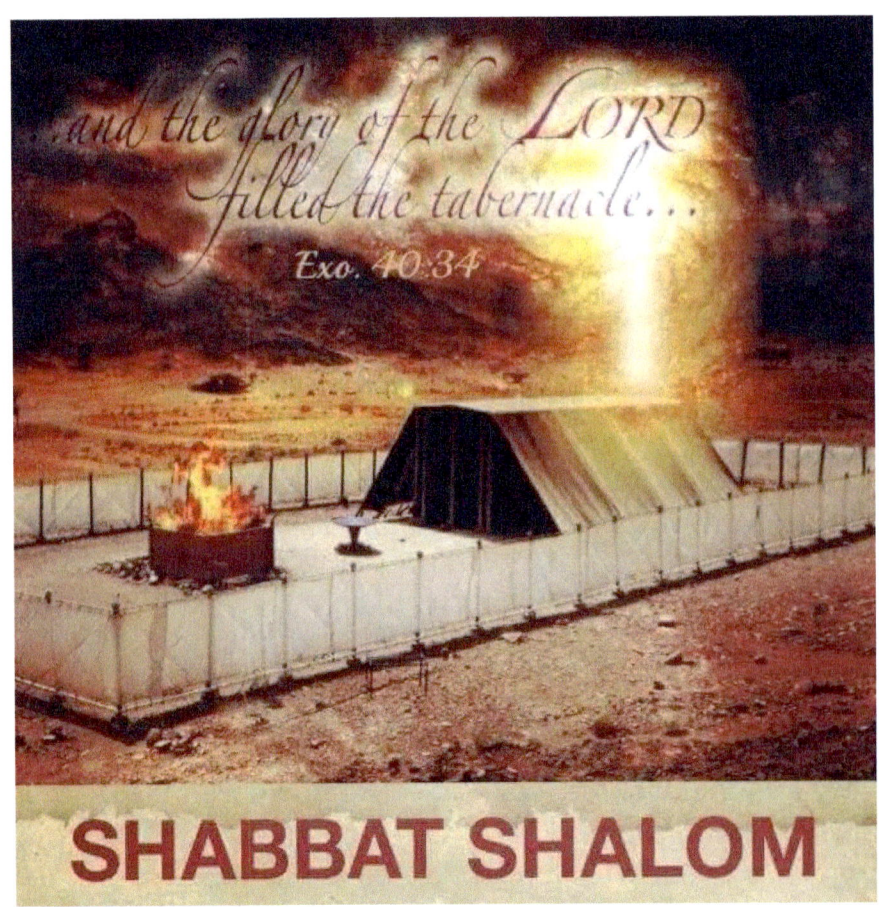

<u>Prayer</u>: *Dear God, we have become such 'human doings' instead of 'human beings' that we no longer even know how to simply sit and rest at Your feet. We have become uncomfortable or anxious when not distracted by work or entertainment.*

Forgive us for breaking this important commandment that you have given us as a gift, by profaning the Sabbath day – or by changing it in a way that You never intended.

Help us to have the grace to cease from all our labors and striving, to come out from among this busy world, and enter into Your rest on the seventh day as we follow in Your footsteps.

May the Sabbath day be a delight – holy, set apart time - that brings refreshment and restoration to our body, mind, soul and spirit.   In Yeshua's name. Amen v'amen.

Leaving Egypt - Mitzraim מִצְרַיִם

Every year at Passover (Pesach), we celebrate the remembrance of the great miracles God performed in order to deliver us from Egypt. With a mighty hand and an outstretched arm, He rescued us from the bondage of slavery into freedom.

"So we called out to the LORD, the God of our fathers; and the LORD heard our voice and saw our affliction, toil, and oppression. Then the LORD brought us out of Egypt with a mighty hand and an outstretched arm, with great terror, signs, and wonders." (Deuteronomy 26:8)

God sent the Ten Plagues upon Egypt until finally, with the last and most terrible plague, Death of the Firstborn, Pharaoh finally agreed to let the children of Israel go free.

Hebrew uses the word '*makot*' מכות for plagues, which means '*beatings or strikes*'. God gave Egypt a mighty beating as He struck the nation with these ten 'makot' in order to bring His people out of their affliction, trouble, and oppression.

Of course we who are followers of Yeshua Hamashiach (the Messiah), understand the deeper spiritual significance of this great historical event. Egypt represents the Kingdom of darkness; and Pharaoh represents Satan, the ruler of his wicked kingdom. The slave masters represent the demons who afflict, torment, and oppress God's people.

The innocent Passover lambs that were slain represent Yeshua, whose blood saves us from the wrath of God. When the Lord passed through Egypt that terrible night to claim every firstborn, it was only the blood of the Lamb that saved the Israelites.

And it is the same for you and for me today. We are saved from God's judgment by one thing alone – not by how good we are, or how much charity we have given; but only by the blood of the Lamb.

"Now the blood shall be a sign for you on the houses where you are. And when I see the blood, <u>I will pass over you</u>; and the plague shall not be on you to destroy you when I strike the land of Egypt." (Exodus 12:13)

Pass - over ('Pesach') פסח

This is where we get the word Passover, which in Hebrew is 'Pesach' פסח – which literally means 'to pass over'. Judgment passes over us; and instead we receive mercy.

Thank God for the blood of the Lamb of God, Yeshua Hamashiach, the Messiah, Lamb of God that protects us from the wrath of God so that Divine judgment may not touch us. He has delivered us from bondage to the powers of darkness; and transferred us into the Kingdom of His beloved son, in whom we have redemption and forgiveness of sins.

"He has delivered us from the power of darkness and conveyed us into the kingdom of the Son of His love, in whom we have redemption through His blood, the forgiveness of sins." (Colossians 1:13-14)

Let My People Go!

God's desire for us to have spiritual freedom from all oppression so that we may serve the Lord with joy and gladness. For this was the whole purpose of Israel's liberation from Egypt. God said to Pharaoh over and over again, **"Let My people go – that they may serve me!"** [1]

Yeshua stood up in a synagogue in Nazareth one Sabbath day and proclaimed His mission as one of 'setting the captives free'. He read from the scroll of Isaiah where it is written, *"The Spirit of the Lord is upon Me, because He has anointed Me to preach the gospel to the poor; He has sent Me to heal the brokenhearted, <u>to proclaim liberty to the captives</u>…<u>to set at liberty those who are oppressed</u>…"*
(Luke 4:18-19)

Yeshua went about doing good; and healing all those who were oppressed by the devil.[2]

Festival of Liberation

We understand Passover to be a celebration of the Israelites' liberation from slavery in Egypt. When we celebrate the Passover, however, we are to consider it not just 'their' liberation, but also a declaration of our own personal freedom.

Egypt can represent much more than a place on the map. In Hebrew, the word for Egypt, 'Mitzrayim' מִצְרָיִם, shares the same root as the word 'metzer' מצר which means <u>boundaries or limitations</u>. Egypt represents the place of limitation that the enemy has placed upon us in order to hinder us from fulfilling our God-given assignment, calling and destiny. The ruler of spiritual Egypt says, "*<u>This is the boundary – this is as far as you go and no further</u>.*"

---

[1] Exodus 7:16, 8:1, 9:13
[2] Acts 10:38

Sometimes we feel that we have gone as far as we can go in life; that this is the end for us. But we need to resist this defeatist mentality. If we are still alive and breathing, then God still has a plan and purpose for our life to give Him glory.

The Hebrew word for narrow, tzar צר, is also contained in the word for Egypt, Mitzraim מִצְרַיִם. It is not God's will for us to live a limited, narrow, pinched existence. Yeshua came to give us life and life more abundantly.

Another derivative of this Hebrew word is **'tzarot'** צרות which means 'troubles'. Troubles will come in this life; as Job said, *"Yet man is born to trouble, as the sparks fly upward."* (Job 5:7) In this world, we will have trouble, but we are created and empowered by the Spirit of God to overcome challenges and live a victorious life.

Another word related to 'narrow' and 'trouble', is the Hebrew name for the anti-Christ **(tzaror)** צרור. This enemy of our souls wants to keep us in a narrow, restricted place of trouble and sorrow; but Yeshua is training us to be overcomers in this spiritual battle with forces of evil. He will teach our hands to battle and our fingers to war.[3]

Yeshua said, *"In this world you will have troubles (tzarot); but be of good cheer, I have overcome the world."* (John 16:33)

Our troubles and trials are not meant to restrict us; but to set us free. The three Hebrew men, Shadrach, Meshach and Abednego, went bound into the fiery furnace; but there was a 4th man in the fire; and when they came out they were <u>unbound</u> and didn't even smell like smoke! [4]

When we go through the fiery furnaces of life; may we know that Yeshua is always the 4th man in the fire with us; and He will bring us through to freedom.

"Therefore if the Son makes you free, you shall be free indeed." (John 8:36)

---

[3] Psalm 144:1
[4] Daniel 3:16-28

Each of us has been 'bound' to some extent by fears and doubts about our abilities; by others' opinions of our worth, and by past abuse or failure. We may see ourselves, as did the ten Israelite spies, as mere 'grasshoppers' in our own eyes and think we could never accomplish anything for God.

We may restrict ourselves with our own lingering 'slave mentality', or live in bondage to selfishness, greed, lust or addictions. Passover is the season of liberation!

It is a time for breakthrough – to break out of our own personal 'Mitzraim' – to transcend the boundaries or limitations that have held us captive, either from others or our own faulty thinking patterns, and to be released into the fullness of God's purpose for our lives. Halleluyah!

"Now the Lord (Ha-Adon) is the Spirit (Ruach); and where the Spirit of the Lord is, there is liberty." (2 Corinthians 3:17)

God doesn't want us walking around dragging our feet, hands hanging limp, heads bowed in shame, looking as if someone's been standing over us with a whip all our lives. He doesn't want us to feel as if we've been stomping in the muck and mire all day, building bricks for the Egyptians' pyramids!

Yeshua said that He came to give us life and life more abundantly! (John 10:10)

The enemy is the one who has come to steal, kill and destroy. He wants to keep us in bondage, in misery, in defeat. But we must rise up as children of freedom, of the living God, and declare our liberty in Messiah!

Setting the Elephants Free [5]

A story is told of an elephant that had its leg tied to a post ever since it had joined the circus as a baby. The young elephant learned that it could walk only so far and no further. As the elephant grew, only a thin rope was needed. Now an adult, it could easily break that rope; but it did not even try. Eventually, it was no longer necessary to even tie the elephant's leg to the post. Even once set free, it would not walk past the previously established limits.

We are sometimes like that elephant. The ruler of 'Mitzraim' has said this is as far as you can go; and we have come to accept these limits. But Yeshua paid the price for us to be set free from sin and all bondage placed upon us by the powers of darkness. Can we believe this truth and embrace the liberty that is our heritage as the redeemed of the Lord?

Let us believe by faith that he or she who the Son has set free is free indeed. (John 8:36)

In order to live out this freedom however, we must first be transformed in our minds. Just as the elephants' feet had worn deep grooves in the earth by tramping down the same path day after day, so too do we carve out neural 'grooves' in our mind, by thinking the same thought patterns day in and day out.

I received a revelation on this one day while watching a science program about the neural and physiological development of babies. The film showed that in order for a baby to learn new behaviors such as smiling, turning over, or grabbing a toy, their brains

---

[5] From my book, Messiah Revealed in Passover
https://www.voiceforisrael.net/product-page/messiah-revealed-in-the-passover-1

must actually develop new neural patterns that accommodate this new behavior. It was one of those 'aha' moments. The scripture about being transformed by the renewing of my mind suddenly took on new meaning

"And do not be conformed to this world, but be transformed by the renewing of your minds, that you may prove what is that good and acceptable and perfect will of God." (Romans 12:2)

Caroline Leaf, communication pathologist and cognitive neuroscientist, as well as New York Times Bestselling Author, writes:

"What you think with your mind changes your brain and body, and you are designed with the power to switch on your brain. Your mind is that switch. You have an extraordinary ability to determine, achieve, and maintain optimal levels of intelligence, mental health, peace, and happiness, as well as the prevention of disease in your body and mind.

You can, through conscious effort, gain control of your thoughts and feelings, and in doing so, you can change the programming and chemistry of your brain.

Breakthrough neuroscientific research is confirming daily what we instinctively knew all along: what you are thinking every moment of every day becomes a physical reality in your brain and body, which affects your optimal mental and physical health. These thoughts collectively form your attitude, which is your state of mind, and it's your attitude and not your DNA that determines much of the quality of your life." [6]

Get Out of the Rut!

In order to 'get out of the rut' that I had already worn down in my brain by thinking the same thoughts over and over again, I needed to actually and consciously think new thoughts; to create new neural pathways in my brain – to blaze a new trail in a sense!

Where I had previously thought about what my emotions dictated, for example, "I can't do it", I must now begin to think and speak in alignment with the Word of God, ***"I can do all things through the Messiah who strengthens me."*** (Philippians 4:13)

This is not as easy as it sounds. Do you think it's easy to budge an elephant? It's much more comfortable and familiar to walk along the same old paths that we have trodden

---

[6] https://drleaf.com/products/switch-on-your-brain

down for years. But in order to enjoy the freedom that our Messiah died for, we must venture beyond the known into the unknown, full of courage and trust in a God who promises to never leave and never forsake us!

Between the Straits

"From the straits* (hameitzar) הַמֵּצַר *I called upon the LORD; He answered me with great enlargement." (Psalm 118:5)

There may come into our lives times of such distress and difficulty, that we may say we are in *'dire straits'*. The three weeks between the 17th Tammuz and the 9th of Av in the Jewish calendar are known as the time period called *'bein hamizrim'* בין המצרים meaning 'between the straits' – a Hebrew phrase which also contains the word 'mitzraim' מצרים (Egypt).

It is used in a Scripture from the Book of Lamentations, read on Tisha B'av: [7]

***"Judah has gone into captivity, under affliction and hard servitude; she dwells among the nations, she finds no rest; all her persecutors overtake her 'between the straits' 'Bein Hamitzrim'* בֵּין הַמְּצָרִים."** (Lamentations 1:3)

It is 'between the straits' that we may be overtaken by the enemy. The phrase 'between the straits' means to go through a time of great peril – threading your way between grave dangers on both sides – like a ship trying to squeeze through a perilously narrow path and trying to avoid the almost inevitable shipwreck.

A few years ago, during a war with Hamas, a missile landed not only in my family's village; but on their very street. The night before, my daughter had felt led by the Holy Spirit to go out and prayer-walk their street.

That missile flew through a very narrow space between two homes and landed to explode harmlessly in a vacant lot. Although the force of the blast blew out their windows; there were thankfully no casualties or fatalities.

---

[7] Tisha B'av (9th of the month of Av) is a day of fasting and mourning in remembrance of the destruction of both the 1st and 2nd Temples
https://www.voiceforisrael.net/_files/ugd/5aa6a5_bdfc5857c1c3400aa5b0b2f027afa3fa.pdf

The emergency workers who came to investigate were amazed! They said that for the missile to fly as it did between these two homes was like threading the eye of a needle. They acknowledged that this must have been the hand of God guiding the missile and they left saying, "*Someone must have been watching out for you*".

Even in perilous times such as these, wars and famines and natural disasters, we can trust that God is watching over us.

The Ruler of This World

Truly we are living in perilous times! Until Yeshua returns, Satan has been given temporary authority upon the earth and is, in fact, called **'the ruler of this world'**. (John 12:31)

Yeshua said, **"*The ruler of this world* approaches. He has no power over me."** (John 14:30)

Satan is also called the god of this world. **"*Satan, who is the god of this world, has blinded the minds of those who don't believe the Gospel.*"** (2 Corinthians 4:4)

Just as Israel suffered under the wicked rule of Pharaoh in Egypt, so do we go through trials and tribulations in this world which is under the temporary rule of Satan. We see evil and wickedness all around us. The only way to walk through this world is to trust in God and obey Him. We are then 'in the world but not of the world'. Yeshua prayed not that God would take us out of the world, but that He would guard us from the evil one. [8]

God did not miraculously deliver the Israelites while pouring out the plagues upon Egypt; but rather guarded them in the shelter of Goshen from the final plagues. The Israelites did suffer through the first plagues along with the Egyptians.

We, likewise, must not expect some kind of miraculous, '*Beam me up Scotty*'[9] type of rapture while God is pouring out His judgment upon the earth; but we can trust Him to provide a hiding place in Goshen for His covenant people.

---

[8] John 17:11, 14–15
[9] Beam me up, Scotty is a catchphrase that made its way into popular culture from the science fiction television series Star Trek. It can be a way of literally saying "get me out of this place" or expressing rhetorical frustration with the world around you by expressing a desire for escape.

Protected in the Secret Place of the Most High

"I will set apart the land of Goshen, in which My people dwell, that no swarms of flies shall be there, in order that you may know that I am the Lord in the midst of the land. I will make a difference between My people and your people..."
(Exodus 8:22–23)

God promises that in the 'evil day', He will hide us in the shelter of His sukkah סֻכֹּה.[10]

Birth Pangs of the Messiah

There is one last secret to be revealed that is hidden in the Hebrew related to 'Mitzraim' (Egypt); and that is the word *'tzirim'* צִרִים – the contractions of a woman in labor. We are now in that time period where we are beginning to experience what is known as the birth pangs of the Messiah's second coming.

The term *chevlei Mashiach*, 'the birth pangs of the Messiah', appears in both rabbinic literature and the New Testament. There will be signs in the heavens and on earth, strange and severe weather and natural disasters, social upheavals, and traumas: plagues, pestilences, and tribulations like the plagues with which God struck the land of Egypt. This time, however, it will happen on a global scale, all leading up to the final redemption and the coming of the Messiah.[11]

Yeshua warned us about these birth pangs: **"Nations will rise against one another, and kingdoms against each other. There will be famines and earthquakes here and there. <u>All this is just the start of the birthpangs.</u>"** (Matthew 24:7-8)

Birth pangs, as any woman who has been in labor knows, can be extremely painful; and as the woman draws closer and closer to the moment of giving birth, the contractions grow increasingly intense and can be excruciatingly painful. The worst time is that of 'transition' – right before the baby's head crowns and the overwhelming desire to push overtakes the woman in labor.

---

[10] Psalm 27:5 A sukkah is a booth or tabernacle
[11] https://ffoz.org/discover/prophecy/birth-pangs-of-messiah-and-covid-19.html

Sometimes it seems like we are watching the birth pangs of the Messiah live every time we tune in to the news. We are seeing wars, famines, earthquakes, fires, race riots, school shootings, terrorism and global pandemics – in short – a world on the verge of collapse. But when we see these things happening, we are to lift up our heads, for surely our redemption is drawing near.

Let us keep watching the clouds for the return of the Master and listening for the sound of His shofar (trumpet call) and truah (shout). As we get closer and closer to the Messiah's return, we can expect these 'tzirim' to grow even stronger and more intense. All of creation groans and suffers in agony along with us:

"For we know that the whole creation groans and suffers the pains of childbirth together until now." (Romans 8:22)

God wants to do a new thing in our lives; but there can be no birthing without pain. And yet the joy of the birth far outweighs the suffering that precedes it.

"A woman has pain in childbirth because her time has come; but when she brings forth her child, she forgets her anguish because of her joy that a child has been born into the world. So also you have sorrow now, but I will see you again and your hearts will rejoice, and no one will take away your joy...." (John 16:21-22)

We should not be surprised by the trials we go through in this world; knowing that nothing is ever wasted, and God uses these difficult circumstances to purify and refine us. We can also have hope that whatever we are going through is temporary – this too shall pass. Ultimately, we will be with Him and He will wipe away every tear from our eyes.

Even in the book of Lamentations, read on the saddest day in the Biblical calendars, we can still find a message of hope, despite the pain of suffering:

"This I recall to my heart— therefore I have hope: because of the mercies of Adonai we will not be consumed, for His compassions never fail. They are new every morning! Great is Your faithfulness.

'Adonai is my portion', says my soul, 'Therefore I will hope in Him'. Adonai is good to those who wait for Him, to the soul that seeks Him. It is good to wait quietly for the salvation of Adonai." (Lamentations 3:21-26)

We must trust the Lord, even through the darkness, honoring Him with unwavering confidence, even in the midst of trials, troubles and tribulations. God will reward this kind of faith; and like the eagle who goes through a period of molting, we will again rise up on wings as an eagle with new strength, new vision and new hope.

God wants to bring us out of our narrow, limited, restricted existence into the broad place He has prepared for us. His intention is to deliver His people from Egypt (mitzraim), and bring us all the way into the Promised Land of beauty and abundance. For this we need faith and courage.

Keep Moving Towards Rehovot

It may take some time; and we may need to keep moving until we find that 'spacious place' – but God has an inheritance in the Land for us to possess. Issac had to keep moving on from the wells of his father when the Philistines strove with him there; but eventually he made it to 'Rehovot' where God made room for him and he could be fruitful.[12]

Rehovot רְחֹבוֹת comes from the Hebrew word 'rachav' רָחָב which means <u>broad or spacious</u>. God has a place of Rehovot for us, where we can breathe again, where we no longer feel restricted or limited or barren; where we can be fruitful for our Father's glory. Let us not settle for life in 'Mitzraim' but leave Egypt and live the abundant life that Yeshua came to give us.

"He also brought me out into a broad (spacious) place (merhav מֶרְחָב);
He rescued me because He delighted in me." (Psalm 18:19)

---

[12] Genesis 26:18-25

Prayer: *Avinu Shebashamayim (Our Father in Heaven), how we long to break out of this limited place in which we have been living for far too long. Deliver us, O God, from our oppression and affliction. Help us to overcome; and keep us from the evil one – for we are Your children. Shelter us in Goshen as You pour out Your judgment upon the earth; and keep us safe as we remain under the blood of the Lamb.*

Show us how to be 'in this world' and yet not 'of the world'. Give us the faith and courage of Joshua to make it into the Promised Land; and guide us to our place of Rehovot where we have room to grow and can be fruitful for Your Kingdom. In Yeshua's name we pray. Amen.

Watchmen on the Walls - netzer נֵצֶר

"I have set (appointed and stationed) watchmen on your walls, O Jerusalem; they shall never hold their peace day or night. You who make mention of the LORD, do not keep silent (take no rest for yourselves): nor give Him any rest until He establishes Jerusalem and makes her the praise of the earth." (Isaiah 62:6-7)

God has set watchmen (and watchwomen) upon the walls of Jerusalem to cry out to the Lord day and night, night and day, until He makes Jerusalem the praise of the earth that she is destined to become. But who are these appointed watchmen?

Did you know that there is a secret hidden in the Hebrew, showing that God has specifically called Christians to be watching over the walls of Jerusalem?

> The Hebrew word **notzri**, נוֹצְרִי means watchman, guardian, or overseer (**notzrim** נוֹצְרִים in the plural). It comes from the **root natzar** – נָצַר, which means to watch, guard, protect or preserve.

This word, natzar, is used to describe how God watches over His people, keeping us protected and safe.

"In a desert land He found him (Jacob), in a barren and howling waste. He shielded him and cared for him; <u>He guarded (natzar) him as the apple of His eye</u>." (Deuteronomy 32:10)

Adonai Is Israel's ultimate Watchman: *"You are my hiding place; <u>You preserve (natzar) me from trouble</u>; You surround me with songs of deliverance."* (Psalm 32:7)

Another meaning of **notzri**, נוצרי however, is a **Christian**. A follower of Yeshua the Messiah became known as a 'notzri' (plural Notzrim) because of the city of Nazareth (Natzeret נצרת in Hebrew), where Yeshua (Jesus) was raised.

The first time that Yeshua's followers were called 'notzrim' is in Acts 24:5 when the Apostle Paul (Shaul) stood on trial and was called **"a ringleader of the Nazarene Sect"** כת הנצרית. Therefore, we can see hidden in the Hebrew an amazing secret – Christians (notzrim) נוצרים are called to be watchmen (notzrim) נוצרים.

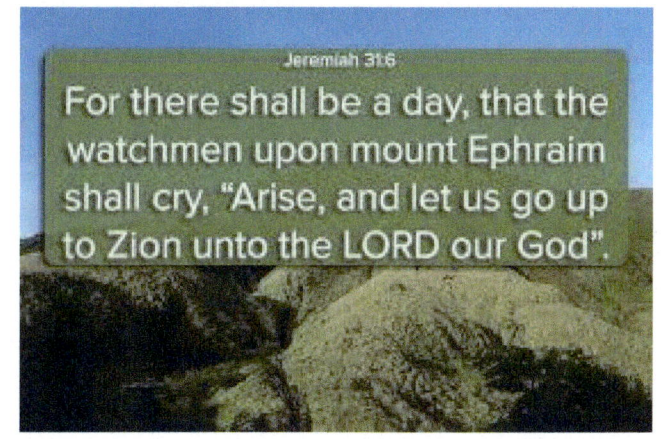

"For there shall be a day when the watchmen (Notzrim) נֹצְרִים will cry on Mount Ephraim, 'Arise, and let us go up to Zion, to the LORD our God.'" (Jeremiah 31:6)

What are Watchmen called to do?

Watchmen Warn of Danger

In Israel, guards or watchmen would be found standing in watchtowers at strategic locations, looking for signs of an enemy approaching, and blowing the shofar to warn people of any danger.

God often calls the prophets His watchmen, such as when He told Ezekiel: ***"Son of man, I have made you a watchman for the people of Israel; so <u>hear the word I speak and give them warning from me</u>."*** (Ezekiel 3:17)

Watchtower at Yad Hashmona, a Messianic moshav (village) in the Judean Hills

When the Prophet Habakkuk complained to God, he appointed himself as a watchman, looking for the answer: ***"I will stand at my watch and station myself on the ramparts; I will look to see what he will say to me, and what answer I am to give to this complaint."*** (Habakkuk 2:1)

Even today, there are guard towers and stations throughout Israel at strategic checkpoints manned by the Israeli Defense Forces, security guards, or local residents of the village. If not for these guards or watchmen, Israel would quickly be overrun by her enemies.

It must be a challenging position, to stand there hour after hour, day after day, in the blazing hot sun, staying ever on the alert – because the consequences of failing to watch can be disastrous – as we have seen in the recent infiltration of hundreds of Hamas terrorists from Gaza into Israel – massacring entire villages of Israel civilians (men, women and children – even babies).[1]

Everyone is asking the question, *"How could this have happened?"* How is it that with the sophisticated Israeli systems of high-tech surveillance and intelligence, that this devastating, pre-planned attack could have been carried out – resulting in 1400 Israeli civilians murdered in the most barbaric manner, gunned down or burned alive in their 'safe rooms'.

Women were raped and then publicly displayed in the most humiliating, degrading manner; people were tortured, mutilated and executed; babies were slaughtered in their cribs and decapitated; over 200 Israeli men, women and children (even babies and the elderly) were kidnapped and taken captive to Gaza.

How did hundreds of terrorists manage to get past the guards on duty? How did they break through the security fence between Gaza and Israel, fly in on hang gliders, and wash ashore by boat without anyone noticing? Where were all our IDF battalions and why did it take hours for them to respond to all the desperate pleas for help?

At the time of this writing, we have questions but no answers…. for now we are still fighting for our survival while the antisemites of the world rejoice at the death of Jews, threaten Jewish students on American university campuses, and Muslim mobs riot in the nations, calling for Jewish genocide.

---

[1] October 7th, 2023

We thank God for faithful Christians – the true 'watchmen on the walls' – who stand with us during this dark and painful time.

What Happens When the Guard Fails to Guard?

Yeshua asked his disciples to watch with Him for one hour; but they fell asleep on the job. ***"Then He came to the disciples and found them sleeping, and said to Peter, 'What! Could you not watch with Me for one hour?'"*** (Matthew 26:40)

Let's look at a couple of other Biblical examples to see what happens when an appointed watchman, guard, or keeper fails to properly guard that which has been entrusted to him (or her).

God placed Adam in a beautiful garden with instructions to tend (work) and keep (guard) it.

There was one stipulation, however. Of every tree he could eat freely; except for one tree, that of the knowledge of good and evil – he was specifically told that it was off limits! [2]

Yeshua Walks into Galilee with His Disciples, by William Hole (1846-1917)

Adam did not faithfully guard his garden – he allowed his helpmeet, Eve, to partake of the fruit of this tree. Not only did he not stop her, but Adam even joined her in disobeying God's express command.

The consequences of Adam's failure to guard his garden were monumentally disastrous – the effects are still suffered by all of humanity today – exile from a perfect, beautiful garden, into a world of sin, pain and hardship.

We see another grave breach of trust with Aaron, brother of Moses, who was left in charge of the unruly mob of Israelites while Moses went up the mountain to commune with God and receive the Ten Commandments.[3]

---

[2] Genesis 2:15-17
[3] https://www.voiceforisrael.net/post/when-moses-is-delayed-on-the-mountain

Rather than guarding the camp, Aaron gave in to the people and actually assisted them in creating a golden calf – Aaron acting as an accomplice to the spiritual treason of idolatry.

The people started getting antsy when Moses was delayed, and so Aaron said to them,

"'Break off the golden earrings which are in the ears of your wives, your sons, and your daughters, and bring them to me.'

So all the people broke off the golden earrings which were in their ears, and brought them to Aaron. And he received the gold from their hand, and he fashioned it with an engraving tool, and made a molded calf." (Exodus 32:2-4)

Moses could see that Aaron had failed to restrain the people (to their shame among their enemies), and so he called the Levites to his side to kill even their brothers and companions; and three thousand died by the sword that day.

When we are placed in charge of a situation, we must guard against all manner of sin, disorder, and every evil thing. For our true struggle is not with flesh and blood; but with principalities and powers of wickedness in high places.[4] We are living in a combat zone – one in which there are many casualties – and so we must constantly be on guard for the approaching of an attack by the powers of darkness against us, our families, and all that has been entrusted to us.

Guard Your Heart

One of the most important things that we have been entrusted to guard is that of our own hearts. King Solomon said it best:

"Above all else, guard your heart, for it is the wellspring of life." (Proverbs 4:23)

---

[4] Ephesians 6:12

Guarding our heart must be our top priority, since it is so precious. We only guard that which is valuable; we don't stand guard over worthless things.

When we throw out our trash at night, we leave it completely unguarded (except for perhaps closing the lid, thereby guarding it from marauding animals – so that we don't end up spending our first hours of the morning cleaning up garbage scattered over the entire neighborhood).

But the point is, that we would not be told to guard our hearts unless our hearts were extremely valuable and precious. Just like our physical heart keeps our whole body alive; our spiritual 'heart' contains the essence of our true being.

Yeshua told us that it is out of our heart that the mouth speaks. Our words reveal what is in our heart. We must guard our hearts against bitterness, unforgiveness, hatred, envy, negative thoughts; and all that would render us unclean:

"For out of the heart proceed evil thoughts, murders, adulteries, fornications, thefts, false witness, blasphemies. These are the things which defile a man, but to eat with unwashed hands does not defile a man." (Matthew 15:18-20)

It is our sacred responsibility to guard our hearts, our thoughts, and the words of our mouth. No one can do this for us; and if we want to live a godly, peaceable, blessed life then it is imperative that we set the right boundaries in these areas.

Guard the Torah

Another treasure we are to faithfully guard is the Torah – the commandments of God. It is this same root word, natzar, which is used to speak of guarding the Torah of God.

"Happy are they that are upright in the way, who walk in the Torah of Adonai.
Happy (blessed/Ashrei) are they that keep (guard) notzrei נֹצְרֵי His testimonies, that seek Him with the whole heart." (Psalm 119:1-2)

The Word of God is so precious; and we have been entrusted with keeping it, guarding it; and passing it on to the next generation.

"These words I am commanding you today are to be upon your hearts. You shall teach them diligently to your children, and shall talk of them when you sit in your house, when you walk by the way, when you lie down, and when you rise up."
(Deuteronomy 6:6-7)

As worshippers of the God of Israel and followers of Yeshua, we have been entrusted to guard the Torah and to ensure that we instruct future generations to keep the ways of the God of Jacob as well. Failure to take this responsibility seriously can result in a faithless, godless generation instead of the generation who seeks the God of Jacob.

We are to diligently guard the Sabbath day, to keep it holy as God has commanded – not to work and not to do our own pleasure on His sacred day of Shabbat. This is the fourth of the Ten Commandments.

"Guard (remember, observe) the Sabbath day, to set it apart, as יהוה your Elohim commanded you. Six days you labor, and shall do all your work, but the seventh day is a Sabbath of יהוה your Elohim."
(Deuteronomy 5:12-14)

Divine Watchman

God also has a 'Divine Watchman' who is ever faithfully and lovingly watching over each one of us; and that is Yeshua Hamashiach (the Messiah). His role as a watchman (Netzer) was foretold by the ancient Hebrew prophet, Isaiah, in this well-known prophetic Messianic verse:

"A shoot will come up from the stump of Jesse (King David's father); from his roots a Branch (Netzer) נֵצֶר *will bear fruit. The Spirit of the Lord will rest on Him – the Spirit of wisdom and of understanding, the Spirit of counsel and of might, the Spirit of the knowledge and fear of the Lord."* (Isaiah 11:1–2)

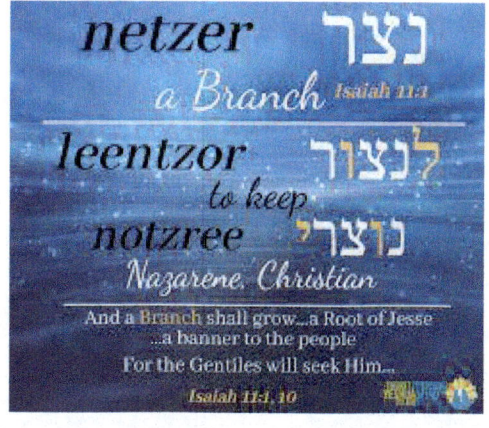

Here, the word **Netzer** means a shoot or branch, which can also refer to descendants. The netzer (branch) here is Messiah Yeshua, the Son of David (Ben David), the Head of the Notzrim. He did not come only for the lost sheep of the House of Israel; but for the salvation of the whole of mankind – for the Jew first and also for the non-Jew.

"And in that day there shall be a root of Jesse, which shall stand for an ensign of the people; to it shall the nations seek: and His rest shall be glorious."
(Isaiah 11:10)

Another related word, **nitzrah,** נצרה means the safety latch on a gun. Yeshua is our 'safety latch' – a secure salvation for all those who repent of their wicked ways and put their trust in Him.

Messiah Yeshua came as a divine watchman warning people to *"repent, for the Kingdom of God has come near."* (Matthew 4:17)

Like the warring angels and the prophets of old, believers in Yeshua today are called to be concerned for the physical and spiritual preservation of Israel – to guard in the Spirit and intercede for Israel against any danger they 'see' approaching.

Believers pray for Jerusalem and the Jewish People from the Mount of Olives.

Believers are called to be the watchmen, ever on the alert; praying for the shalom (peace) of Jerusalem and all Israel; helping the world to understand God's plan for His people and His land, and defending us from the battles waged against us on a daily basis.

As Messianic believers and Christians, we are also called to speak the Word of God to the Jewish People, helping them to understand that Messiah Yeshua is the prophesied **Netzer (Branch) of David**, the 'mashiach'[5] they have, for so long, been waiting and longing for to bring peace to this troubled land and to our hearts.

Prayer: *Dear God, may we be ever diligent to guard that which You have given us to guard, and watch over all that You have entrusted into our care. Thank you for all the faithful watchmen and watchwomen in the nations of the earth - Christian followers of Yeshua of Nazareth - who stand faithfully at their post, day and night, night and day, giving the Lord no rest until He makes Jerusalem a praise in the earth. Halleluyah!*

"Listen! Your watchmen lift up their voices; together they shout for joy. When the LORD returns to Zion, they will see it with their own eyes." (Isaiah 52:8)

---

[5] Mashiach is the Hebrew word for Messiah

A Right Heart - Lev Nachon לב נכון

"My heart is steadfast, O God, my heart is steadfast; I will sing and give praise."
(Psalm 57:7)

The one writing this Psalm had obviously been facing intense battles: calamities, danger and persecution. He says, "My soul is among lions…" as He pleads for God's mercy; and yet in the midst of it all, he declares, "My heart is steadfast, O God, my heart is steadfast". What does this mean in the original Hebrew?

The Hebrew word used for 'steadfast' is 'nachon' נכון which means literally 'right'. If we want to acknowledge something (or someone) as being right or correct, then we say, 'nachon'. The Psalmist is declaring that he has a right heart (lev nachon) לב נכון before God. Knowing that our heart is right with God is of immeasurable value.

"Great beauty, great strength, and great riches are really and truly of no great use; a right heart exceeds all."
— **Benjamin Franklin**

We have heard people saying, *"God knows my heart"*; but what does it actually mean in Hebrew to have a right heart? What is the condition of our heart before God? It is important to take the time to examine our hearts; for out of it flows all the issues of life.[1]

---

[1] Proverbs 4:23

What are some of the characteristics of a 'right heart'?

1. <u>A right heart trusts in God</u>: ***"Trust in the Lord with all your heart, and do not lean on your own understanding."*** (Proverbs 3:5)

Especially in this day and hour, as we approach the return of the Lord, we cannot simply 'follow our heart' for, as the prophet Jeremiah said, ***"The heart is deceitful above all things."*** (Jeremiah 17:9)

In the book of Proverbs, which contains so much wisdom, King Solomon wrote that whoever trusts in his own heart is a fool.

"He who trusts in his own heart is a fool, but whoever walks wisely will be delivered." (Proverbs 28:26)

Even above what our own heart is telling us about our situation or circumstances, we must trust in the Lord and walk in wisdom. We cannot make decisions only on the basis of what our heart or emotions are compelling us to do. We also need wisdom from above.

To ensure the survival of the species, Noah brought a male and a female of each species into the ark. The male represents the logical mind; and the female represents the emotional heart. Both are needed for survival. A right heart is very important; but we must also listen to wisdom in order to survive these perilous times.

2. <u>A right heart is filled with praise, thanksgiving and peace</u>: ***"And the peace of God, which surpasses all understanding, will guard your hearts and your minds in Messiah Yeshua."*** (Phillipians 4:7)

It's so easy to complain about our lot in life, the weather, the economy, the government, the traffic, our boss, our nosy (or noisy) neighbor.... There is no end to things to complain about; and yet we need to guard our hearts against murmuring, grumbling and complaining which only gives the enemy more ammunition to use against us.

Intentionally filling our hearts with praise and thanksgiving will keep us in a place of rest and peace, knowing that God is fighting our battles and we can be still.

3. A right heart is joyful! *"A joyful heart is good medicine, but a crushed spirit dries up the bones."* (Proverbs 17:22)

Not only does a merry heart keep us in good health and bring forth healing, it also gives us strength; for the *'joy of the Lord is our strength'*. No one wants to be around an 'Eyore' kind of pessimistic, miserable person; we need to have a smile on our face and go out into the world, and shine with the joy that comes from the presence of the Lord.

4. A right heart is filled with faith, hope and love; it is not fearful, fretful or anxious. Fretting, according to the Word of God, not only does not help anything; it actually makes things worse. We are exhorted not to fret, but to rest in the Lord:

"Cease from anger, and forsake wrath; do not fret – it only causes harm." (Psalm 37:8)

Yeshua told us not to allow our hearts to be troubled; and not to be afraid. This is a choice whether or not we allow our hearts to be troubled.

"Do not let your heart be troubled (afraid, cowardly). Believe [confidently] in God and trust in Him, [have faith, hold on to it, rely on it, keep going and] believe also in Me." (John 14:1)

If our hearts are not filled with faith; then they can be fearful – a heart condition that is running rampant in these troubled times. We are called to encourage those with fearful hearts:

"Say to them that are of a fearful heart: 'Be strong, fear not; behold, your God will come with vengeance, with the recompense of God He will come and save you.' " (Isaiah 35:4)

In the original Hebrew Scripture, it describes this heart as *'quick hearted'*, 'nimharei lev', נִמְהֲרֵי-לֵב. A fearful heart is going to be impulsive; quick to jump into something before considering wise counsel or praying about it. A right heart is patient – willing to wait upon the Lord for wisdom, guidance and direction.

5. <u>A right heart is one that listens for God's voice</u>. When King Solomon asked God for wisdom, what he actually asked for was a 'listening heart' (lev shomea) לֵב שֹׁמֵעַ – a heart that hears the still, small voice of God. We don't try to figure it all out on our own; we keep the 'ears of our heart' open to listen for what God has to say about the matter that concerns us. This is how we receive wisdom.

In order to serve the Lord effectively, we need to have a heart full of wisdom. Biblical artisans Betzalel, Ohaliab and others who created artistic works for the mishkan (tabernacle) were said to be 'wise-hearted'.

"And Moses called Bezalel and Oholiab, and every wise-hearted man, in whose heart the LORD had put wisdom, even every one whose heart stirred him up to come unto the work to do it." (Exodus 36:1)

The Hebrew word for 'wise-hearted' is 'haham lev' חֲכַם-לֵב

It is God who puts wisdom in our heart in order to serve Him: whether we are sewing curtains for a tabernacle or a home, creating works of silver and gold for the temple, or simply cooking a meal – we need to be 'wise-hearted'.

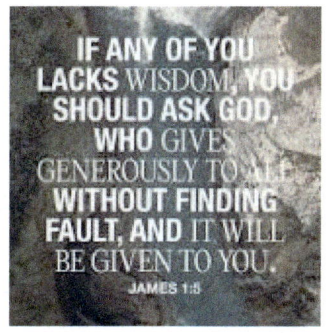

"The wise woman builds her house, but the foolish pulls it down with her hands." (Proverbs 14:1)

How do we make sure that we are building our house with a wise heart and not pulling it down with our own foolish hands? We ask God and He will give it to us generously because He is a good God!

6. <u>A right heart is generous</u>: When Moses called for offerings to build the wilderness tabernacle, the Israelites responded with generous hearts.

"And they came, both men and women, as many as were willing-hearted, and brought nose-rings, and ear-rings, and signet-rings, and girdles, all jewels of gold; even every man that brought an offering of gold unto the LORD." (Exodus 35:22)

> In Hebrew, the word used for 'willing-hearted' is nediv נָדִיב, which means 'generous, benevolent, or open-handed. In fact, the people were so generous that they actually had to be restrained from giving! (Exodus 36:6-7)
>
> The Israelites understood that every material blessing they had came from the hand of God and therefore they were more than willing to give back. God's word promises that those who are generous will prosper. Halleluyah!

7. <u>A right heart keeps the commandments of God</u>:

> ***"But this is the (new) covenant that I will make with the house of Israel after those days, says the Lord: I will put My law in their minds, and write it on their hearts; and I will be their God, and they shall be My people."***
> (Jeremiah 31:33)

Under the new covenant (brit chadashah), God's laws (Torah) are not thrown in the garbage or tossed to the wayside as some believe; but rather are now written on the tablets of our heart – to keep them.

Create in me a pure heart (lev tahor) לֵב טָהוֹר

We are the ones in charge of our hearts. We have been given the responsibility of guarding our own heart and keeping it pure. No one else is going to come along and keep our heart pure for us. We need to guard our heart from all that would harm it.

If we want to experience the presence of God, then we need to purify our hearts from all that may defile: ***"Blessed [anticipating God's presence, spiritually mature] are the pure in heart [those with integrity, moral courage, and godly character], for they will see God."*** (Matthew 5:8)

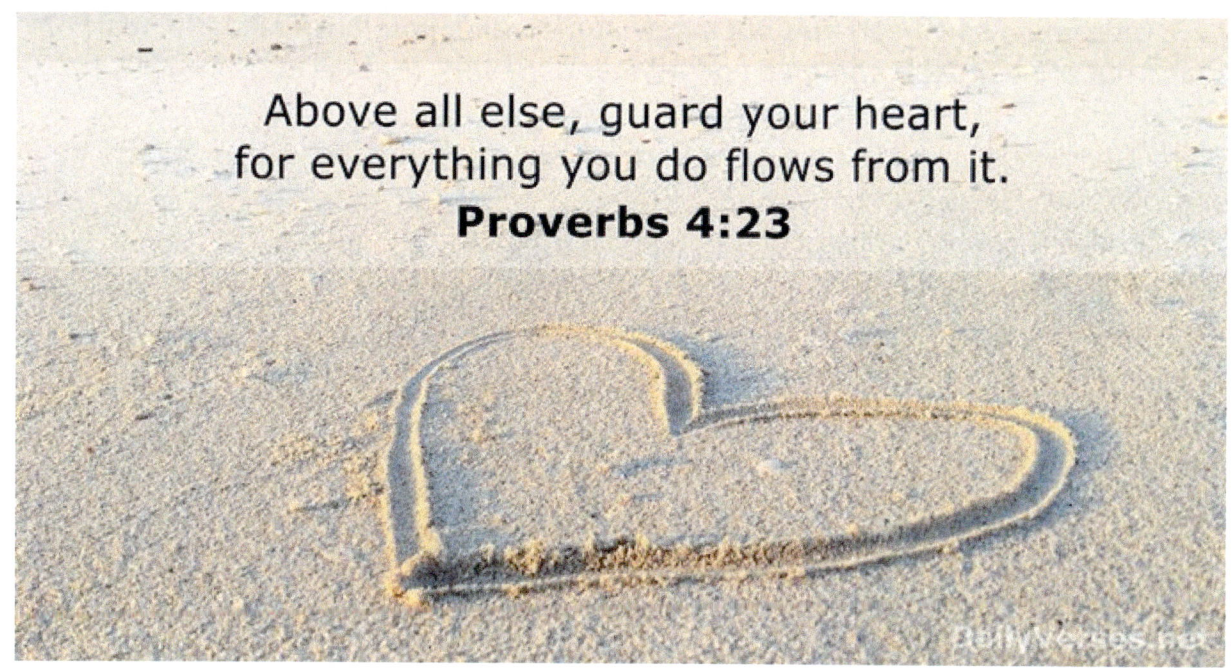

After the prophet Nathan confronted King David with his sin of adultery with Bat Sheba, David humbled himself before God, repented, and pleaded for a 'pure heart' (lev tahor) לֵב טָהוֹר.

"Create in me a clean (pure) heart, O God; and renew a steadfast spirit within me." (Psalm 51:10)

A pure heart doesn't mean we will be perfect; but it does mean that we want to do what is right and pleasing in God's sight; and that we have the humility to admit when we have messed up. <u>A right heart is humble</u>.

David knew that he could not, in himself, purify his heart; he needed God to create in Him a whole new heart – one that would be pure and clean. Because the very first place we see God is as 'Creator of the Universe' in the book of Genesis (Breisheet).

God makes many beautiful promises to those who return from out of exile into the Land of Israel: renewal of the land, fertility, fruitfulness, restoration, and vindication. However, one of the greatest blessings of all is God's promise to create in us a new heart.

"For I will take you from among the nations, gather you out of all countries, and bring you into your own land. Then I will sprinkle clean water on you, and you shall be clean; I will cleanse you from all your filthiness and from all your idols.

I will give you a new heart and put a new spirit within you; I will take the heart of stone out of your flesh and give you a heart of flesh." (Ezekiel 36:24-26)

When God brings us out of the exile of unbelief; and into the 'good land' of faith, hope and love, then He also gives us a new heart – removing our heart of stone and giving us a heart of flesh. Before I came to faith in Yeshua, my heart had become hardened by all the hardships I had lived through; but once I came to faith, God gave me a new heart of flesh that is sensitive to His Spirit and weeps with those who weep – having compassion for those who suffer – whether animals or people.

A right heart is a soft heart.

We can see that the heart and the spirit need to be working in harmony together. Along with a new, pure heart, we need a new, right spirit as well. When David pleaded with God to create in him a pure heart, he also asked for God to renew a 'steadfast spirit' within him.

"Create in me a clean (pure) heart, O God; and renew a steadfast spirit within me." (Psalm 51:10)

If we look into the Hebrew, we will see again that the Hebrew word for steadfast is 'right' (nachon). David asked God to renew in him a 'right spirit' (rua'ch nachon) רוּחַ נָכוֹן. How are the spirit and the heart connected? When God gives us a 'new heart', His Spirit causes us to keep His commandments. A right spirit is obedient.

"I will put My Spirit within you and cause you to walk in My statutes, and you will keep My commandments and do them." (Ezekiel 36:27)

Many Christians believe that the sign of being filled with the Spirit is evidenced by speaking in other tongues; however here we see that when God gives us His Spirit, then we seek to keep God's commandments and do them, not just talk about them. Before I came to faith, I had absolutely no desire to keep God's commandments. I lived like the world and did basically whatever I wanted to do; but when I came to faith in Yeshua, something changed. I no longer wanted to live to please myself; I wanted to live to please my Heavenly Father. I wanted to 'love what He loves' and hate what he hates.

It was not something I tried to do by my own will; it was just a supernatural transformation. I stopped using curse words; they were suddenly just no longer part of my vocabulary. I didn't want to live like the world anymore, committing sexual immorality; breaking Shabbat and eating unclean foods. I began to read the Bible and put it into practice – because God had given me a new heart and a new spirit within.

A right heart and spirit is a gift from God that we need to guard and protect from sin, stubbornness and rebellion. The Bible tells us about the children of Ephraim, who turned back on the day of battle. They lacked faith and courage; they did not keep the Torah. Their hearts were not right with God; and their spirits not steadfast.[2]

"For their heart was not steadfast (not right) loh nachon לֹא־נָכוֹן with Him, neither were they faithful in His covenant." (Psalm 78:37)

We can talk a lot about the condition of our hearts – and whether or not our heart is right with God – but perhaps the most important sign of a right heart is <u>love</u>. Because God is love; and without the love of God in our hearts we are nothing.

Paul wrote that even if we have faith that can move mountains; speak with tongues; understand all the mysteries of the universe; and even if we give away all that we have

---

[2] Psalm 78:8-10

to the poor, but if we have not love then we are like a clanging cymbal - an irritation to those around us.[3]

Under the New Covenant, the Torah of God has been written upon our hearts.[4] Let us, therefore, love God with all of our hearts; and love our neighbor as ourselves.

These, Yeshua tells us, are the two most important commandments. And with this we will fulfill the entire Torah.[5]

"Let not steadfast love and faithfulness forsake you; bind them around your neck; write them on the tablet of your heart." (Proverbs 3:3)

Prayer: *We thank you Adonai for filling our hearts to overflowing with Your steadfast love; that we may love You and love others as You do. We desire to have a 'right heart' before You. Cleanse our hearts of all pride and rebellion, and renew in us a right spirit that we may obey You and walk in a way that is pleasing unto You. Perform heart surgery on us, Holy Spirit, and remove our stony heart, replacing it with a heart of flesh - a tender 'lev shomeah' that hears Your Voice. In Yeshua's name. Amen.*

---

[3] 1 Corinthians 13:1–3 (ESV)
[4] Jeremiah 31:33
[5] Matthew 22:37-40

The Almond Tree (Shaked) שָׁקֵד

"Then said the LORD to me, 'You have seen well, for I am alert and active, watching (shoked) שֹׁקֵד *over My word to perform it.'"* (Jeremiah 1:12)

It is a beautiful sight to see the almond trees blossoming in Israel each year, right around the time of Tu Bishvat (Festival of Trees). This is the first tree to blossom after a cold, damp winter and it is always a welcome sign of the soon coming arrival of spring.

It was actually this realization that sparked our desire to return to the Land from out of Canadian exile. Troubles and trials had driven us out of the Land of Israel; and we had been living in Canada for a season. During this time, I had gotten divorced and my eldest son had passed away. It was not an easy time, to say the least.

My children went to a Jewish day school in Canada called Talmud Torah; and as usual, they received a little potted plant in honor of Tu Bishavat.

It was February, and we still found ourselves in the throes of the freezing cold Alberta winter; the entire landscape covered with snow and ice. It was not unusual for winter to linger in this part of the country until well into May! I began to think about how the Land of Israel would now be warming with the spring sunshine; and that the almond trees would already be flowering – decorating the Land with their beautiful blossoms.

I thought to myself, *"What are we still doing here when our home in Israel awaits our return?"* So we decided to pack away the ski hats and mitts and scarves and snow pants and sweaters – and head back home to see the almond trees blossoming in the Land of Israel.

Almond tree blossom Photo by Liat Nesher

There is a word play hidden in the Hebrew about the almond tree that we miss completely in any translation. God asked the prophet Jeremiah, *"What do you see?"*

And Jeremiah answered, *"I see a rod of an almond-tree."* (Jeremiah 1:11)

An almond tree in Hebrew is a called a 'shaked' שָׁקֵד.

So God was using a clever Hebrew word play when He said, ***"You have seen well, for I am alert and active, watching (shoked)*** שֹׁקֵד ***over My word to perform it."*** (Jeremiah 1:12)

Yes, God is watching over His own Word to perform it in our lives. Another Hebrew prophet, Ezekiel, said that whatever word God יְהוָה would speak, it would surely come to pass.[1]

"For He spoke, and it was done; He commanded, and it stood fast." (Psalm 33:9)

God's Word is the ultimate truth; and His word will not return void but will accomplish its purpose: ***"So shall My word be that goes forth from My mouth; it shall not return to Me void, but it shall accomplish what I please, and it shall prosper in the thing for which I sent it."*** (Isaiah 55:11)

We can learn an important lesson from the almond tree (shaked) – that the Word of God is true – no matter what our senses perceive to the contrary. God is watching over His Word to perform it.

God does not lie or change His mind like man is prone to do. God will act upon His Word; He will fulfill His promises to us.

"God is not a man, that He should lie, or a son of man, that He should change His mind. Does He speak and not act? Does He promise and not fulfill?" (Numbers 23:19)

It may seem, at times, that God is taking an awfully long time to act on His word or to fulfill a promise in our life. When a negative situation has gone on for a long time; and we don't see any change, we can begin to doubt God's word and lose heart.

---

[1] Ezekiel 12:25

But we need to remember that God will act in His time, not according to our own timetable. God sees the big picture while we have a limited human understanding.

Until The Time…

We may have to wait a lot longer than we would like, to see God's word come to pass; but we can look at some of the heroes of faith in the Bible for inspiration.

Abraham and Sarah had to wait a long time to see the fulfillment of the promised son, Issac. Abraham was 75 years old when he first received the promise, and Genesis 21:5 tells us he was 100 years old when Isaac was born. Sarah was 90. So Abraham and Sarah waited 25 years for the fulfillment of God's promise.

Joseph was given a dream from God that he would one day be in a position of leadership. His father gave him a coat of many colors that signified leadership over his brothers. In his prophetic dreams, Joseph saw his brothers bowing down to him; but instead, they threw him into a pit and sold him to Ishmaelite slave traders.

Rather than ruling and reigning, Joseph worked as a servant of Potipher, and later languished for years, forgotten in an Egyptian dungeon, imprisoned on false charges. This certainly doesn't look like God performing His word to Joseph or fulfilling His promise – and yet it did come to pass – in God's perfect time.

"…Joseph – who was sold as a slave. They hurt his feet with fetters, he was laid in irons. Until the time that His word came to pass…" (Psalm 105:17-19)

Moses had destiny as a deliverer of his people, Israel, but spent forty years on the back side of the Midian desert, just tending his father in law's sheep, before God called him out of a burning bush and sent him to deliver the children of Israel out of slavery in Egypt.

The prophet Samuel anointed a young, shepherd boy named David to be the King of Israel at the age of 15; but it would be another 15 years of waiting and being persecuted by the murderous King Saul before David was finally crowned the King.[2]

God has a proper time for His word to come to pass; and we need to wait patiently for His timing. The Land of Israel lay desolate for thousands of years while the people remained in exile, always hoping for a return to Zion.

---

[2] 2 Samuel 5:4-5

By the rivers of Babylon, the people of Israel sat and wept. They hung their harps on the willows, unable to sing the songs of the Lord in a foreign land.[3]

The exiles of Israel said, *"If I forget you, Jerusalem, may my right hand forget its skill."* (Psalm 137:5)

The Israeli national anthem, Hatikvah (meaning 'The Hope'), reflects this longing, for two thousand years, to live free in our Land again. And now here we are today, singing Hatikvah at every national gathering or event:

As long as deep in the heart,
The soul of a Jew yearns,
And forward to the East
To Zion, an eye looks
Our hope will not be lost,
<u>The hope of two thousand years</u>,
To be a free nation in our land,
The land of Zion and Jerusalem.

The Word of God promises that one day, in His mercy, God would bring His people out of exile and restore the fertility of the land. It took two thousand years; but that day has finally come! God is gathering us out of all the nations to which He has scattered us and is bringing us back into our own Land.

"Then it shall be, after I have plucked them out, that I will return and have compassion on them and bring them back, everyone to his heritage and everyone to his land." (Jeremiah 12:15)

Hannah with children & grandchildren planting trees on Tu Bishvat in the Land of Israel

---

[3] Psalm 137:1-4

The fertility of the Land has been restored; and Israel now exports fruit all over the world!

"But you, O mountains of Israel, you shall shoot forth your branches and yield your fruit to My people Israel, for they are about to come." (Ezekiel 36:8)

Indeed, the land that lay desolate is now glorious in its beauty like the Garden of Eden. The deserts are blooming and blossoming just as God promised in His Word through the ancient Hebrew Prophets. How privileged we are to be the generation to witness the fulfillment of God's promises to Israel with our very own eyes!

Darom Adom - Red South Festival in the Negev when the desert is covered by beautiful red poppies (calanit flowers)

"The wilderness and the wasteland shall be glad for them, and the desert shall rejoice and blossom as the crocus; it shall blossom abundantly and rejoice, even with joy and singing." (Isaiah 35:1-2)

The Promise Fulfilled

When tempted to become discouraged and lose hope; when we begin to doubt if God's word will ever come to pass in our lives, we need to think about Israel; think about the heroes of our faith; and think about the almond tree.

We need to remember that God makes all things beautiful in *His* time. For God's ways are not our ways and His thoughts not our thoughts; but God is faithful to His word.

When Joshua led the children of Israel across the Jordan River, they took possession of the Land after fighting many battles; and God kept every promise that He had made to Joshua and His people, Israel. Not one word failed of all that He had spoken: it all came to pass just as He had promised.

"So the Lord gave to Israel all the land <u>of which He had sworn to give to their fathers</u>, and they took possession of it and dwelt in it.

The Lord gave them rest all around, <u>according to all that He had sworn to their fathers</u>. And not a man of all their enemies stood against them; the Lord delivered all their enemies into their hand.

<u>Not a word failed of any good thing which the Lord had spoken to the house of Israel. All came to pass</u>." (Joshua 21:43-45)

There are not many things that we can count on in these last days when everything is being shaken. People come and go; friends or family can decide to move away, our health or finances can take a nosedive; our spouse may come home one day and ask for a divorce. The circumstances of our life are always subject to change.

But the one thing that we can rely upon is the eternal Word of God which will never pass away. *"Heaven and earth will pass away, but My words will never pass away."* (Matthew 24:35)

Remember the lesson of the almond tree (shaked) שָׁקֵד: God is always watching (shoked) שֹׁקֵד over His Word to perform it.

Hoping Against all Hope

"Hoping against all hope, Abraham kept hoping – believing that he would become the father of many nations. For God had said to him, 'That's how many descendants you will have!'" (Romans 4:18)

I would like to end this chapter on the almond tree with a personal story – not my own – but a very precious testimony related to me by my dear friend and editor of this book, Sue Socci[4] about her sister, Julie Cameron-Hall:

A few days after her first husband passed away suddenly from a heart attack, a tree was delivered to her house from a dear friend, with a gift tag tied to it reading, "*The almond tree will blossom again*". Julie was in no state at the time to plant the tree so she left it on the patio in its plastic bag.

Two or three days later, a huge freeze arrived in the UK, later nicknamed, "*The Beast from the East*", when temperatures dropped to -16 degrees centigrade! (Not normal in the UK!). It stayed around for about ten days and afterwards, the poor little tree was just a stick. Julie was so sad, "*Oh no, I've managed to kill the tree*".

All winter it was just a twig, and in the spring she decided to plant it anyway. All summer and the following winter it remained a twig and did nothing at all, then the following spring a few little leaves started to sprout.

After some time went by, her now-husband, Nigel, a man she had known from years prior, proposed! On the day that he gave her the ring, she looked out of the window and the almond tree was COVERED with blossoms!

Then she remembered the promise that had been written on the tag years earlier: "*The almond tree will blossom again*".

The very next day, a friend of Julie's came up to her in a prayer meeting, saying that in her devotional time that morning, the Lord had given her bible verses and instructed her to give them to Julie. It was exactly the verses from Jeremiah 1:11-12!!!

"'Jeremiah, what do you see?' And I said, 'I see the branch of an almond tree.' Then the Lord said to me, 'You have seen well, for I am alert and active, watching (shoked) שֹׁקֵד over My word to perform it.'" (Jeremiah 1:11-12)

---

[4] Jim & Sue Socci are anointed musicians and worship leaders who have recorded several albums, including their latest - Soon Coming King. http://www.jimandsuesocci.com/

God reminded her that He was watching over His word to perform it ... hope for Julie's future ... and NOTHING can stop it. These days, Julie and Nigel travel the world together as "musicianaries"![5]

"The grass withers and the flowers fall, but the word of our God stands forever."
(Isaiah 40:8)

Prayer: *Dear God, there are many times when we look at our circumstances and determine that, in the natural, there is no reason to hope. And yet You are the God of all hope, and Your desire is that Your people will always be filled with joy and peace, abounding in hope through believing – not in what we see – but in Your faithful promises in Your unfailing Word.*

Thank you that You are always watching over Your Word to perform it, and that You have given us the almond tree with its beautiful spring blossoms to remind us of Your faithfulness. Help us to be patient as we wait for you to fulfill Your plans and purposes in our lives. Strengthen us, O Lord, to be people who live by faith and not by sight. Amen v'Amen.

Almond Blossoms in Israel You Tube Video (Link)

---

[5] Celtish - Nigel Cameron & Julie Cameron-Hall

Get in the Ark (Tevah) תבה

"Then the Lord said to Noah, "Get in the ark, you and all your household, because I have seen that you are righteous before Me in this generation."
(Genesis 7:1)

After Adam and Chava (Eve) were exiled from the Garden of Eden, they became fruitful and multiplied; but the wickedness of mankind also increased upon the earth. In those days, as is now, the earth was filled with every kind of sin, vulgarity and violence.

This descent into darkness began with the murder of Abel by his brother Cain; but the wickedness of mankind markedly increased by the union of daughters of Adam with fallen angels (called 'nephilim' נְפִלִים from the Hebrew root word 'nafal' נפל which mean 'fallen'). The children created from these unions were giants (anakim) upon the earth.[1] The DNA of humankind had become corrupted by the seed of fallen angels.

When God saw their wickedness, His heart was grieved; and He was sorry that He had ever created mankind. He decided to send a Great Flood upon the earth that would destroy every living thing He had created and cleanse the world from evil.

"The earth also was corrupt before God, and the earth was filled with violence (hamas). So God looked upon the earth, and indeed it was corrupt; for all flesh had corrupted their way on the earth." (Genesis 6:11-12)

No More Violence (Hamas)

The Hebrew word for violence in these scriptures is 'hamas' חָמָס. This is the name for one of the terrorist organizations in the Middle East which has vowed to destroy Israel through violence. It was because of this hamas חָמָס (violence) that God decided to destroy every living thing from the face of the earth except Noah and his family.

"And God said unto Noah, 'The end of all flesh has come before Me; for the earth is filled with violence (hamas) חָמָס *through them; and, behold, I will destroy them with the earth.'"* (Genesis 6:13)

---

[1] Genesis 6:1-4

Some may want to perceive Hamas or other Islamic terrorist organizations as simply engaged in a political battle to 'liberate' their rightful territory from the Israeli 'occupiers'. Many people (and even some Christians) are deceived into agreeing with this skewed point of view; but nothing could be further from the truth.

The Word of God clearly reveals the truth about the Arab-Israeli conflict, if we only have eyes to see. We must not fear calling Hamas what it is – a violent force of darkness whose goal is to bring death and destruction to God's people everywhere.

Violence and strife continue even unto today, just as it was in ancient times. The Psalmist lamented how he wanted to grow wings and fly away, since, *"I have seen violence (hamas)* חָמָס *and strife (riv)* רִיב *in the city."* (Psalm 55:9)

Since first writing this chapter, war has recently broken out in Israel after Hamas terrorists attacked innocent, peace-loving Israeli civilians living in communities around Gaza, murdering, raping, and kidnapping men, women and children – even babies! Hamas terrorists gunned down hundreds of Israeli young people celebrating the end of sukkot at an outdoor music festival.[2]

Entire villages were massacred; bodies of forty babies were found decapitated. Whole families were burned alive in their 'safe rooms', unable to escape the fires set by the

---

[2] October 7th, 2023

terrorists. The horrors perpetrated by these evil, wicked people is unimaginable and too much for the heart to bear.

Our hope is found in the prophetic promise that one day, violence (hamas) will no longer be heard in our land: **"Violence (hamas) חָמָס shall no longer be heard in your land, neither wasting nor destruction within your borders; but you shall call your walls Salvation (Yeshuah) and your gates Praise (Tehillah)."** (Isaiah 60:18)

But amidst all the violence and corruption of Noah's day, God found this one man worth saving. Noah was in his generation the only 'ish tzadik' (righteous man). We don't have to give in to peer pressure and follow the crowd to do evil. The account of Noah tells us that we and our children do not need to conform ourselves to the immorality and corruption of the world all around us.

In response to the horrific, unprovoked attack on innocent Israeli civilians, masses of people are now marching in the streets in pro-Hamas, pro-Palestinian rallies, calling for the destruction of Israel and the Jews; and anti-semitism is rising in the nations.

Just like in the time of Hitler and Nazi Germany, when the majority of the population supported the annihilation of the Jewish people; or at best, did nothing to stop it, we see the same thing happening today. These people who curse the Jews and Israel have placed themselves under the curse of God who has promised, **"I will bless those who bless you and those who curse you I will curse."** (Genesis 12:3)

And yet, there is always a faithful remnant who chooses to be set apart from the crowd and take a stand for righteousness. Theirs will be the reward promised by the King of Kings and Lord of Lords, *"Come, you blessed of My Father, inherit the kingdom prepared for you from the foundation of the world."* (Matthew 25:34)

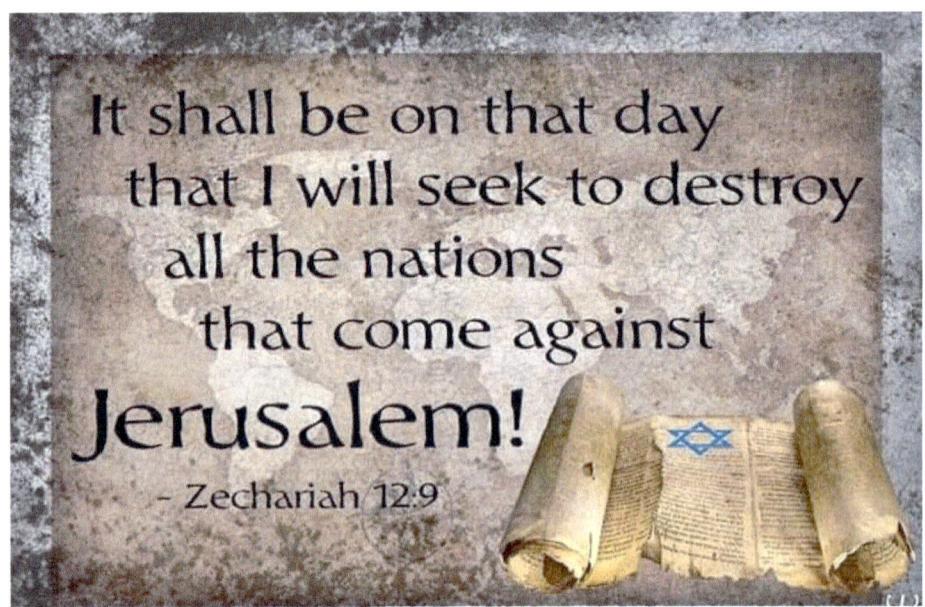

It's okay to be different than our peers; it's more important to be righteous before God than to be popular with people. The Word of God tells us that in the last days, the wickedness of man will again flourish and increase upon the earth:

"But know this, that in the last days perilous times will come: for men will be lovers of themselves (selfish), lovers of money (greedy), boasters, proud (arrogant), blasphemers, disobedient to parents, unthankful, unholy, unloving, unforgiving, slanderers, without self-control, brutal, despisers of good, traitors, headstrong, haughty, lovers of pleasure rather than lovers of God, having a form of godliness but denying its power. And from such people turn away!"
(2 Timothy 3:1-5)

God found one righteous man on earth who found favor in His eyes; and his name was Noach. The Hebrew Scriptures describe him as tzadik צַדִּיק (righteous) and tamim תָּמִים (pure, innocent, complete and faultless).[3] He was one of only two Biblical men to 'hithalech' (walk) with God, the other being Enoch.

---

[3] Genesis 6:9

God instructed Noach to build an ark to save him and his household, along with a pair of every animal – and enough food to sustain them all through the time of the terrible flood.

Saved in the Ark (Tevah)

The Hebrew word for 'ark' is a 'tevah' תֵּבָה. It is used in only one other place in Scripture and that is to describe the basket that Yochebed placed her baby Moses in to save him from Pharaoh's wicked directive to throw all Hebrew male infants into the Nile River. When, after three months, she could no longer hide him, she set her son in a basket (ark – teivah) and placed him into the hands of God on the Nile.

"But when she could no longer hide him, she took an ark of bulrushes for him, daubed it with asphalt and pitch, put the child in it, and laid it in the reeds by the river's bank." (Exodus 2:3)

When the daughter of Pharaoh came to bathe at the river, she spotted the ark (tevah תֵּבָה); had compassion on the Hebrew baby boy within and saved him. The ark, therefore, is a means of salvation for one marked for certain death.

Sealed with Atonement

God gave Noach specific instructions and dimensions for the construction of the ark. It was to be sealed inside and outside with 'pitch'.

"Make yourself an ark of gopherwood; make rooms in the ark, and cover (kapartah) כָּפַרְתָּ it inside and outside with pitch (kofer) כֹּפֶר."
(Genesis 6:14)

I had always imagined this pitch to be some kind of waterproof sealant, like perhaps tar. However, the Hebrew uses a specific word which surprised me כפר – K-P-R – which comes from the Hebrew word for <u>atonement</u> 'kaparah' כפרה.

The saving ark was sealed with 'atonement'; just as we are saved through the atoning sacrifice of Yeshua our Messiah! We are sealed, inside and out, with the blood of Yeshua, that atones for all of our sins and saves us from death and eternity in hell.

"He (Yeshua the Messiah) is the atoning sacrifice for our sins, and not only for ours but also for the sins of the whole world." (1 John 2:2)

Yeshua is our ark and protection as the storm accelerates upon the earth. We are truly living in the days of Noah again; and we must know where to find our place of safety inside the ark of salvation when the end-time storm strikes the earth.

It is God who told Noah how to prepare for the flood; and Noah moved with 'godly fear' to build the ark for the saving of his household. **"By faith Noah, being warned by God about things not yet seen, in reverence prepared an ark for the salvation of his household, by which he condemned the world, and became an heir of the righteousness which is according to faith."** (Hebrews 11:7)

We need to be praying earnestly, and being willing to move with godly fear in obedience as God directs us for the saving of our households through the coming 'time of Jacob's trouble'.

Beyond physical preparations, however, we can prepare spiritually by maintaining a sacred ark of 'shalom' (peace) in the midst of the storm.

Noah's Ark (New Beginning II)
Artist: David Miller, Art for Wildlife Galleries

Noach Means Rest נח

It is not a coincidence that the name Noach נח means rest. Spelled backwards, his name would mean 'grace or favor' {chen} חן.

"But Noah found grace (chen חן) in the eyes of the Lord." (Genesis 6:8)

Noah had truly entered into a place of blessed rest through his absolute faith in God which led to his obedience. He was not a man who 'leaned on his own understanding' of the situation but he trusted wholeheartedly in the Word of the Lord and simply obeyed.

We will also come to this place of peace and rest when we learn to simply trust and obey God at His Word instead of trying to reason everything out and make sure something makes sense or agrees with our theology before complying with God's commands.

We are, each of us, saved not through works, but by the grace of God through faith. And faith means resting in the Lord through believing. As the storms intensify, we need to become even more firm and resolute in our determination to 'cast our cares' upon the Lord and rest in Him through faith.

"Rest in YHVH יהוה and wait patiently for Him. Do not fret ..." (Psalm 37:7)

Resting in the Lord requires an attitude of faith that knows God is fighting our battles for us. Rather than panicking when we face a challenge, we are commanded to fear not – *"Be still and know that I am God."* (Psalm 46:10)

God is still in control. Just as He sat enthroned at the flood, He is still enthroned above every storm that will come upon us in these end times. He will give us all the strength we need; and He will bless His people with peace (shalom).

"The Lord sat enthroned at the Flood, and the Lord sits as King forever. The Lord will give strength to His people; the Lord will bless His people with peace." (Psalm 29:10-11)

Just as the flood was a purifying force upon the earth – to cleanse the earth from wickedness, corruption and violence; so too will the coming storms serve God's good purposes. Let us not panic when 'flooded' with negative experiences at this time, but know that a cleansing and purifying is taking place in our lives.

We can 'hold our peace' and know that God will bring good somehow out of every situation. We can build an ark of peace, rest, calmness and tranquility, through trusting in the Lord, that will get us through every storm.

Even though Yeshua seemed to be asleep in the boat when the disciples faced what seemed to be a life-threatening storm; even though they felt that He no longer even cared that they were perishing, Yeshua still got them safely through to the other side! [4]

Just Like in the Days of Noah

Most of us know that a great judgment and destruction is coming upon the world. But many people still continue on with life as usual, completely unaware of what is coming, just as it was in the days of Noah before the flood.

"But as the days of Noah were, so also will the coming of the Son of Man be. For as in the days before the flood, they were eating and drinking, marrying and giving in marriage, until the day that Noah entered the ark, and did not know until the flood came and took them all away, so also will the coming of the Son of Man be." (Matthew 24:37-41)

Our relationship with God must be securely founded upon the Rock of our Salvation or we will not endure to the end and be saved; but if we ask, God is faithful, and He will prepare us and see us through. Just as Joseph acted in Divine wisdom to prepare for a time of famine in Egypt, and Noah was divinely warned of things not yet seen to prepare an ark for the saving of his household, God will also warn us and give us wisdom if we will ask.

We must keep our ears open to the voice of His Spirit. We cannot be complacent or asleep, going about 'life as usual'; but we must be about our Father's business and work while there is yet light.

"Watch, therefore, and pray always that you may be counted worthy to escape all these things that will come to pass, and to stand before the Son of Man."
(Luke 21:36)

---

[4] Mark 4:35-40

It is time to prepare physically and spiritually for the storm to come; to wear the full armor of the Lord and be covered with the protection of the blood of Yeshua.

For those who refuse to bow down to Baal and the demonic agenda, the Lord will be the fourth man in the fire just as He was with Shadrach, Mishach & Abednego. He will protect us and will miraculously deliver us. We must know that God will never leave us or forsake us; so let us be strong and very courageous! (Joshua 1:6-9)

We must be prepared to go into hiding when the time comes if the Lord so directs:

"A prudent man foresees evil and hides himself, but the simple pass on and are punished." (Proverbs 22:3)

God has an ark (tevah) תֵּבָה for us and our households if we will do, as Noach did, all that God commands. *"Thus Noah did; according to all that God commanded him, so he did."* (Genesis 6:22)

Just as He told Noach when to enter the ark, so too will He set us safely inside; and then it is God Himself who will shut us in. **"So those that entered, male and female of all flesh, went in as God had commanded him; and the Lord shut him in."** (Genesis 7:16)

In the end times, judgment will come suddenly, just like the flood in the days of Noah (Matthew 24:36-41); but we need not fear, for the Lord will provide a safe shelter, an ark (a tevah), to protect us from the raging storms of tribulation to come – just as He provided the ark for Noah and his family.

"You are my hiding place; You preserve me from trouble; You surround me with songs of deliverance. Selah." (Psalms 32:7)

The prophet Isaiah wrote, **"Come, my people, enter your chambers, and shut your doors behind you; hide yourself, as it were, for a little moment, until the indignation is past."** (Isaiah 26:20)

May we emerge from the ark to establish the new heavens and the new earth of peace, righteousness and justice, under the rule of the Messiah, Yeshua in the New Jerusalem.

Prayer: *Dear God, it's starting to feel, more and more these days, like the world is spinning totally out of control, and yet we know that You are still in control and that Your plans and purposes will surely come to pass. But when we see the evil, wickedness and corruption all around us, we sometimes wonder where we can find a safe place of shelter to hide until all these calamities pass us by?*

So we thank you, Adonai, that You are our shelter, our refuge and our hiding place. You have provided an ark to save us for eternity through the atoning sacrifice of Yeshua the Messiah. Help us to clearly hear Your voice and be willing to move with godly fear when you say "move", and give us the wisdom to stay when you say "stay", because You have promised that those who listen to the voice of wisdom will be safe and secure without any fear of evil.[5] Amen v'amen.

THE PROMISE, NOAH'S ARK (2010) Painting by **Sonia Finch**

---

[5] Proverbs 1:33

Preparing for the Bridegroom - Elul אֱלוּל

The Hebrew month of Elul אֱלוּל precedes the God appointed times (mo'ed) of the Fall Feasts: Yom ZikaronTruah (Feast of Trumpets), Yom Kippur (Day of Atonement) and Sukkot (Feast of Tabernacles). During the entire month of Elul, the shofar (ram's horn) is blown every morning and evening, as a call to prepare for these great festivals.

How do we prepare ourselves spiritually for these holy, God Appointed Times (Moadim)? Elul is observed as an opportunity <u>to search our hearts</u> in preparation for the coming days of Judgment – when it is traditionally believed that God opens the **Book of Life** and examines our deeds.

Why is this so crucial? It is prophesied in the book of Daniel that a time of trouble is coming such as never has been experienced on earth before; and that only those whose names are <u>written in the book</u> will be delivered.

"And there shall be a time of trouble, such as never was since there was a nation...And at that time your people shall be delivered, <u>everyone who is found written in the book</u>." (Daniel 12:1)

Slichot - Prayers of Forgiveness

During this time, special psalms are read and prayers recited called Slichot (forgiveness). The Hebrew word 'slichah' סְלִיחָה means forgiveness, sorry, absolution or pardon.

Although we strive to live a pure and holy life before God, all of us sin and fall short of the glory of God, therefore we need to examine our hearts, repent and return to the Lord.

"Let us examine our ways and test them, and let us return to the LORD." (Lamentations 3:40)

Hebraic Concept of Repentance

> The Hebrew word for repentance is 'hazarah be t'shuvah'. חזרה בתשובה.
>
> The word, hazarah חזרה means to 'return'.
>
> T'shuvah תשובה means to 'answer'. Shuvah שובה means 'to take captive';
>
> and Shuv שוב means 'again'.

What a beautiful message on repentance is hidden in this Hebrew word. God wants us to return to Him; and He will answer us when we call out to Him. Yeshua's mission is to set the captives free; and we need to come to Him again and again and again and again… to receive His mercy and forgiveness.

Even the Hebrew letter symbolizing the name of God, ה, is a picture of this beautiful truth. This letter is pictured as a door with a perpetual opening at the top.

The arms of Yeshua on the cross were open wide to receive all who would come to Him and receive forgiveness.

Yeshua proclaimed himself 'the door' (opening) for the sheep, saying, **"I am the door. If anyone enters by Me, he will be saved, and will go in and out and find pasture."** (John 10:9)

It is through Yeshua the Messiah that we come to the Father in repentance. He is the way, the truth and the life and no one comes to the Father but through Him. (John 14:6)

Just as the Father ran to meet the prodigal son when he saw his son returning from the pig pen, having wasted his inheritance, having nothing to offer his Abba but his remorse; so too does our Abba Father run to meet us when we begin our journey back to Him through repentance. The door is always open.

God doesn't desire our burnt offerings of ritual sacrifices and vain traditions; but the sacrifice that God desires is a broken and contrite heart.

"The sacrifices of God are a broken spirit, a broken and a contrite heart— These, O God, You will not despise." (Psalm 51:17)

We are all being purified, refined, and prepared for the return of our Messiah Yeshua. This is the message of the Fall Feasts: upon the shout (tru'ah) and the blast of the shofar, the Messiah is returning to judge the world; and to save Israel from our enemies. Now is the time to prepare our hearts for the soon coming return of the Lord.

"For the Lord Himself will descend from heaven with a shout (tru'ah), with the voice of an archangel, and with the trumpet (shofar) of God." (1 Thess. 4:16)

Elul - A Time for Love

Elul is not a time to fear, however; but to remember how much God loves us!

God loved the world so much that He sent His only son, so that whoever believes in Him will not perish but have eternal life (John 3:16). Yeshua gave his life for us so that through the New Covenant (Brit Chadashah), we have forgiveness of our sins – a promise sealed with His own blood.

There is a secret hidden in the Hebrew; that is, the word "Elul" אֱלוּל can be interpreted an acronym for "Ani L'dodi V'dodi Li" אֲנִי לְדוֹדִי וְדוֹדִי לִי

"I am my beloved's and my beloved is mine."
(Song of Solomon 6:3)

Elul is the month of love and relationships – the perfect time to renew our covenant relationship with our Beloved Bridegroom. In the month of Elul, let us draw near to God, seeking a more intimate relationship with our Beloved; and He will draw near to us in love and faithfulness.

Elul - A Time for Reconciliation

Elul is also a season to renew and reconcile our human relationships with one another. My mother (may she rest in peace) had a beautiful tradition of approaching each one of us children during the month of Elul to ask for our forgiveness in case she may have done (or not done) something that hurt or wounded us. This is a beautiful tradition she passed on to us.

Yeshua calls us to love one another, to forgive, and to be kind-hearted towards each other, forgiving one another just as God, in Messiah, has forgiven us. (Ephesians 4:32)

Elul - A Time for Forgiveness

It is forbidden in the Torah to hold a grudge against anyone. *"You shall not hate your brother in your heart. You shall surely rebuke your neighbor, and not bear sin because of him. You shall not take vengeance, nor bear any grudge against the children of your people, but you shall love your neighbor as yourself: I am the LORD."* (Leviticus 19:17-18)

Even in the New Testament it is written that if we do not forgive all others from our heart; then our Father in Heaven will not forgive us.

"Therefore if you are offering your gift at the altar and there remember that your brother has something against you, leave your offering there before the altar and go; first be reconciled to your brother, and then come and present your offering." (Matthew 5:23-24)

Prayer: Dear God, during the month of Elul, may we make a special effort, by Your grace, to bring healing, restoration and reconciliation in all of our relationships. Let there be a complete release of all unforgiveness and grudges that we may be holding in our hearts against anyone in our life.

Draw us closer to You, that we may know true intimacy with our Beloved Bridegroom. Give us the wisdom to know what changes we need to make in the coming season, especially in our relationship with You, O God, and with one another so that there may be peace, love and unity in our midst – for Your glory. Amen.

Blow the Shofar in Zion שׁוֹפָר

"Blow the shofar in Zion, and sound an alarm in my holy mountain: let all the inhabitants of the land tremble: for the day of the Lord comes, it is right at hand."
(Joel 2:1)

God has commanded His people to blow the shofar and shout (Tru'ah) at an appointed time

– a day called in Hebrew Yom Zikaron Tru'ah

יום זכרון טועה (literally translated as 'Day of remembering the shout – or blast of the shofar').

"Speak to the children of Israel, saying: 'In the seventh month, on the first day of the month, you shall have a sabbath-rest, a memorial of blowing the shofar, (Shabbaton Zikaron Tru'ah) a holy convocation (mikreh kodesh).'"
(Leviticus 23:24)

We know this is a commandment; but why do we blow the shofar and shout on this day? What are we to be remembering? The reasons are not actually spelled out, but through the Hebrew Scriptures, we can glean full understanding.

Most Jewish people call this day Rosh Hashanah (Head of the year) and consider it a 'Jewish new year'. A Jewish custom is to eat the head of a fish (rosh dag) at the festive meal, bringing to mind the promise that God will make us the "head and not the tail; above and not beneath." [1]

Other customs are to eat pomegranates (which become ripe in Israel at the time of the Fall Feasts); and to dip apples in honey as well as eating honey cake to symbolize the hope of a sweet and fruitful 'new year' ahead.

Most Jewish people greet one another with the words, "Shana Tovah u'metukah". "Have a good and sweet year."

---

[1] Deuteronomy 28:13

The True Head of the Year

But is this concept of 'Rosh Hashana' actually true?? According to the Hebrew, Biblical calendar, the head of the year is the month of Nissan, during which we celebrate the Passover. This tells us that all time is reckoned from the day of our salvation through the blood of the Lamb. Halleluyah!

"This month (Nissan/Aviv) shall be your beginning of months; it shall be the first month of the year to you." (Exodus 12:2)

Yom Zikaron Tru'ah (also called the Feast of Trumpets or Feast of the Shofar) is clearly observed and celebrated in the seventh month of the year called Tishrei on the first day of the month.

The true meaning of this special day is not in any way, shape or form about it being a 'new year'; but rather a day to remember that the day of the Lord is at hand. The King is coming and the day of His return is drawing near; therefore we are to make ourselves ready.

This true meaning of Yom Zikaron Tru'ah has been obscured by yet another Rabbinical, man-made distortion of the truth, designed to deceive the masses of Jewish people and to hide from them the real significance of this festival – which is the imminent return of the Messiah, Yeshua.

It is with the blast of a shofar and with a great shout (tru'ah) that Yeshua will come from the clouds! The King is coming and the Bride needs to make herself ready.

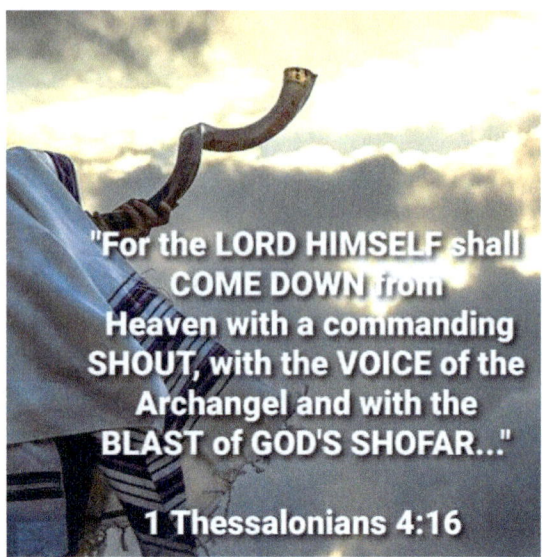

We all need to come up higher – to be purified from everything that we have allowed to defile us; and to turn away from all the ways that our conduct, attitudes, thoughts and words do not bring glory to God. There is not one who has not sinned and fallen short of the glory of God.

The Hebrew word, shofar שופר comes from the root word shaper לשפר, which means *'to improve'*. The shofar reminds us to improve! Each year when the shofar blows, we are to examine our hearts and listen for the voice of God telling us how we may improve our character in order to be more and more conformed into the image of Yeshua.

As the shofar is blown, let us hear with spiritual ears the voice of God showing us where we can come up higher and improve our character.

The Voice of God

Not many have heard the audible voice of God; but the blast of the shofar represents the voice of God to His people. On Mount Sinai, on the third day, amidst the thunder and lightning and thick cloud on the mountain,

"The sound of the shofar was very loud, so that all the people who were in the camp trembled." (Exodus 19:16)

We can only imagine the intensity of such a scene. Who blew the shofar from that thick cloud on Mt Sinai with all the people of Israel gathered below? Was it a man or could it have been Elohim Himself blowing on the shofar? Moses had brought the people out to meet with their God at the base of the mountain.

Mt. Sinai became completely engulfed in smoke as the Lord descended upon it in fire. Its smoke was like the smoke of a furnace and the whole mountain shook. The voice of the shofar sounded long and became louder and louder! Moses spoke, and God answered him by voice.[2] Wow!

---
[2] Exodus 19:18-19

Purposes of the Shofar

Obviously, the shofar is an instrument of extraordinary spiritual significance; and has been used for several purposes in Scripture including:

* to mark the arrival of a new moon

* to celebrate a simcha (joyous occasion)

* to proclaim liberty

* to hail a king

* to warn of impending judgment

* to gather troops to battle

* to sound an alarm

* to call a sacred assembly and time of fasting

* to confuse the enemy camp

* to draw God's attention

Constructed out of a ram's horn, the shofar is blown in synagogues around the world during the entire month of Elul preceding Yom Zikaron Tru'ah. It is also blown throughout the fall feasts and especially on Yom Kippur (Day of Atonement).

Somehow, even as a young girl, without hearing the loud tru'ah of the shofar during the fall feasts, I felt that I had missed something incredibly significant. One year, due to circumstances beyond my control, I arrived at the shule (synagogue) too late to hear the shofar. I was so disappointed; but God is so merciful.

Shortly afterwards, I attended a teacher's convention at a mountain hotel. I walked into the lobby only to see several men dressed in Dutch costumes blowing on these incredible instruments that resembled a huge, elongated shofar! Our heavenly Father is so gracious to give His children the desires of our hearts.

To miss the shofar is like sleeping past our alarm clock which was set for an important event. The primary purpose of the piercing sound of the shofar is to remind God's people to wake up out of their spiritual slumber, to see the signs of the times, and to examine the spiritual condition of our lives.

This is the message of t'shuvah, which translates literally 'to return' in Hebrew. Its meaning is to turn from our sins in repentance and return back to God.

"Return (shuvu) שׁוּבוּ *to me with all your heart, with fasting and weeping and mourning. Rend your heart and not your garments."* (Joel 2:12-13)

The Shofar in Sounding an Alarm

An alarm has been going out in the spirit all across the Land; and in all the nations of the earth to prepare for a time of trouble which is to come. Called the Time of Jacob's trouble,[3] it will be like nothing we have ever seen before; but we will be saved out of it – everyone whose name is written in the Book of Life.[4]

The shofar calls us, like sounding an alarm, to get ready for the day of the Lord which is very near.

"Blow the shofar in Zion; sound the alarm on my holy hill. Let all who live in the land tremble, for the day of the Lord is coming. It is close at hand – a day of darkness and gloom." (Joel 2:1-2)

One of the things that each one needs to do is to make sure that they are on the right side of this battle – and that means standing with Israel! For God has vowed to destroy all the nations that come against Jerusalem. He will make Jerusalem a heavy stone and all who try to move it will be cut to shreds!

---

[3] Jeremiah 30:7
[4] Daniel 12:1

I thought of this verse as I watched some Israeli school children at the Jerusalem Science museum, trying to move the heavy stone standing at the entrance - but no matter how hard they tried - it would not budge. So too shall it be with Jerusalem. No matter how many people try to come against her, she shall not be moved.

Israeli children trying to move stone in front of Jerusalem Science Museum

"And it shall happen in that day that I will make Jerusalem a very heavy stone for all peoples; all who would heave it away will surely be cut in pieces, though all nations of the earth are gathered against it." (Zechariah 12:3)

A Global Holocaust?

Although we often lightly say, "*Come Adonai Yeshua…*" we must realize that the day of the Lord will be a day of wrath, judgment, trouble and distress for the inhabitants of the earth.[5] It is actually described in Hebrew as the day of **'Shoah'** יוֹם שֹׁאָה which is Hebrew for 'Holocaust Day'.

It is a day of 'shofar and alarm' (tru'ah)! [6]   יוֹם שׁוֹפָר, וּתְרוּעָה

---

[5] Zephaniah 1:14-16
[6] Zephaniah 1:16

Now is the time to hear the alarm, wake up and get ourselves ready – spiritually and physically – for the coming of the day of the Lord. No amount of silver or gold will save us from the wrath of God; but only righteousness which we have obtained through the perfect sacrifice of Yeshua the Messiah.

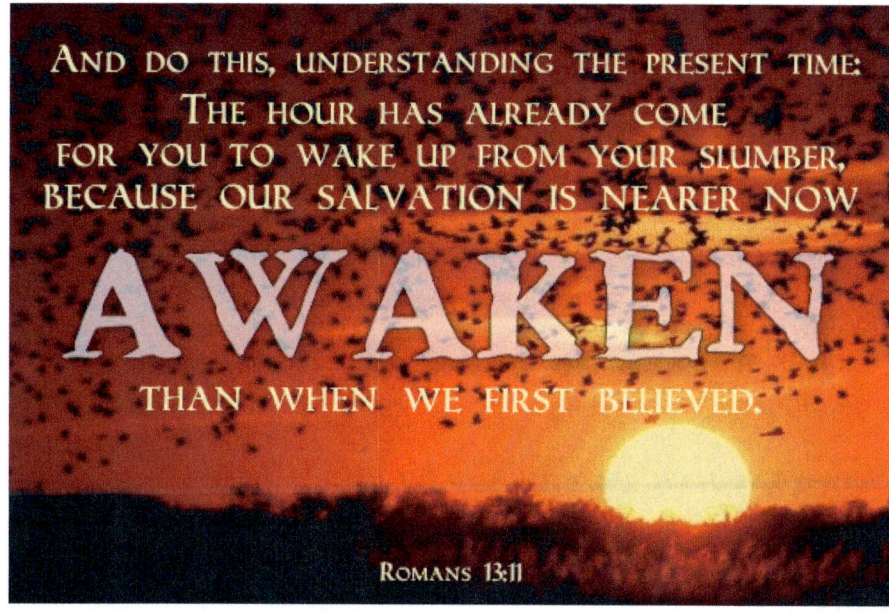

"*Awake, O sleeper, Arise from the dead, And the Messiah will give you light.*"

"See then that you walk carefully, not as fools but as wise, redeeming the time, because the days are evil." (Ephesians 5:14-16)

The Shofar in Calling an Assembly

"Blow the shofar in Zion, declare a holy fast, call a sacred assembly. Gather the people, consecrate the assembly…" (Joel 2:15-16)

Whoever has heard the intensity of the blast of a shofar can testify that it is definitely a sound that carries. When we went camping in the mountains, the children and I wandered off on some trails, taking in the beauty and majesty of God's creations in the Canadian Rockies. When my husband wanted us to come back, all he had to do was blow the shofar and no matter where we were, we knew we were to come back to camp. The sound really carries like no other. The faithful remnant in the nations, in Jerusalem and across the Land of Israel, are blowing the shofar to rally God's people to fasting, prayer and repentance, knowing that the day of the Lord is at hand.

Liat with shofar in Canadian Rocky Mountains

The Shofar in Mercy

The shofar as a ram's horn may also represent God's mercy by sparing the life of Issac. Abraham, in obedience to God's command, prepared to offer up his son on the altar as a sacrifice; but instead of taking Issac's life, God Himself provided the sacrifice with a ram caught in the thicket.

"And Abraham said, "My son, God will provide for Himself the lamb for a burnt offering." (Genesis 22:8)

We blow the ram's horn to remind us of this example of God's mercy, but God has further revealed His greater mercy through Yeshua (Jesus). He did not spare the life of His only son, Yeshua, but gave it up for us in order that we may have eternal life. How can we even doubt God's goodness?

"He who did not spare His own son, but gave Him up for us all – how will He not also, along with Him, graciously give us all things?" (Romans 8:32)

The Shofar in Warfare

Today, the shofar is being re-discovered as an instrument of spiritual warfare and is being blown, not only in Jewish synagogues, but also in Christian Churches and Messianic Congregations all over the world.

The Bible contains many references to the shofar being used in battle. Joshua and his Israelite army took the enemy city of Yericho with the sounding of the shofar.

"When the shofarot [7] sounded, the people shouted, and at the sound of the shofar, when the people gave a loud shout, the wall collapsed; so every man charged straight in, and they took the city." (Joshua 6:20)

In another example, Gideon and his small band of men blew their shofarot, held in their right hands and broke the pitchers holding the torches in their left hands. *"When the three hundred blew the shofarot,[8] the Lord set every man's sword against his*

---

[7] Shofarot is plural for shofar
[8] Shofarot is plural for shofar

companion through the whole camp...All the Midianites ran, crying out as they fled." (Judges 7:19-22)

How does this relate to us as people of the God of Abraham today? In our family, we regularly blow the shofar when we experience an attack of the enemy, basing our hope for divine help on the promise in the book of Numbers:

"When you go to war in your land against the enemy who oppresses you, then you shall sound an alarm with the shofarot and you will be remembered before the Lord your God, and you will be saved from your enemies." (Numbers 10:9)

Of course we know that He hears even the tiniest whisper and knows even our unspoken thoughts, but in the heat of battle, there is something about blowing that shofar to draw God's attention! We have used it especially in times of sickness and demonic oppression. If you find yourself, your family, or your congregation under attack, I strongly recommend using the shofar as an instrument of spiritual warfare.

The Prophetic Shofar in the Rapture

One of the most significant prophetic scriptures with regards to the shofar relates to the rapture (or lifting of the Believers to be with the Lord in heaven). This subject creates much debate. What we sometimes forget is that the issue of rapture is not some strange phenomenon mentioned only in the New Testament. The Hebrew prophet Eliyahu (Elijah) was also 'raptured'.

"...suddenly a chariot of fire appeared with horses of fire, and separated the two of them; and Elijah went up by a whirlwind into heaven." (2 Kings 2:11)

A popular book and video series has popularized the concept of a pre-tribulation rapture – that is, that the Believers will also be suddenly swept into heaven without warning. But scripture tells us that this event will happen at the sound of the shofar. When? – when the Lord returns and the resurrection of the dead occurs...

"For the Lord himself will come down from heaven, with a loud command, with the voice of the archangel and <u>with the shofar call of God</u>, and the dead in Messiah will rise first. After that, we who are still alive and are left will be caught up together with them in the clouds to meet the Lord in the air. And so we will be with the Lord forever. Therefore encourage each other with these words."
(1 Thessalonians 4:16-18)

At the Last Shofar

The Word also makes reference to the shofarot of the Tribulation in the book of Revelation. Again, we read that the resurrection and rapture will occur together. When? <u>At the last shofar.</u>

"Listen, I tell you a mystery. We will not all sleep, but we will all be changed – in a flash, in the twinkling of an eye, <u>at the last shofar</u>. For the shofar will sound, the dead will be raised imperishable, and we will be changed." (1 Corinthians 15:51-52)

The Shofar in Judgment

The sounding of the shofarot begins in Revelations 8:7 with the outpouring of God's judgment upon the earth. Seven angels standing before God in heaven are given seven shofarot to sound. *"So the seven angels who had the seven shofarot prepared themselves to sound."* (Revelation 8:6)

The earth is struck with plagues similar to the plagues God used to destroy Egypt, forcing Pharaoh to finally agree to God's command through Moses, "Let My people Go"!

The first shofar: Hail and fire mixed with blood; a third of the earth burned up; a third of the trees burned up, and all the green grass burned up.

The second shofar: a mountain ablaze thrown into the sea; a third of the sea turned to blood; a third of the living creatures in the sea die; a third of the ships destroyed.

The third shofar: a great star, Wormwood, blazing like a torch falls on the waters, which turn bitter and many people die from the bitter waters.

The fourth shofar: a third of the sun, moon, and stars, struck and turn dark.

The fifth shofar: The sun and sky darkened by smoke. Locusts come upon the earth and sting and torture the people on earth who do not have the seal of God on their foreheads for five months. People will long to die but won't.

The sixth shofar: Four angels are released to kill a third of mankind by the three plagues of fire, smoke and sulfur. The rest of mankind still does not repent of their worship of demons, idolatry, sorcery, sin, and immorality (The Pharaoh syndrome).

The seventh and final shofar: (Revelation 11:15-18) The seventh shofar signals the rule and reign of the Messiah on earth, **"The kingdoms of this world have become the kingdoms of our Lord and of His Messiah, and He shall reign forever and ever!"** (Revelation 11:15)

At this time, the dead will be judged and rewards given to the servants of the Lord, prophets and saints. (Revelation 11:18) This also fulfills the spiritual meaning behind the Feast of Tabernacles, when the Lord will finally 'tabernacle' with us. (Revelation 21:3-4)

Sukkot (or the Feast of Tabernacles or Booths) will be the first feast of the millennium. It will not only be Israel or the Jewish people who will be celebrating, but all the nations will be called to celebrate this appointed time of the Lord or be cursed with drought. (Zechariah 14:16-19)

Babylon will be destroyed (Isaiah 13:19-20) as well as Israel's enemies (Zechariah 14). Finally, we will experience the longed for peace on earth during the millennium under Yeshua's reign. (Isaiah 11:1-9)

The International global kingdom of the Messiah, as prophesied in Isaiah 9:6-7, will be established; with Israel the head of the nations and Jerusalem the capital and center of worship of the One True God.

At this time, all denominations and double standards will be wiped away as Believers come from all nations to learn how to live according to the ways and laws of God, written in the Torah, which go forth out of Zion.

"Many nations shall come and say, 'Come and let us go up to the mountains of the Lord, to the house of the God of Jacob; He will teach us His ways and we shall walk in His paths.' For <u>out of Zion</u> the Torah shall go forth, and the word of the Lord from Jerusalem...Nation shall not lift up sword against nation, neither shall they learn war anymore." (Micah 4:2-3)

Sound of the Shofar[9]

May the sound of the shofar shatter our complacency
And make us conscious of the corruption in our lives.
May the sound of the shofar penetrate our souls
And cause us to turn back to our Father in Heaven.

May the sound of the shofar break the bonds of the evil impulse within us
And enable us to serve the Lord with a whole heart.
May the sound of the shofar renew our loyalty to the one true King
And strengthen our determination to defy the false gods.

May the sound of the shofar awaken us to the enormity of our sins
And the vastness of God's mercy for those who truly repent.
May the sound of the shofar summon us to service
And stir us to respond, as did Abraham, "Here am I."

May the sound of the shofar recall the moment
When we stood at Mount Sinai and uttered the promise:
"All that the Lord has spoken, we will keep and obey."

May the sound of the shofar recall the promise of the ingathering of the exiles
And stir within us renewed devotion to the Land of Israel.
May the sound of the shofar recall the vision of the prophets,
Of the day when Egypt, Syria, and Israel will live in peace.

May the sound of the shofar awaken us to the flight of time
And summon us to spend our days with purpose.

---

[9] Sound of the Shofar poem from the High Holy Days Supplement at Orthodox synagogue

May the sound of the shofar become our jubilant shout of joy
On the day of the promised, long-awaited redemption.

May the sound of the shofar remind us that it is time
to "proclaim liberty throughout the land
to all the inhabitants thereof."

May the sound of the shofar enter our hearts;
For blessed is the people that hearkens to its call.

**"Happy (blessed) are the people who know teruah תְּרוּעָה;
they walk, O LORD, in the light of Your countenance."** (Psalms 89:15)

Prayer: *Dear God, we know that we have only so much time left of daylight while we may still work; for soon the night and the darkness will be upon us. Help us to be wise, to know Your perfect will, and to make the most of the time we have left to serve You with all our hearts.*

As we hear the sound of the shofar, may we hear Your voice speaking to our hearts. Reveal to us any ways that we need to come up higher and improve in our walk with You. Most of all, help us to remember, as we hear the sound of the shofar, that You are coming soon. Make us ready to meet You as Your Bride. Come Adonai Yeshua….

When a Kiss is a Weapon - Neshek נֶשֶׁק

"Faithful are the wounds of a friend, but the kisses (neshikot) נְשִׁיקוֹת *of an enemy are deceitful."* (Proverbs 27:6)

The Hebrew word for weapon is 'neshek'. נֶשֶׁק

This root word is also found in the Hebrew word 'neshikah' נְשִׁיקָה
- which means 'a kiss'.[1]

How are these two words related? This is a secret hidden in the Hebrew. The word for kiss (nashak) means to put two mouths together; but it can also mean 'to array oneself for battle'.

---

[1] Plural neshikot

I had to laugh when we drove into the underground parking at the mall, rolled down the window and the security guard asked, "*neshek*?" It was one of those 'only in Israel' moments. What he was really asking me was whether or not I was carrying a weapon; but I thought he was asking me for a kiss!

In Hebrew, these two words, *neshek* and *neshika*, are closely related, but why? A kiss can be a sign of love and affection; but can also be used as a weapon. The Proverbs are full of warnings to young men to avoid becoming entangled with immoral women.

The Crafty Harlot

In Proverbs chapter 7, a father is warning his son to stay away from a seductress who uses her kiss as a weapon to lure him into his destruction. A young man takes the path to her house....

***"And there a woman met him, with the attire of a harlot, and a crafty heart....
So she caught him <u>and kissed him</u>."*** (Proverbs 7:10-13)

She seduced him with a kiss and he went with her, not knowing that it would cost his life! This father warns his son to beware, for she has slain many strong men, and ***"her house is the way to hell, descending to the chambers of death."*** (Proverbs 7:26,27)

This path of destruction all started with a kiss! Yes, a kiss can definitely be used as a weapon. All we need to do is to remember the story of Samson and Delilah. Samson was physically the strongest man on the face of the earth, but he was emotionally immature and morally weak.

Because he succumbed to the deceitful kisses of an immoral woman, he lost his gift of strength and almost forfeited his destiny. Samson ended up a pathetic captive of the Philistines who gouged out his eyes and robbed him of his dignity. In the end, he did succeed in delivering Israel from the Philistines but it cost Samson his life.

A sober warning indeed! It is not only men who need to beware; women also need to use wisdom, discernment and good judgment in relationships. The Word of God tells us that in the last days, some men will be evil; they will worm their way into the homes of gullible women.[2] Many a wolf has disguised himself, even in a congregation, as a sheep, only to prey upon and devour an innocent but unaware lamb.[3]

---

[2] 2 Timothy 3:1-6
[3] See Hannah's testimony <u>Grafted in Again</u>

Kiss the Son

A kiss is generally an expression of romantic love, sexual passion and affection; but can mean something quite different in other cultures. European and Middle Eastern people often greet one another with a kiss on both cheeks.

In the Psalms, we are told to 'kiss the son', meaning to give Him reverence and honor:

"Kiss the Son (nashku bar נַשְּׁקוּ־בַר), lest He be angry and you perish from the way, when His wrath is kindled but a little. Blessed are all those that put their trust in Him." (Psalm 2:12)

Paul exhorted the early believers to **greet one another with a holy kiss** (neshikah).[4] A kiss of greeting between believers implied that everyone was equal. All were equally loved and accepted – not only by God – but by one another.

A Judas Kiss

When does a kiss become a weapon? I am reminded that it was with a kiss that Judas betrayed Yeshua. The kiss given by Judas in the Garden of Gethsemane after their Passover supper led directly to Yeshua's arrest by the police force of the Sanhedrin.

This prearranged signal was that the person Judas kissed was to be arrested and taken away.[5] In this way the Son of Man was betrayed with a kiss.[6] Since then, a 'Judas Kiss' has become a common expression meaning, *"an act appearing to be one of friendship, which is, in actuality, harmful to the recipient".*

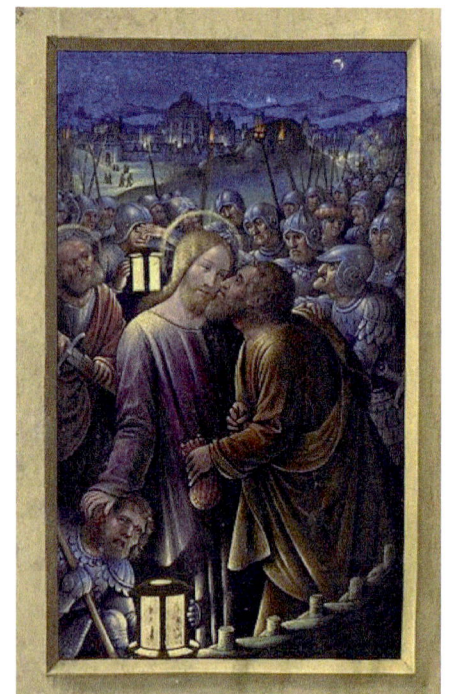

Judas betraying Jesus with a kiss Grandes Heures, Anne de Bretagne 1500-1520 Public Domain, https://commons.wikimedia.org

---

[4] 2 Corinthians 13:12
[5] Mark 14:44
[6] Luke 22:48

In the culture of first-century Israel, a kiss on the cheek could be a common greeting, a sign of deep respect, honor, and brotherly love. It would have been entirely appropriate for Judas to give Yeshua a kiss on the cheek as a sign of his love, devotion and respect for Yeshua as his teacher and rabbi.

For Judas to use a kiss as a weapon, however, was the ultimate betrayal. His actions were saying, *"I love and honor you"*; but his intentions were to give Yeshua over to be murdered.

As it is written, **"Faithful are the wounds of a friend, but the kisses (neshikot) נְשִׁיקוֹת of an enemy are deceitful."** (Proverbs 27:6)

We need to be wise as serpents and gentle as doves. Enemies can disguise themselves as friends. Even the devil can masquerade himself as an angel of light. [7]

I heard an interesting sermon recently at a Messianic congregation in Be'er Sheva. The pastor, Eduardo, exhorted us to use our heads and not just our hearts with regards to our intimate relationships. He said that in the animal kingdom, predators know that the best time to catch their prey is during mating season, because while they are so 'preoccupied', they become easy prey. It's like they totally lose their minds.

We need to keep our wits about us and be careful that we too do not become 'easy prey' for the enemy of our souls. With all of our relationships, but especially with our romantic ones, we need to use discernment.

My daughter seems to have this intuitive discernment about people; she will often say, *"I just got a 'funny vibe' from them."* She has learned to trust this intuitive gift and avoid people like this – which has saved her a lot of trouble! When she grew up, she married a wonderful, godly man who cherishes her and treats her like a queen. Praise God!

I, on the other hand, have not been similarly gifted. After three failed marriages, I have come to conclude that I am not really a very good judge of character. The problem is that unless someone is obviously strange, dysfunctional or downright mean, I usually assume that most people are good-hearted and honest – which is why I tend to get ripped off a lot in Israel. They have a word for people like me – a 'frier'.

A 'frier' means a person who has a tendency to be gullible and is easily taken advantage of. I have learned (and am still learning), to go slowly, set healthy boundaries, use wisdom, and take time to get to know someone's true character.

---

[7] 2 Corinthians 11:14

The truth is that someone can speak and act very kindly, but in actuality, they may be hiding hatred and multiple abominations in his (or her) heart. Talk is cheap, and anyone can present a good face in public, but eventually, their true nature will be revealed.

"He who hates, disguises it with his lips, and lays up deceit within himself; when he speaks kindly, do not believe him, for there are seven abominations in his heart; Though his hatred is covered by deceit, his wickedness will be revealed before the assembly." (Proverbs 26:24-26)

Several years ago, I met a man in a church who seemed like 'Mr. Wonderful' - kind, thoughtful, generous, attractive, and intelligent – a prosperous professional man who loved kids (which seemed an answer to prayer, as a single mother with three children).

When he pursued me and eventually proposed, I thought this was my dream come true – but my dream soon turned into a nightmare. After we married, his wickedness was publicly revealed. He was, in reality, a treacherous deceiver who had physically assaulted women and had been imprisoned for molesting his adopted daughter.

Eventually, I escaped to a women's shelter where I found refuge, but I learned some important (though painful) lessons. I now teach young people and singles how to spot the signs of a potentially abusive or toxic personality in both men and women in my 'Red Flags' seminars.[8]

Yes, a kiss (neshikah) can be a delightful expression of love, honor, and affection; but a kiss can also be used as a weapon (neshek). So let us guard our hearts and love one another with the pure, holy love of God in Messiah Yeshua.

Prayer: *Dear God, we want to honor and glorify You in all of our relationships: friendships, business partnerships, as well as love and marriage. It can be confusing and difficult to discern whether someone is using a kiss as a healthy expression of love and affection, or as a weapon the enemy is using for our destruction.*

We have a tendency to completely lose our minds, especially when involved in a romantic relationship. Help us to notice and pay attention to the red flags, Lord, but truly only You know a person's heart.

---

[8] https://youtu.be/JDj6KWv86wc   https://youtu.be/rCixzg9OpU0
▶ From Red Flags To Green Lights (Part 2 of a relationship seminar) A Message from Jerusalem

Speak to us by Your Holy Spirit and help us to listen to Your voice. Send the right people into our lives – true friends who will love us enough to speak the truth in love if they see that we are headed towards a disaster.

As our sons and daughters grow into maturity, deliver them from traps that the enemy sets to trip them up and steal their destiny through wrong or immoral relationships. Dear God, "Lead us not into temptation and deliver us from evil." (Matthew 6:13)

Thank You for the gift of healthy, supportive, relationships that encourage us to be all You have created us to be.

In Yeshua's name. Amen v'amen.

"Two are better than one…" (Ecclesiastes 4:9)

Going Lower to go Higher - Humility - Anavah עֲנָוָה

The Dead (Salt) Sea - The Lowest Place on Earth

The **Dead Sea,** known in Hebrew as Yam Ha-Melakh (the Sea of Salt) is the lowest point on earth. Surrounded by the stunning landscape of the Negev Desert, it is a popular tourist attraction in Israel due to its renowned health and healing properties.

Because of its salty water, fish cannot survive, but the other result of the high salt content of the water is that you can also float naturally – a uniquely Israeli relaxing and healing experience which everyone should try at least once in their lifetime!

Like the Salt Sea of Israel, in order to be the 'salt of the earth', we may need to go through experiences that humble us, bring us lower, and set us free from the bondage of pride. One of life's paradoxes is that in order to rise higher, one must first sink lower.

We must choose to, *"humble ourselves under the mighty hand of God, and in due time, He will exalt us."* (1 Peter 5:6)

And if we are not willing to voluntarily humble ourselves, then God has His ways of teaching us humility, since God is seeking humble vessels whom He can use for His glory.

If we want to experience God's grace in our lives and stop being blocked at every turn, then we need to become humble, since: *"God resists the proud but gives grace to the humble."* (James 4:6)

MESSIAH SAID

"Whoever **exalts** himself shall be **humbled**; and whoever **humbles** himself shall be **exalted**."

Matthew 23:12

The Hebrew word for humility is 'anavah' עֲנָוָה and it is related to the word, 'anah' ענה, which means to 'answer'. When we walk in humility with God, He answers our prayers. *"If my people, which are called by my name, shall humble themselves, pray and seek my face and turn from their wicked ways, then I will hear from heaven, and will heal their land."* (2 Chronicles 7:14)

This word is also related to 'anav' עָוִי which means 'meek', and 'ani' עני which means 'poor'. Yeshua, in the Sermon on the Mount, said,

"Blessed are the poor in spirit, for theirs is the kingdom of heaven…Blessed are the meek, for they shall inherit the earth." (Matthew 5:3,5)

A Definition of Humility

One definition of humility is: *'a modest or low view of one's own importance'*.

In simple terms, humility means giving up what you rightfully deserve for another purpose that benefits the other person. The best example is that of Yeshua giving up His glory in heaven to come down to earth and give His life for our eternal salvation.

"And being found in appearance as a man, He (Yeshua) humbled Himself and became obedient to the point of death, even the death of the cross."
(Philippians 2:8)

Most of us will not be required to sacrifice our lives for the sake of another; but every day we are presented with opportunities to walk in humility and consider others – or to walk in pride and think only of ourselves.

Philippians 2:4 instructs us, ***"Let each of you look out not only for his own interests, but also for the interests of others."***

The Beauty & Rewards of Humility

Humility is one of the most beautiful fruits of the Holy Spirit;[1] God promises to beautify the humble with salvation.[2] If we want a beauty treatment from God Himself, then we need to learn to walk in humility.

The rewards of humility are so great that it is no wonder our flesh resists it so fiercely.

"The reward of humility (anavah) and fear of the Lord is <u>riches, honor and life</u>." (Proverbs 22:4)

Humility Comes Before Honor

Most of us desire to be honored, valued, and appreciated. The desire to be significant is an inborn human trait; but the Word tells us that ***"humility comes before honor."*** [3]

We may want to become an honored minister, or a famous worship leader, or a successful business person, but we may first need to occupy a lowly position without complaining. Someone with aspirations of becoming a great spiritual leader may need to faithfully shepherd his own family before he can be trusted to shepherd the flock of God.

Both David and Moses served as lowly shepherds before being promoted to their destined position as shepherds over the entire nation of Israel.

---

[1] Galatians 5:22,23
[2] Psalm 149:4
[3] Proverbs 18:12, Proverbs 29:23

One of the Hebrew words for humility or *'lowliness'* is *'shefel'* שפל which can also mean *'low tide'*. Like the tide, it goes out; but will also come back in again. We may need to go through a season of being brought low before rising to a position of honor.

God often uses afflictions, trials and tribulations – leading us into a sometimes lengthy 'wilderness season' – in order to teach us humility. The purpose of the wilderness, a 'dry and thirsty land of snakes and scorpions' is to humble and test us; not to harm us – but to prepare us for the Promised Land!

"And you shall remember that the Lord your God led you all the way these forty years in the wilderness, to humble you and test you, to know what was in your heart, whether you would keep His commandments or not." (Deuteronomy 8:2)

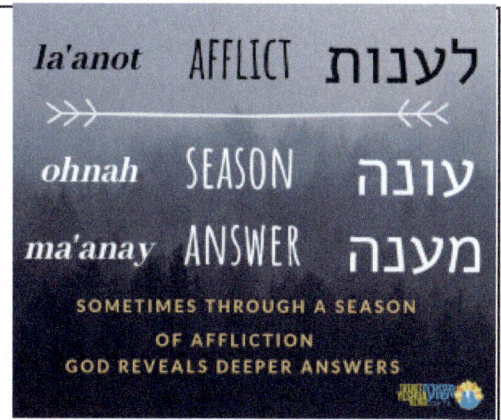

The Hebrew word for afflict is *'la'anot'*.
It is related to the word for season: *'ohnah'*, as well as *'ma'ane'* which means *'answer'*.

God may take us through a season of affliction in order to reveal answers to the questions we hold in the depths of our hearts.

Seasons of Affliction

We can see throughout the Bible that most of the great men and women of God went through a deeply humbling season in their lives before God used them in any significant way. It is not a punishment; it is part of the process of fulfilling our destiny.

Moses, self-confident and sure of himself as a youth, tried to deliver his brethren, the Israelites, from the brutal oppression of their Egyptian slave masters. But in his arrogance, Moses failed, and ended up running away to the Midianite desert where he spent the next forty years on the back side of nowhere, simply tending his father in law's sheep.

God may keep us hidden in obscurity for a season, simply serving in mundane ways without any recognition or acclaim; but this is how He shapes our character.

It was only once Moses had become sufficiently humbled, that God appeared to him in a burning bush and commissioned him to go back to Egypt to deliver His people. This time, Moses understood that he couldn't do it in his own strength, but God said, **"I will be with you."** (Exodus 3:12) A humble person knows that without God he or she can do nothing; but with God all things are possible.

Moses was called *'the most humble man on the face of the earth'* [4] He definitely had a lowly opinion of himself and doubted if he could even carry out his God given mission. He also put others' needs before his own, often interceding for the Israelites who brought judgment upon themselves by their sins, and even pleading for his very own sister whom God struck with leprosy after criticizing Moses and his Cushite wife.

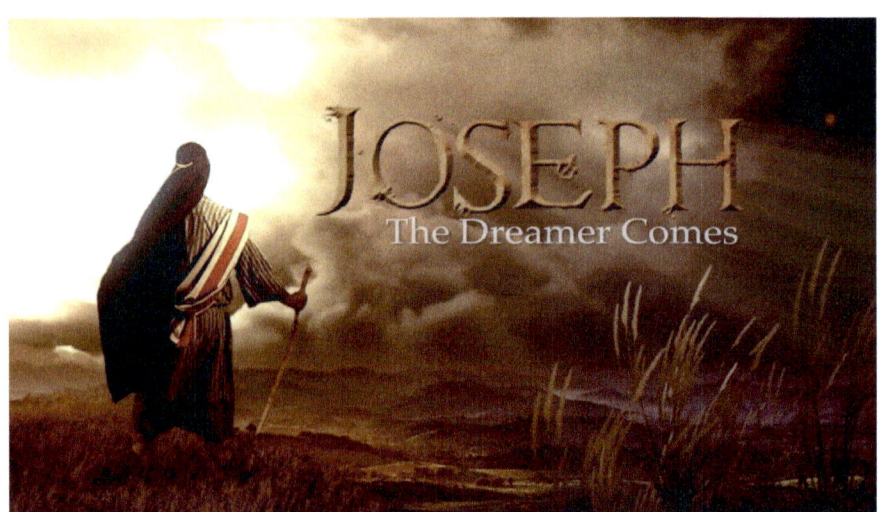

Joseph also showed a streak of arrogance as a youth; tattling on his brothers and boasting about his dreams of greatness. It was only after he was thrown into a pit and sold to slave traders by his very own brothers; served as a slave to Potipher; and thrown into an Egyptian dungeon for a crime he didn't commit – that God finally exalted him to become ruler of all Egypt, just under Pharaoh.

---

[4] Numbers 12:3

After being humbled through these long, painful trials and afflictions, Joseph emerged as a man of humility who not only forgave his brothers, but also spoke kindly to them and provided for his entire family in Egypt. His humbling wilderness season prepared Joseph for his destiny – to save an entire nation!

David also went through a long season of persecution by King Saul, who had gone crazy with jealousy and was therefore troubled by evil spirits. Although David had been anointed by the prophet Samuel to be the next King of Israel, he was first hunted down like a fugitive, hiding in the caves of Ein Gedi for years before God delivered him from the hand of Saul.

We can see the humility of David, that when presented with an opportunity to kill King Saul, he refused to allow his men to touch the Lord's anointed. He said to his men,

"God forbid that I should do such a thing to my master, the LORD's anointed, or lift my hand against him; for he is the anointed of the LORD (mashiach YHVH). With these words David rebuked his men and did not allow them to attack Saul. And Saul left the cave and went his way." (1 Samuel 24:6,7)

It was David's humility that caused God to call him a 'man after His own heart'. We can see a huge contrast between King David and King Saul when it came to receiving correction.

When King Saul was confronted by his sin of disobedience, he did not receive the correction and became immediately defensive.[5] David, however, who had committed far graver moral sins than Saul, immediately acknowledged his sin, repented and sought God's forgiveness.[6]

David also received the correction of a woman, Avigail, when he was about to kill all their workers because of anger against her husband, Naval,[7] a fool. Refusal to receive correction is the mark of a fool: ***"Whoever loves instruction loves knowledge, but he who hates correction is stupid."*** (Proverbs 12:1)

Moses demonstrated his humility by receiving the correction of his father in law, Jethro[8]. Hating correction is a sign of pride which leads to destruction, ***"Harsh discipline is for him who forsakes the way, and he who hates correction will die."*** (Proverbs 15:10)

---

[5] 1 Samuel 15:10-20
[6] Psalm 51
[7] The name, Naval, in Hebrew means 'fool'. As his name was, so was he. 1 Samuel 25:23-35
[8] Exodus 18:14-26

God can and often does use a person who is not perfect; but He cannot use someone who is filled with pride. David demonstrated humility; whereas King Saul showed his pride – a sinful trait which led to his downfall.

Pride Comes Before a Fall

"Pride goes before destruction, and a haughty (arrogant) spirit before a fall." (Proverbs 16:18)

We need to be so careful to guard our hearts from pride, because pride always leads to destruction, and those walking in an arrogant spirit will surely stumble and fall. In fact, we are warned that *"It is better to be lowly in spirit among the humble than to divide the spoil with the proud."* (Proverbs 16:19)

One of the human characteristics that God hates is pride! He says, *"I hate arrogant pride, evil conduct, and perverse speech."* (Proverbs 8:13)

Pride leads to eventual disgrace, but humility brings us wisdom: *"When pride comes, disgrace follows, but with humility comes wisdom."* (Proverbs 11:2)

Pharaoh's Pride Became his Downfall

Stubborness is another face of pride; and it was Pharaoh's stubborn pride that brought about, not only his own destruction – but that of all Egypt!

The Hebrew word for '**Pharaoh**' is פַּרְעֹה

If we switch these same letter around, we get '**Orpah**' עָרְפָּה

This comes from the Hebrew word '**Oref**' עוֹרֶף

which means 'the back of the neck' (in other words, 'stiff-necked' or stubborn).

It was Orpah, in the story of Ruth, who gave her Jewish mother-in-law, Naomi, the back of the neck after kissing her goodbye. We never hear from Orpah again.

Ruth, however, vowed to never leave or forsake her; and although a Moabite, ended up in the lineage of the Messiah! Our Redeemer always rewards those who choose the lowly path of standing with Israel and the Jewish people.[9]

Stubbornness Leads to Brokenness

Stubborness is strongly linked to pride; usually the two ride together in tandem. The Word of God equates stubbornness to the sin of idolatry. Saul was not only prideful; he was also stubborn – and for this reason God rejected him as king of Israel.

"For rebellion is as the sin of witchcraft, and stubbornness is as iniquity and idolatry. Because you have rejected the word of the Lord, He also has rejected you from being king." (1 Samuel 15:23)

Stubbornness can lead to brokenness; and if the person persists in being stubborn and resisting correction, they can be broken without any hope of healing (as with Pharaoh who resisted rebuke over and over again).

"He who is often rebuked, and hardens his neck (becomes stiff-necked or stubborn), will suddenly be destroyed and that without remedy." (Proverbs 29:1)

Some people seem to be born with a strong will, and usually these individuals possess a God-given gift of leadership to be used for His glory; but being naturally 'strong-willed' must be tempered with humility in order to remain soft clay in the hands of the Potter.[10]

"But now, O Lord, you are our Father; we are the clay, and you are our potter; we are all the work of your hand." (Isaiah 64:8)

Your Pride has Deceived You

Not only is pride destructive; it is also deceitful. In a chilling prophecy against Edom, the descendants of Esau, God warns them that, in fighting against Israel, they are on the wrong side of the battle and will be destroyed.

God declares, ***"Because of your violence against your brother Jacob (Israel), shame shall cover you, and you shall be cut off forever."*** (Obadiah 1:10)

---

[9] https://www.voiceforisrael.net/product-page/ruth-a-righteous-gentile-1
[10] See "The Strong Willed Child' by Dr. James Dobson

In fact, the prophecy goes on to reveal the tragic end of Edom: ***"'But the house of Esau shall be stubble; ... and no survivor shall remain of the house of Esau,' for the Lord has spoken."*** (Obadiah 1:18)

The prophet explains what will cause this terrible destruction. In ancient times as it is even up until this very day – the reason is – pride! ***"The pride of your heart has deceived you."*** (Obadiah 1:3)

If allowed to remain in our heart, pride can lead to deception, and therefore cause us to do many foolish and destructive things which are completely out of the will of God.

How many Christian individuals and churches support anti-semitic theologies, attitudes and actions, such as boycotting Israel and sympathizing with the Palestinians, when the Word of God clearly states that the Land belongs to the descendants of Abraham, Isaac and Jacob (Israel) - not to the descendants of Ishamael or Esau.

Where was the majority of the Christian Church in the Holocaust? Where is the Church today as hundreds of thousands of anti-semitic, pro-Palestinian protestors march in the streets of the nations and take over university campuses, calling for genocide of the Jews and the annihilation of Israel following the horrendous massacre and kidnapping of hundreds of innocent Israeli civilians by Hamas terrorists.[11]

We thank God for His faithful remnant who stand on the truth and refuse to keep silent, but instead, have been taking to the streets to show their support and solidarity with Israel and the Jewish people in the nations – however these are a minority.

The people of God need the humility to bow to the Word and will of Almighty God and accept the leadership of Israel among the nations rather than resisting the truth out of stubbornness and pride.

God speaks this about Israel: ***"For the nation and kingdom which will not serve you (Israel) shall perish, and those nations shall be utterly ruined... Also the sons of those who afflicted you shall come bowing to you, and all those who despised you shall fall prostrate at the soles of your feet; and they shall call you 'The City of the LORD Zion of the Holy One of Israel.'"*** (Isaiah 60:12,14)

It takes real humility to accept the plan of God for Israel and the nations. Paul warned the Church not to be ignorant of this mystery lest they become arrogant (prideful).[12]

---

[11] October 7th 2023
[12] Romans 11:25

The Fruits of Pride

How can we detect and recognize pride in our hearts? Here are some common signs:

I am demonstrating the fruits of pride when I am...:[13]

- Selfishly ambitious: wanting to make a name for myself, wanting to be well known and important; to have a title and high position.

- Overly competitive: always wanting to win and come out on top in everything.

- Dominating conversations; interrupting people to make my own ideas heard.

- Refusing to receive correction: becoming angry and defensive when corrected, seeing it as an invasion of my privacy; I resent the person correcting me.

- Insisting on having the last word in an argument; to prove I am right.

- Wanting to impress people and making my accomplishments known.

- Wanting to be the center of attention and mostly talking about myself; wanting to be in the spotlight and have a hard time serving 'behind the scenes'.

- Not fulfilled serving others; wanting to be served rather than serve.

- Envious, jealous or critical towards those who are doing well or being honored.

- Wanting to be independent, self-sufficient and not ask people for help.

- Anxious about my life and my future; have a hard time trusting God.

- Self focused and overly self-conscious: I am very concerned about my appearance and what people think of me.
- Often comparing myself to others, "performance oriented". I feel that I have greater worth if I do well.

- Self-critical and tend to be a perfectionist. I have a hard time accepting when I make mistakes.

---

[13] https://www.scribd.com/document/362237721/50-Fruits-of-Pride

- Self-serving. When asked to do something, I find myself asking, "How will doing this help me?" or "Will I be inconvenienced?" I am more focused on my own interests than on the needs and interests of others.

- Thinking highly of myself in relation to others. I typically see myself as more mature and more gifted than most people.

- Tending towards self-righteousness. Pointing out people's sins and looking down on them for not being as 'holy'.

- Feeling deserving of everything I have; and that the world 'owes' me.

- Often feeling ungrateful. Instead of appreciating other people, I tend to complain about them; and grumble about what I don't have in life.

- Wallowing in self-pity: consumed with how I am treated by God and others. I tend to feel mistreated and misunderstood.

- Demonstrating a know-it-all attitude. I am impressed by my own knowledge and understanding of things. I have an answer for everything and have to make my opinions known.

- Being contentious and argumentative, easily angered and offended. I don't like being crossed or disagreed with. I find myself thinking, "I can't believe they did that to me". I often feel wronged.

- Continually having 'personality conflicts' with others. I have a hard time getting along with certain kinds of people. People regularly tell me I am 'difficult'.

- Critical of others: feeling or talking negatively about people. I subtly feel better about myself when I see how bad someone else is.

- Self-willed and stubborn. I have a hard time cooperating with others. I really prefer my own way and often insist on getting it.

- Unsubmissive. I don't like being under the authority of another person or being told what to do. I always like to be in charge.

- Thinking I don't need this list because I'm pretty humble already!

This is, admittedly, a very comprehensive list of the fruits of pride; and likely most of us can see ourselves in some (perhaps several) of these points. Some personality types are created with a God-given gift of leadership as well; and so this list is not meant to condemn; but only to bring awareness of areas where pride may have taken up residence in our heart.

Many of these are also the symptoms of low self-esteem, but ironically, this insecurity usually goes hand in hand with pride – a compulsive need to prove oneself.

False Humility

As with most issues, there needs to be a balance. When some people hear a message about humility; they think it means becoming passive, timid and fearful – living a small, limited life of poverty and mediocrity – never attempting anything great for God.

This is far from the truth. God even rebuked Moses for his false humility, losing patience when Moses kept coming up with one excuse after another for why he could not do what God was calling him to do:

"Moses said, 'O my Lord, please send by the hand of whomever else You may send.' So the anger of the Lord was kindled against Moses..." (Exodus 4:13-14)

We must not allow false humility to keep us from stepping out in faith to fulfill our calling and destiny when God has commissioned us to go…. We may not use 'humility' as a cover for fear, passivity or laziness.

Humility does not give us license for self-deprecating attitudes or self-hatred.

Nor does humility mean that we should hide our light under a bushel, or bury our God-given gifts and talents in the dirt out of fear.

God wants us to rise up and let our light shine!

What Pride is Not:

- Shining the light of God into the world.
- Acknowledging and using our God-given gifts and abilities.
- Walking in our leadership gifting and calling.
- Pursuing godly dreams and desires.
- Taking purposeful action to achieve noble goals.
- Standing up for truth, justice and righteousness.

The Remedy

Wherever we find ourselves on the spectrum of the fruit of pride, the only remedy for its work of destruction in our lives is to repent and walk in the opposite spirit. If we find it difficult to receive correction, then we must purposely find opportunities to be corrected, and even invite people to do so.

If we always need to be in the spotlight and spout off all our opinions, then perhaps we should intentionally serve behind the scenes for a while, and listen to others instead of talking so much.

If people find us difficult, we can work on getting along with others, seeing everyone as a worthy child of God, practicing grace for people's flaws and weaknesses, knowing that, as my Dad often said, *"But for the grace of God, there go I."*

Crucifying the flesh that desires to rebel against any kind of authority, we can choose instead to submit ourselves to the godly authorities over us. Instead of complaining with an entitled attitude, we can realize that everything we have is by the grace of God; therefore we can walk in gratitude, servanthood and gentleness.

When we seek to walk in deeper humility, who better to model ourselves after than Yeshua, the humble King, who rode into Jerusalem on the foal of a donkey:

"Rejoice greatly, O daughter of Zion! Shout, O daughter of Jerusalem! Behold, your King is coming to you; He is just and having salvation, Humble (ani) עָנִי and riding on a donkey, a colt, the foal of a donkey." (Zechariah 9:9)

Yeshua fulfilled this Messianic prophecy with His triumphant entry into Jerusalem on the foal of a donkey:

"And a very great multitude spread their clothes on the road; others cut down branches from the trees and spread them on the road. Then the multitudes who went before and those who followed cried out, saying:

'Hosanna to the Son of David! Blessed is He who comes in the name of the Lord! (Baruch Haba B'shem Adonai) Hosanna in the highest!'"
(Matthew 21:8-9)

Yeshua invites us to come to Him, in all of our weariness, and with all of our heavy burdens; to lay down all of our prideful striving for acclaim, and to simply rest upon His humble heart.

"Come to Me, all you who labor and are heavy laden, and I will give you rest. Take My yoke upon you and learn from Me, for I am gentle and lowly (humble) in heart, and you will find rest for your souls. For My yoke is easy and My burden is light."
(Matthew 11:28-29)

At the end of the day, the only way to truly conquer pride in our lives and to walk in humility is to receive a divine revelation of God's unconditional love for us personally – to know that we know that we know that we have nothing to prove to anyone – not to ourselves, not to the world and not even to God.

Our inner security rests on the solid truth that we are 'accepted in the beloved' right here and right now; and that God's approval does not depend on our performance. We are His sons and daughters in whom He is well pleased.

Prayer: *Dear God, many of us have grown up with parents, teachers or other authority figures that seemed impossible to please; and so we have come to feel that we always have to achieve in order to be 'good enough'. Open the eyes of our understanding, dear God, to receive a divine revelation of Your unconditional love for us in Messiah Yeshua.*

Help us to be content where You, in your wisdom, have placed us in life so we are not always striving for a position we are not even anointed for; but keep us from shrinking back from shining our light in the world out of false humility. Heal us from the sin of pride, so that we may love others with humble hearts, knowing that everything we have and all that we are is only because of Your amazing grace. Amen v'amen.

The Early and Latter Rains - Geshem גֶּשֶׁם

"He shall come down like rain upon the grass before mowing, like showers that water the earth." (Psalm 72:6)

I woke up the other morning to the sound of rain and rejoiced. Halleluyah! After immigrating to Israel, I discovered that, unlike Canada where I grew up (and where it often rained during the summer), not a drop of rain falls upon the ground during the entire, scorching hot, long, dry summer here in the Land. So whereas I used to consider rain a general nuisance in Canada, responsible for ruining any chance of outdoor plans; the early rains in Israel are always a cause to celebrate!!

We are so excited to feel the first drops of rain, that most Israelis stand outside and shout, sing, and dance. Our very survival depends on the presence of rain falling upon the Land of Israel during the fall, winter and spring seasons.

> These first rains are called 'yoreh' יוֹרֶה, a word that also means 'to shoot'. The word of God, the Torah תּוֹרָה, comes from this word as well as well as 'moreh' מוֹרֶה (teacher). Just as the first rains (yoreh) are sent down from heaven to soften the ground and prepare it for the seeds that the farmers will plant; so too is the word of God sent like an arrow to a target. The 'rain' of the Holy Spirit softens the soil of our hearts so that the seeds of the Word of God may take root and bear good fruit.

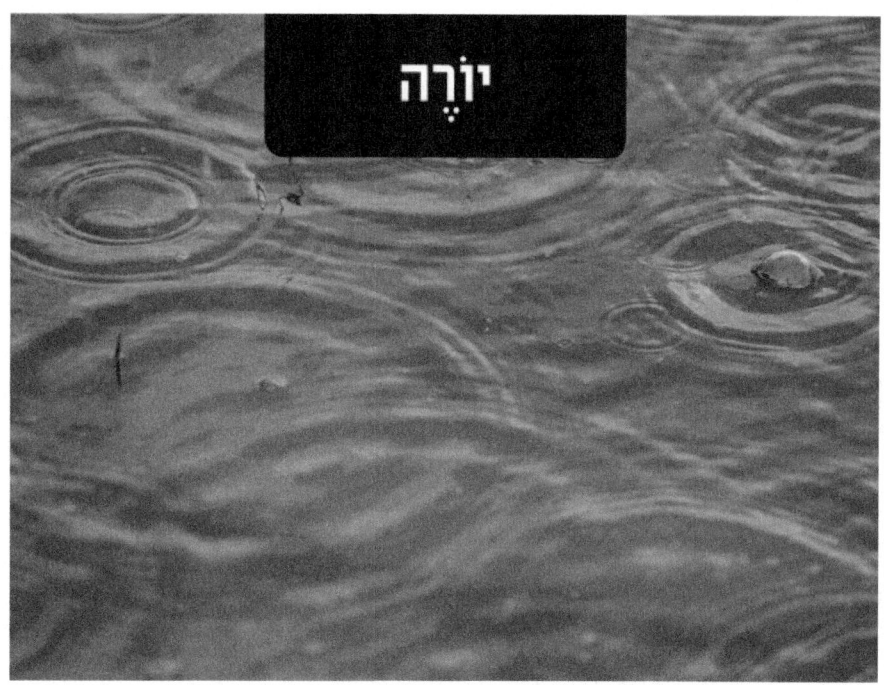

Yoreh - First rain - well, any rain - is cause for celebration in Israel. Credit: Eyal Hershkovitz

This is the meaning of the parable of the sower that Yeshua told to his disciples. Just as a planted seed starts to grow, the word of God starts to deepen and grow within a person whose heart has been prepared to hear and understand.

"But he who received seed on the good ground is he who hears the word and understands it, who indeed bears fruit and produces: some a hundredfold, some sixty, some thirty." (Matthew 13:23)

Moses also compared his teachings to the sending of rain:

"May my teaching drop as the rain, my speech distill as the dew, like gentle rain upon the tender grass, and like showers upon the herb." *(Deuteronomy 32:2)*

Although the most common Hebrew word used for 'rain' is 'geshem', Moses uses the word, 'matar' מָטָר in this Scripture.

Just as the Eskimos have several words for snow, Hebrew uses four distinct words to describe rain: '*geshem*' גֶּשֶׁם , '*matar*' מָטָר, '*yoreh*' יוֹרֶה and '*malkosh*' מַלְקוֹשׁ.

God's word promises that if we will obey His commandments to love Him with all our heart and soul, *"...then I will give you the rain (matar)* מְטַר *for your land in its season, the early rain (yoreh)* יוֹרֶה *and the latter rain (malkosh),* מַלְקוֹשׁ *that you may gather in your grain, your new wine, and your oil. And I will send grass in your fields for your livestock, that you may eat and be filled."*
(Deuteronomy 11:14-15)

Israel is a land that drinks rain from Heaven, and is continually watched over by the eyes of the Lord who cares for it. Unlike Egypt with its Nile River or Assyria with its Euphrates, Israel does not have a plenteous water supply; therefore we must always look up to God who faithfully waters and enriches the earth with rain.[1]

"But the land you are crossing the Jordan to take possession of is a land of mountains and valleys that drinks rain (matar) מָטָר *from heaven. It is a land the Lord your God cares for; the eyes of the Lord your God are continually on it from the beginning of the year to its end."* (Deuteronomy 11:11-12)

It is by sending rain that God confirmed His inheritance:

"The heavens also dropped rain at the presence of God; ... You, O God, sent a plentiful rain ('geshem' גֶּשֶׁם*), whereby You confirmed Your inheritance."* (Psalm 68:8-9)

---

[1] Psalm 65:9

Counting it all Joy!

Caught in a downpour in Jerusalem during the rainy season, I felt (and looked) somewhat like a drowned rat! I was wet, cold, and uncomfortable; and yet I knew better than to curse the rain or to even complain about it. Rain is so very precious in these hot, dry climates; and so even though our flesh may not like it, our spirit rejoices, because it is the rain that brings life!

Geshem and Lehitgashem

The Hebrew word for rain, geshem גֶּשֶׁם is the root of the word, lehitgashem להתגשם which means to materialize or make come true. It is the rain that causes tiny, shriveled seeds to grow and materialize into plants and mighty oak trees. Similarly, the trials of life, those difficulties and challenges that seem to 'rain on our parade', are often the very things that cause our hopes and dreams to come true.

In fact, the Hebrew word for the latter rains, malkosh מַלְקוֹשׁ, comes from the words, 'koshi' קוֹשִׁי which means 'difficulty or hardship'; and 'mal' מל which means to 'circumcise or purify the heart'. The one who performs the ritual circumcision (brit millah) on the eight day old male infant is called a 'moel' מוהל.

This Hebrew word for the latter rains, malkosh מַלְ-קוֹשׁ, is showing us a hidden secret in the Hebrew – that *the difficulties or hardships of life (represented by the rains), are the very circumstances that purify or circumcise our hearts to love God and keep His commandments.*

> The latter rains מַלְקוֹשׁ are the harder downpours which can more easily penetrate the soil which has already been softened by the first rains of the yoreh, in order to bring forth a second harvest in the spring.

We may wonder why we are going through such severe storms, but these 'latter rains' can thoroughly soak the barren places in our lives, in order that we may become even more fruitful and flourishing – for our Abba Father's glory. Every life that is to be fruitful needs these heavy rains of trials and challenges to overcome.

Just like with the rain, we may feel uncomfortable in the midst of the downpour, but if we keep a right attitude and 'count it all joy', then these trials and tribulations of life can become '<u>showers of blessing</u>'.[2]

"I will make them and the places all around My hill a blessing; and I will cause showers to come down in their season; there shall be showers of blessing."
(Ezekiel 34:26)

---

[2] ▶ Showers of Blessing! - Rain in Israel

Prayers for Rain - Simchat Beit Hasho'eva

Starting on the last day of the Feast of Tabernacles (Sukkot), Jewish people add a special phrase to their daily prayers, praising God who *"sends the wind and brings down the rain"* – *Mashiv Ha'Ruach u'morid Hagashem* הגשם.

Rain at Jaffa Gate, Jerusalem

Water is a recurring theme throughout the festival of Sukkot; but why is there such an emphasis on water on the last day? Rabbinic Tradition teaches that on the eight day of assembly, called **'Shemini Atzeret'**, God judges the earth for water, deciding on the amount of rainfall for the coming year, therefore the Jewish people recite special prayers for rain on this day.

At this time, the people of Israel also hold a special ceremony called '*Simchat Beit Hashoeva*' (Rejoicing of the House of Drawing of Water). This ceremony originates from a Second Temple period custom in which the Cohen (priest) would draw water from the Pool of Siloam and pour it out upon the altar.

After a long, hot, dry summer in Israel, the people must have felt their desperate need of water; and yet they did not withhold the water, but poured it out on the altar before the Lord. This sacrificial act demonstrated their faith in God to provide the rains they would need in the upcoming year.

The Temple Institute in Israel[3] performs a re-enactment of this ceremony each year on the last day of Sukkot. The Cohen (priest) fills his silver flask with the waters of the Shiloach spring in the City of David. With the flask held high, he ascends the steps of the spring and leads a gathering of more than 1000 people into the Churva Plaza of Jerusalem's Old City Jewish Quarter. In Temple times, the cohen would lead the

procession up to the Holy Temple into the inner courtyard where they would pour out the water upon the great stone altar.

---

[3] The Temple Institute, known in Hebrew as Machon HaMikdash, is an organization in Israel focusing on the endeavor of establishing the Third Temple. Its long-term aims are to build the third Jewish temple on the Temple Mount, on the site occupied by the Dome of the Rock, and to reinstate animal sacrificial worship.

The Miracle Waters of the Shiloach Spring

Why did the Jewish priests (cohanim) draw water from this specific place? The pool of Siloam (in Hebrew called Shiloach Spring), still exists today. It is a rock cut pool, fed by the waters of the Gihon Spring, located on the southern slope of the City of David, outside the walls of the Old City.

The Shiloach Pool filled with rain water and an illustrated reconstruction of the pool in the Second Temple period

Blind man healed at Pool of Siloam

This pool also has Messianic significance. It is the very site where Yeshua performed one of his greatest miracles. He sent a man who had been blind from birth to this pool to wash in the waters and be healed: **"'Go', He told him, 'wash in the Pool of Siloam'. So the man went and washed, and came home seeing."** (John 9:7)

The waters from this pool were believed to have miraculous healing properties, therefore it is no coincidence that it is from the waters of this very pool that the Jewish priests (cohanim) would draw water to pour out upon the altar of the Holy Temple in this special ceremony with such great spiritual significance.

Poured Out Like Water

Yeshua was also 'poured out like water', as described in the Messianic prophecy:

"I am poured out like water, and all my bones are out of joint. My heart has turned to wax; it has melted within me." (Psalm 22:14)

However, it was after He **poured out His soul even unto death** on a cross, that God poured out the **'rain of the Holy Spirit'** upon the earth. Halleluyah!

The Rain of the Spirit

Water is often connected in Scripture with the Spirit of God. His promise is not only to pour out physical water upon our Land; but also to pour out His Spirit (Ruach) along with His blessing upon our offspring.

"For I will pour water on the thirsty land, and streams on the dry ground; I will pour out My Spirit on your offspring, and My blessing on your descendants." (Isaiah 44:3)

It was on this last day of the Feast, that Yeshua stood up and invited everyone who was thirsty to come to Him and drink of the Living Waters of the Spirit of God.

Hope of the Messiah

This ceremony, Simchat Beit Ha'shoevah, was much more than just a prophetic act demonstrating hope for the coming Yoreh (first rains) after Sukkot; but it also expressed the eternal faith of the people of Israel for the coming of the Mashiach (Messiah), as it is written:

*"**He shall come down like rain** upon the grass before mowing, like showers that water the earth. In His days the righteous shall flourish, and abundance of peace...He shall have dominion also from sea to sea."* (Psalm 72:6-8)

Can we picture this? At the same moment that the Cohanim (Jewish priests) were pouring out the waters upon the altar of the Holy Temple, with all this great expectancy of the Messiah, Yeshua stood up and proclaimed Himself to be the source of Living Water – by which He meant the Spirit!

"On the last day, that great day of the feast, Jesus stood and cried out, saying,'If anyone thirsts, let him come to Me and drink. He who believes in Me, as the Scripture has said, out of his heart will flow rivers of living water.' But this He spoke concerning the Spirit." (John 7:37-39)

Never Thirst Again

Yeshua invites us to come to Him and drink of the Living Waters only He can give us. He spoke to a Samaritan woman at the well who had been married five times and was living with another man. Notice that it was not to the religious Jewish people of His day, but to this broken Samaritan woman that He clearly declared Himself to be the Messiah they were all waiting for.

Yeshua promised that if she would drink of the water He would give her, she would never thirst again.

If we've made too many poor choices because of our seemingly insatiable thirst to be loved, then we are prime candidates for Yeshua to reveal Himself to us.

"Everyone who drinks of this water will be thirsty again, but those who drink of the water that I will give them will never be thirsty. The water that I will give will become in them a spring of water gushing up to eternal life." (John 4:13-14)

So many are dying of thirst in this dry and weary world, trying to find satisfaction in broken cisterns of relationships, power or pleasures; not knowing that our thirst can only be quenched by the Spirit of the Living God through Yeshua the Messiah.

In this hot, dry country of Israel, it is easy to become dehydrated if we don't drink enough water. Sometimes our bodies may become thirsty without even realizing it. We can live for quite a while without food, but life quickly withers and dies without water.

People who become lost in the desert without water can even die from dehydration. There are spiritual vultures from hell continually circling overhead, watching for their next meal – waiting for someone to collapse from spiritual sunstroke and dehydration.

We need to drink deeply from the wells of living water that Yeshua provides through relationship and fellowship with Him. Yeshua said, *"Come to me, all you who are weary and heavy burdened and I will give you rest."* (Matthew 11:28)

If we will accept Yeshua's invitation to come to Him when we are weary or full of sorrow, and drink from the Spirit, then we can prevent a spiritual collapse.

None of us are camels; we humans cannot travel for long distances without drinking water. We can only walk from oasis to oasis in this wilderness. We may not necessarily feel thirsty, but we need to come daily and drink deeply from the fountain of living waters to quench our thirsty soul.

"Come, all you who are thirsty, come to the waters; and you who have no money, come, buy and eat! Come, buy wine and milk without money and without cost." (Isaiah 55:1)

Just as the Jewish people followed the cohanim (priests) to the altar to pour out the waters from the pool of Siloam, so too may we joyously sing and dance in the rain.

"Ushavtem mayim besason Mimaynei hayeshua."

"With joy you will draw water from the wells of salvation (Yeshuah)." (Isaiah 12:3)

Yeshua, the word used in this verse is also the Hebrew name for Jesus the Messiah. It means '<u>God is salvation</u>' or God saves.

Let us rejoice and be glad in YHVH יהוה our God, who has poured down upon us abundant rain for our salvation:

"Be glad, O children of Zion, and rejoice in the LORD your God, for He has given the early rain for your vindication; He has poured down for you abundant rain, the early and the latter rain, as before." *(Joel 2:23)*

May we celebrate the rain of the Holy Spirit into our lives; and trust that God will cause ALL things to turn out for our good in the end. May the gentle early rains of the yoreh soften the hard soil of our hearts, bringing showers of blessing into our lives. And may the harder, more piercing latter rains of the malkosh flood the dry ground of our hearts, cleansing away sin, and causing the barren places in our lives to become fresh, fruitful and flourishing.

Just as the farmer waits patiently for the early and the latter rains, may we also be patient as we wait for the coming of the Lord which is so close at hand.

"Be patient, therefore, brothers, until the coming of the Lord. See how the farmer waits for the precious fruit of the earth, being patient about it, until it receives the early and the late rains. You also, be patient. Establish your hearts, for the coming of the Lord is at hand." *(James 5:7-8)*

Prayer: *Dear God, our soul longs for You in a dry and thirsty land where there is no water. We need the early and latter rain of Your Holy Spirit (Ruach Hakodesh) to refresh our weary souls and bring life! Forgive us for trying to quench our thirst by drinking from broken cisterns and sources which can never satisfy. May the rain of Your Spirit cleanse us from the filth of this world, and water the barren places of our hearts – that we may bear much good fruit – for Your glory, Amen.*

The Lord Our Banner - Yehovah Nissi יְהוָה נִסִּי

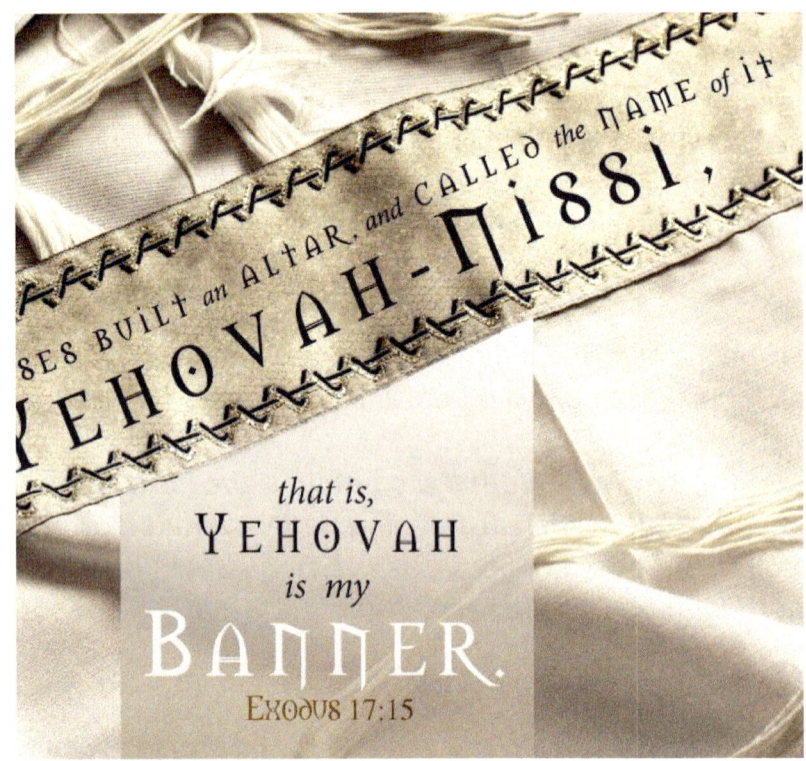

"And Moses built an altar, and called the name of it Yehovah-Nissi."
(Exodus 17:15)

God delivered the children of Israel from slavery in Egypt, but that didn't mean that their troubles were over – far from it – there were still battles to fight and enemies to defeat in the wilderness as well as once they entered the Promised Land.

Israel's exodus from bondage in Egypt represents our spiritual deliverance from the Kingdom of darkness. Pharaoh, who enslaved and oppressed the descendants of Jacob (Israel), represents Satan, whose desire is to keep us in bondage.

We have been saved from 'Egypt' and are no longer under the dominion of sin, but that doesn't mean that we are instantly transported to lala land. This is a 'false gospel' message that is sometimes preached – that once we 'get saved', we will experience continual peace, love and joy.

The truth is, that we will still face battles and need to overcome, just as Israel continues to fight against her many enemies even today.

Banner of Victory

A sworn enemy of Israel, the Amalekites, in an unprovoked attack, came out to fight against Israel just after they had finished crossing the Red Sea. Joshua chose men to fight Amalek, while Moses stood on a hill with his hands raised to heaven, calling upon the aid of Yehovah Tzeva'ot – Captain of the Host of Heavenly Armies.

As long as Moses held up his hands, Israel prevailed, but when he lowered his hands, Amalek began to win. We can imagine this became tiring for Moses, so Aaron and Hur supported Moses on either side to keep his hands raised to heaven. And so, Joshua defeated Amalek and Israel won the victory.

The Lord swore to *"utterly blot out the remembrance of Amalek from under heaven."* (Exodus 17:14)

"And Moses built an altar and called its name, The-Lord-Is-My-Banner (Yehovah Nissi) יְהוָה נִסִּי; for he said, 'Because the Lord has sworn: the Lord will have war with Amalek from generation to generation.'" (Exodus 17:15-16)

We are still at war with this ancient spirit of Amalek today, since our true battle is not with flesh and blood but with principalities and powers of darkness and wickedness in high places. This spirit of Amalek has been operating through different people groups throughout the centuries to attack and attempt to destroy Israel and the Jewish people.

Haman, in the book of Esther, was a descendant of Amalek. His hatred of the Jews caused him to attempt genocide – a disastrous plot which backfired on him, as God turned what was to be a day of slaughter and defeat for the Jews into a day of <u>victory, feasting and rejoicing</u>. We still celebrate this every year as the Festival of Purim.

Haman was hung on the very gallows he built for Mordechai, the Jew.[1] Even Haman's advisors and his wife, Zeresh, told him that if Mordechai was of Jewish descent he would not prevail against him.[2] Why? Because God is in covenant with the Jewish people forever!

This same spirit operated through the Nazis during World War II, but the end result of this attempted genocide was that out of the ashes of the holocaust was birthed the beautiful, modern state of Israel. God has given us beauty from ashes. Halleluyah!

Today, this same spirit of Amalek is attempting another genocide of the people of Israel through radical Islamic Jihad, Hezbollah, Hamas and the affiliated terrorist groups.

In a similarly unprovoked attack against Israel, hundreds of Hamas militants infiltrated Israel on October 7th, 2023, on the last day of the Festival of Sukkot (Feast of

---

[1] Esther 7:10
[2] Esther 6:13

Tabernacles), murdering, beheading, pillaging, raping and kidnapping hundreds of Israeli civilians in the peaceful villages and communities around Gaza.

But just as Moses kept his hands raised to Heaven, our Israeli military forces also look to God in Heaven for the strength, courage and resilience needed to win the victory in this battle against evil.

"I will lift up my eyes unto the mountains: where shall my help come from?

My help comes from Yehovah יְהוָה, who made heaven and earth."
(Psalm 121:1-2)

IDF soldiers seeking God during morning prayers in Gaza

The presence and power of God were the banner under which the Israelites waged warfare against Amalek, and we too must raise up our banners in the name of Yehovah Nissi in order to walk in triumph.

There is, however, a secret hidden in the Hebrew about this Divine name.

The word, Nissi נִסִּי (my banner) derives from the Hebrew root word 'nes', נֵס which means **'banner'** or **'miracle'** or to **'flee for refuge'**. In order to defeat our enemies, we need more than a banner, we need a miraculous demonstration of the power of God.

The Miracles of Chanukah

At the season of Chanukah (Feast of Dedication), we celebrate the miraculous victory of the heroic Jewish freedom fighters, the Maccabees, against the Greek-Syrian army.

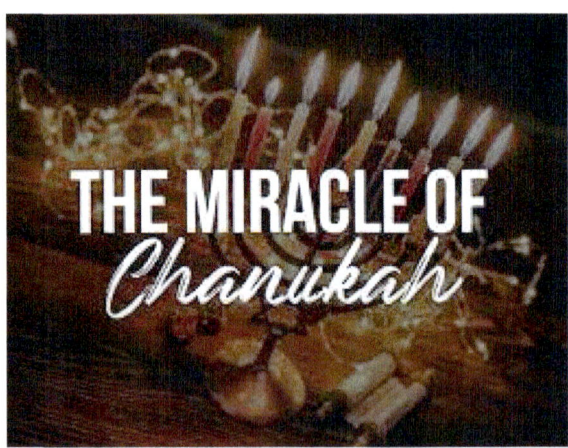

Under the iron rule of Antiochus, in 165-163 B.C., they persecuted and oppressed the Jewish people, forbidding us from practicing our biblical faith under penalty of death.

Although greatly outnumbered, untrained and ill-equipped militarily, the Maccabees succeeded in overthrowing their oppressors, and reclaiming the Holy Temples which had been defiled with statues of Greek gods and blood sacrifices of swine on the altar.

Therefore, each year at Chanukah time, we recite blessings on the candles praising God, not only for the miracles He performed for our forefathers, but also for the miracles He is still doing today in our lives. We serve a God of Miracles!

A Jewish family celebrating the miracle of Chanukah

The children also play a game with spinning tops called dreidles (or sivivon in Hebrew) with four Hebrew letters on it, an acronym for the phrase: **Nes Gadol Haya Poh** (A Great Miracle Happened Here). נס גדול היה פה[3]

For the first forty years of my life, I had to play with a different dreidel that read, "Nes Gadol Haya *sham*", נס גדול היה שם which means "A Great Miracle Happened *There*",[4] until I made aliyah (immigrated to Israel) and to my joy, I could say that the miracle actually happened here, in this very nation where we now live, in a place called Modiin.

Chanukah is the season of miracles (Nissim) ניסים, and Hebrew shows us that there is a direct connection between a banner and a miracle.

What is a Banner?

What do banners symbolize in a biblical, Hebraic context? In ancient times and throughout Scripture, banners were ensigns or standards declaring allegiance to God, a

---

[3] The first letter of each word, *nun-gimel-hey-pey,* is found on the Israeli *sevivon* [spinning top] we play with on Chanukah in Israel.
[4] The first letter of each word, *nun-gimel-hey-shin,* is found on the *sevivon* [spinning top] used for Chanukah by those located outside of Israel.

nation or an army. Banners helped lead the Israelites into battle; they were used to declare the majesty of Adonai, and to beckon the lost to find refuge in Him.

1. Banners Call Us to Gather and Proclaim the Truth

In the Scriptures, banners were often raised as a rallying point – to gather or assemble the people – or to announce that something significant was about to happen:

"The Root of Jesse will stand as a banner (nes נֵס) for the people; the nations will rally to him and His resting place shall be glorious... He will raise a banner (nes נֵס) for the Gentiles and collect the exiles of Israel and gather the dispersed of Judah from the four corners of the earth..." (Isaiah 11:10-12)

A banner was also raised to announce the downfall of Babylon;[5] and to proclaim to all nations to the ends of the earth: *"See, your Savior comes!"* (Isaiah 62:10-12)

Let us display our banners to proclaim the truth that God is faithful, He is good and His mercy endures forever: *"You have given a banner to those who fear You, that it may be displayed because of the truth."* (Psalm 60:4)

2. Banners Give us Identity

The first mention of banners in Scripture occurs when God commanded the children of Israel to camp in tribal groups around the tabernacle and to erect banners, standards or

---

[5] Jeremiah 50:2

ensigns to identify their clans. The colors of their banners may have corresponded to the colors of the tribal stones represented in the priest's ephod (Exodus 28:15-21). The other word used for banner (nes) is a flag (degel) דָּגֶל and everyone was to camp by their own flag.

"The children of Israel shall pitch their tents, everyone by his own camp, everyone by his own standard (his flag – degelo) דִּגְלוֹ, according to their armies." (Numbers 1:52)

The Levites camped closest to and all around the Tabernacle while the remaining tribes were divided into three camps. Each camp consisted of three tribes, with one being the lead tribe and serving as the ensign, or standard, by which they were identified.

The lead tribes were Ephraim on the west, Judah on the east, Reuben on the south and Dan on the north. God chose the ensigns (flags or banners), all of which point prophetically to Yeshua.

The Ensigns of the Camps of Israel

On the west, Ephraim was given the ensign of an ox, an animal of service and submission, yet strong and able to bear a load. On the north side, Dan was represented by an eagle, often used as a symbol of God who carries His people on wings as an eagle. On the south side, Reuban's ensign was a man, and Judah, on the east side, was a lion (the Lion of Judah roaring out of Jerusalem).

Each ensign represented something about Yeshua's character.

The tribes of Israel were organized and assembled according to their family's flag or banner; therefore a banner represents identity.

The people of Israel today come from many different nations, but we all live under the flag of Israel, standing as a banner that identifies and unites us as Israelis – no matter our ethnicity or country of origin.

It is under this flag (banner) that we stand, march, celebrate, dance, compete in world competitions, wage war, pray, worship, mourn, and even bury our dead!

Mother of fallen IDF soldier at the funeral of her son

IDF soldiers with Israeli flag after completing grueling 40 km training march

Jerusalem March

Praying at the Kotel (Western Wall)

Israeli Independence Day

His Banner Over me is Love

What is our identity in Messiah? Under what banner do we gather and unite to proclaim our allegiance to Yeshua? His banner over us is love and as His disciples, we are to be known by our love for one another.

"He brought me to the banqueting house (House of wine - Beit ha'Yayin בֵּית הַיָּיִן) and His banner (His flag - deglo דִּגְלוֹ) over me is love." (Songs of Solomon 2:4)

3. Banners Symbolize Joy and Victory!

"We will shout for joy in Your victory, and in the name of our God we will set up our banners! May the Lord fulfill all your petitions." (Psalm 20:5)

It has been the custom of armies throughout history, to hoist flags of victory after conquering a town or territory in battle. As 'more than conquerors',[6] we can lift up our banners in celebration of the victory that Messiah Yeshua has already won for us.

IDF soldiers raise a flag and sing Hatikvah, the Israeli national anthem on conquered Gaza beach

4. Banners Rally us to Battle

"Lift a banner in the land! Blow the shofar among the nations! Prepare the nations for battle against her…" (Jeremiah 51:27)

Flags or banners would be raised up high, often glistening in the sun, so that they could be seen from a far distance as a rallying point for troops. In times of war, banners were used to guide soldiers in battle and civilians to safety. The prophet Jeremiah warned the people of Israel of a coming invasion from the North, saying, **"Raise a banner to go to Zion! Flee for safety without delay."** (Jeremiah 4:6)

---

[6] Romans 8:37

As God's people, we are all engaged in fierce spiritual battles; and banners can serve as visual reminders to encourage us in our daily battles against our enemy, that we can find refuge, shelter, strength and victory in the Lord of Hosts, Yehovah Tzeva'ot, Captain of the Heavenly armies.

5. Banners in Worship

We can use banners in worship with music and dance, as well as hanging them in our churches and our homes as reminders of God's presence, His truth and His promises.

Artistic banners may be displayed in colors symbolizing various aspects of God's character: white for purity, orange for fire, red for Yeshua's blood, blue for Heaven, purple for royalty and gold for His kingdom. Flags add beauty and glory to the worship experience. They can be powerful tools for spiritual warfare.

DIY Worship Flags https://worshipdanceministries.com/2015/08/20/diy-worship-flags/

Banners can also incorporate biblical words such as the Hebrew names of God, and symbols like the dove (peace, Holy Spirit), the lion (of Judah) and the lamb (Passover sacrifice) to help proclaim God's truth. Used creatively, they may become a meaningful part of our gatherings, praise and worship experiences.

Flags and banners used in worship are an outward expression of the inner praise we hold in our hearts. They express God's love, purity, grace, holiness and power. They symbolize the security, hope and freedom we have in Messiah Yeshua. As we minister with flags, we declare that the Lord is Our Banner, and we identify ourselves as God's children, His messengers, ambassadors, servants and Light of the world.

Banners of Darkness

It's not just the people of God who display their flags and banners, however; the enemies of Israel and supporters of terrorism also identify themselves and proclaim their allegiance to the Kingdom of darkness by their flags and banners. Many who have been protesting against Israel since the invasion of settlements around Gaza by Hamas, raise Islamic Jihad & Palestinian flags and banners.

Some are not even aware of the evil and wickedness that they are supporting, but by aligning themselves with these flags and banners, they are identifying themselves as children of darkness, agents of Satan and enemies of the God of Israel.

Pro-Palestinian Protestors display banners

The Nazis, under the leadership of Hitler in World War II, carried out their attempted genocide of the Jewish people of Europe under the banner of the swastika (the twisted cross), which is originally a Hindu Symbol.

"Your enemies roar in the midst of Your meeting place; they set up their banners for signs." (Psalm 74:4)

Homosexuals also march in gay pride parades under the 'twisted' banner of the rainbow which was God's symbol of mercy. God set the rainbow in the sky as a sign that He would never again destroy the earth with a flood, but it has been perverted into a banner proudly proclaiming their sexual sin – that which God calls an abomination!

What does it mean for God to be our Yehovah Nissi, our Banner?

Banners proclaim the ideals and allegiance of those who carry them; they announce their devotion to a nation, a cause or a leader. Moses held up his arms like a banner to Heaven in the battle with the Amalekites, appealing to God's power to give them victory.

Moses then built an altar, naming it Yehovah Nissi – the Lord is My Banner – as a memorial of God's power and protection over His people, Israel, in their first battle after their great deliverance from Egypt. Not only was Moses proclaiming God as their banner (nes נֵס) but also that God had performed another miracle (nes נֵס) in giving these Israelites, a ragtag group of former slaves, the victory over an entire Amalekite army of warriors.

What battles are you facing right now? No matter what we may face, God is walking right alongside us. He is our strength, our shelter and our shield. He will guide us and give us His wisdom as we surrender our lives to Him. So let us march forth, carrying the banner of His victory and joy to the very front of the battle, holding it high for all to see His salvation (Yeshuah).

God longs to be our Banner, our Miracle worker and our place of refuge!

What miracle do you need in your life?? Yehovah Nissi wants to demonstrate His miracle working power in order to bring about a great victory! He wants to gather us together under the banner of His name; to find our identity, our security, and our refuge under the shelter of His wings.

"When the enemy comes in like a flood, the Spirit of the Lord (Ruach Yehovah רוּחַ יְהוָה) will lift up a standard (nes) against him." (Isaiah 59:19)

Prayer: *Dear God, thank you that Your banner over us is love. When we feel lost, like we can't find our tribe or where we belong, help us to remember that we stand under the banner of Your holy name and that our identity is secure in You.*

We need a miracle in our lives, Lord, so we lift up our hands to Heaven, calling upon your power, beseeching You for the victory that we so desperately need. Lion of Judah, come and save us! We flee to You for refuge from our enemies, trusting that since You are fighting our battles, we will emerge victorious. Amen v'amen.

The Wells of Satisfaction - Sheva שבע

"Therefore he called that place Be'er Sheva, because the two of them swore an oath there. Thus they made a covenant at Be'er sheva." (Genesis 21:31-32)

I am currently living in the Negev desert of Israel in a city called Be'er Sheva[1] – a modern, bustling city filled with people, cars, buildings and businesses. It's not particularly the city of my choice, as it is scorching hot in the summer, full of garbage (in my mixed Arab-Jewish neighborhood at least) and is fairly isolated from the rest of the country. But it seems that this is where the Holy Spirit has led me for now and I am learning to appreciate this 'wilderness experience.'

David Ben Gurion, primary founder of the State of Israel as well as the state's first prime minister, carried in his heart a great vision for developing the Negev.

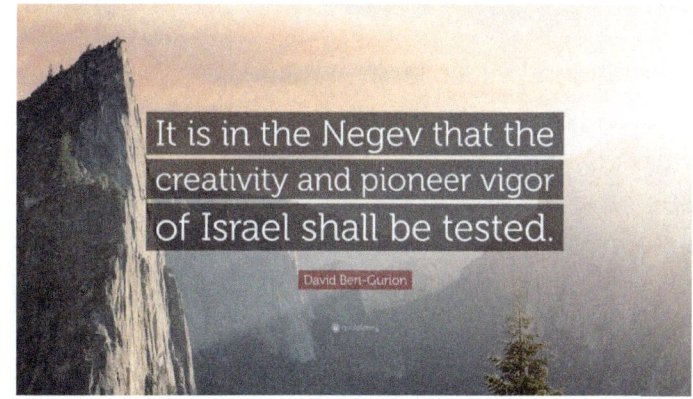

He said, *"It is in the Negev that the creativity and pioneer vigor of Israel shall be tested."*

---
[1] At the time of this writing March 2024

The desert truly is a place of testing. Even Yeshua was led into the desert for 40 days to be tested by the devil.[2]

In 1953, Ben Gurion and his wife, Paula, moved to Kibbutz Sde Boker to fulfill his vision of settling the Negev and seeing the desert bloom as the Hebrew prophets foretold,

"The desert will rejoice, and flowers will bloom in the wastelands.

The desert will sing and shout for joy; it will be as beautiful as the Lebanon Mountains and as fertile as the fields of Carmel and Sharon.

Everyone will see the Lord's splendor, see his greatness and power." (Isaiah 35:1-2)

Today, we are witnessing the blooming of the Negev desert with our very own eyes!

Paula and David Ben-Gurion's home is open to the public and has been preserved exactly as it was left in 1973, according to the instructions in his will. It is now part of the Ben-Gurion Heritage institute to preserve his legacy throughout generations.

Ben Gurion University in Beersheva is named after this visionary Israeli leader who, it seems to me, would be astounded to see the miraculous growth, development and prosperity of the Negev today, and especially its capital city of Be'er sheva.

---

[2] Matthew 4:1-11 See chapter Walking in the Wilderness - Midbar

Abraham's Well

I recently had the pleasure of visiting a fascinating place called Abraham's Well (Be'er Avraham באר אברהם) where I discovered more of the ancient biblical history and significance of Be'er Sheva where I now reside. I highly recommend it as a point of interest when you visit Israel.[3]

Abraham first gravitated towards the region of Be'er sheva to find water which flowed down a stream from Mount Hermon in the North. Water represents life, blessing and prosperity. In a place where there is an average of only ten rainy days per year, resulting in a mere 200 mm of precipitation, obviously finding life-sustaining water is essential to survival.

The Psalmist, David, cried out to God in the wilderness of Judah, *"O God, You are my God; early will I seek You; my soul thirsts for You; my flesh longs for You in a dry and thirsty land where there is no water."* (Psalm 63:1)

Since the ground in the area was fairly soft, Abraham went underground to fulfill the critical need for a source of water by digging several wells.

A well in Hebrew is called a 'be'er' באר.[4]

Sheva שבע means seven 7. This is the first reason for the name Be'er Sheva באר שבע; it is the location of the seven wells that Father Abraham dug to provide water for his household and livestock.

An old photograph of Abraham's Well, Beersheba
Courtesy of the New York State Library, Manuscripts and Special Collections.

---

[3] https://www.beer-sheva.muni.il/Eng/Tourism/pages/abrahamswell.aspx
[4] See chapter From the Pit to the Well (Bor to Be'er)

The number seven has special significance in the Bible. It symbolizes <u>completion and perfection</u>, for in six days God created the heavens and the earth and all that is in them, and on the seventh day he rested.[5] There are seven spirits of God as written in the Scriptures.[6]

Joshua and seven priests (cohanim) marched around Jericho seven times with seven shofars and on the seventh day, the walls came tumbling down![7] Halleluyah!

Be'er Sheva - the Well of Oath

In the Book of Genesis (Bereisheet), we read that the servants of Abimelech, the Philistine King of Grar, had seized Abraham's wells. *"Then Abraham rebuked Abimelech because of a well of water which his servants had seized."* (Genesis 21:25)

This is not the first time we see an altercation between Abimelech and Abraham; they have a history together. It was not so long prior that Abimelech had abducted Sarah, Abraham's wife, taking her into his harem after being told by Abraham that she was his sister – a lie confirmed by Sarah in obedience to her husband. Oye vey!

After God told Abimelech the truth that Sarah was actually Abraham's wife, Abimelech confronted Abraham over his lies, restored to him his wife, gave him livestock, servants, silver and his choice of land to dwell.

"Then Abimelech took sheep, oxen, and male and female servants, and gave them to Abraham; and he restored Sarah his wife to him. And Abimelech said, 'See, my land is before you; dwell where it pleases you.'" (Genesis 20:14-15)

Abimelech could see that God was with Abraham, and so he asked him to <u>swear an oath</u> that he would not lie again, but would deal truthfully from now on. Abimelech said,

"'God is with you in all that you do. Now therefore, <u>swear to me by God</u> that you will not deal falsely with me, with my offspring, or with my posterity; but that according to the kindness that I have done to you, you will do to me and to the land in which you have dwelt.' And Abraham said, '<u>I will swear</u>.'" (Genesis 21:22-24)

---

[5] Genesis 1; 2:1-2
[6] Revelation 3:1, Isaiah 11:2
[7] Joshua 6:8-20

Our forefather, Abraham, was not a perfect man; he had human weaknesses such as a tendency towards fearfulness and deception. One of Abraham's more noble qualities, however, was that of being a peacemaker. Instead of arguing over the well, Abraham gave back to Abimelech some of the livestock he had previously given him; and they made a covenant together.

"So Abraham took sheep and oxen and gave them to Abimelech, and the two of them made a covenant. And Abraham set seven ewe lambs of the flock by themselves. Then Abimelech asked Abraham, 'What is the meaning of these seven ewe lambs which you have set by themselves?'

"And he said, 'You will take these seven ewe lambs from my hand, that they may be my witness that I have dug this well.' Therefore he called that place Be'er sheva, because the two of them swore an oath there." (Genesis 21:27-31)

Here we have the second meaning of the word 'sheva' – to swear an oath. It is the second reason they called the place Be'er Sheva באר שבע – the Well of Oath.

It's interesting that Abraham used seven lambs as witnesses to his rightful possession of the wells. Abraham likely did so with full understanding of the symbolism of the number seven being that of completion or perfection.

Abraham planted a **tamarisk tree** (eshel אֶשֶׁל) in this place of Be'er Sheva as a sign to all travelers that they could find water here in the desert. The tamarisk tree is always green and stands as a sign of life. It was here that Abraham called on the name of **Yehovah, El Olam** יְהוָה, אֵל עוֹלָם (God of the Universe), thereby proclaiming his faith in the One True God.

Hannah standing next to tamarisk tree at Abraham's well

For this reason, Be'er Sheva may be considered the birthplace of Monotheism, the belief that Yehovah, the God of Israel is the God of the whole Universe!

Biblical Significance of a Well

What do wells symbolize in the Bible? What are their purposes?

1. Wells Represent Supply, Provision & Opportunity

When Sarah considered Ishmael a threat to her son, Isaac, the child of promise, she told Abraham to banish him and his mother, an Egyptian slave woman named Hagar, into the desert. Feeling hopeless, Hagar sat a ways off, not able to bear the sight of her son dying of thirst.

"Then he sent her away with their son, and she wandered aimlessly in the wilderness of Be'er sheva. When the water was gone, she put the boy in the shade of a bush. Then she went and sat down by herself about a hundred yards away. 'I don't want to watch the boy die,' she said, as she burst into tears." (Genesis 21:14b -16)

But then something amazing happened – something miraculous! God opened her eyes and she suddenly noticed a well of water!

"Then God opened Hagar's eyes, and she saw a well full of water. She quickly filled her water container and gave the boy a drink." (Genesis 21:19)

Perhaps we can identify with Hagar – her shock and despair, her sense of betrayal and abandonment. The ones we were counting on have let us down. Our supply has run out and we don't know how we're going to survive. We start to wander aimlessly. The future stretches out before us, barren and desolate, with no water in sight. We feel hopeless...

This is when we need to <u>open our eyes to see the well in the desert</u>. God sees us in our helpless state; He hears our cries. He is a God of compassion with a special soft spot in His heart for those who are most vulnerable: the lost, the weary, the oppressed, the weary and the broken ones.

The well represents more than just provision; it brings promise of hope to the hopeless. Just as with Hagar and Ishmael, He will come to our rescue:

"But God heard the boy crying, and the angel of God called to Hagar from heaven, 'Hagar, what's wrong? Do not be afraid! God has heard the boy crying as he lies there. Go to him and comfort him, for I will make a great nation from his descendants.'" (Genesis 21:17-18)

The well existed all along, but Hagar just didn't see it. We need to pray for God to reveal the well that exists for us – the creative ideas and solutions that we haven't yet thought of – to open the eyes of our understanding to perceive the hope and the future He has for us.

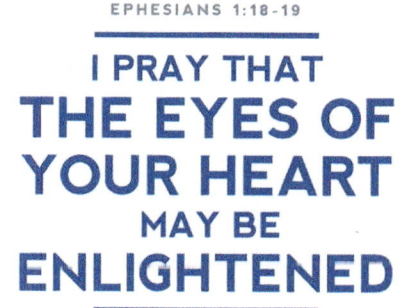

We can trust in God, a faithful Father, who has ample supply and provision for His children. Our God shall supply all of our needs according to His riches in glory in Messiah Yeshua.[8]

A well can also represent an opportunity. The well in itself may be small in size and yet it is connected to a vast underground water supply. May God reveal to us new wells of supply.

Let us drink deeply from the well of provision right in front of us; and bring comfort to those around us feeling lost and hopeless. We can pray that God will reveal the good future He has for each and every one of us in Yeshua – the living water.

2. Wells Represent Salvation

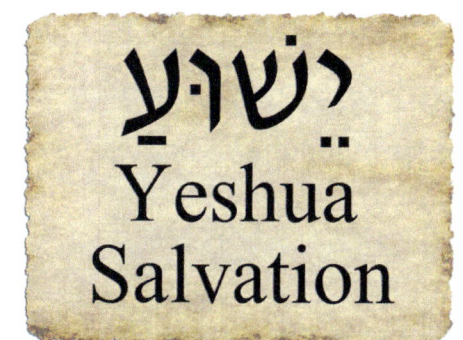

When Hagar saw the well, she knew they were saved. Wells not only provide life- saving water, they also represent eternal salvation.

Yeshua's very name means 'salvation'. It is a gift of God. ***"For by grace you have been saved through faith, and that not of yourselves; it is the gift of God."*** (Ephesians 2:8)

---
[8] Philipians 4:19

By Yeshua's death on the cross, through faith, we have been saved for eternity from sin, death and hell. This should be ample reason to 'rejoice always'.

"Therefore with joy you will draw water from the <u>wells of salvation</u> (Yeshuah)." (Isaiah 12:3)

Salvation means that our names are written in the Lamb's book of life. Yeshua rebuked his disciples for rejoicing that the demons were subject to them; but to rejoice that their names were written Heaven.[9]

After repenting for his sin with Batsheva, King David prayed that God would create in him a clean heart and restore to him the joy of His salvation. He said, ***"Restore to me the joy of Your salvation, and uphold me by Your generous Spirit."*** (Psalm 51:12)

There are times when the cares of this world so weigh us down that we forget how great a benefit we have in Yeshua. He is the resurrection and the life; and though our bodies will one day die, our soul shall never die.

Yeshua said, ***"I am the resurrection and the life. He who believes in Me, though he may die, he shall live. And whoever lives and believes in Me shall never die. Do you believe this?"*** (John 11:25-26)

This is the real question – do we have faith to believe this? To believe that whoever believes in Him shall not perish but have eternal life?[10]

Salvation is so much more than just our 'ticket out of hell' card in some Heavenly monopoly game. Salvation represents deliverance, emancipation, liberation, pardon, protection, redemption, and restoration. Salvation is also closely connected to healing.

We read in the New Testament, ***"Nor is there salvation in any other, for there is no other name under heaven given among men by which we must be saved."*** (Acts 4:12)

If we read it in context, however, Peter and John were arrested for healing a lame man and making him whole. There is no other name under heaven by which we may be

---

[9] Luke 10:20
[10] John 3:16

healed and made whole. Healing and salvation go hand in hand.

Let us gather at the well and drink deeply from the living waters to walk in wholeness, peace, joy, and in the end, eternal life.

*"From there they went to Be'er, which is the well where the L*ORD* said to Moses, 'Gather the people together, and I will give them water.' Then Israel sang this song: 'Spring up, O well! All of you sing to it—'"* (Numbers 21:16- 17)

Let us sing and rejoice, bringing forth the living waters of the Spirit of God.

3. Wells Represent Community

Wells have traditionally functioned as gathering places where the community would come together to draw their daily supply of water. The Hebrew word for community is kehila קהילה and it is what we call our Messianic congregations in Israel. Being part of a community of faith is essential to our spiritual life, health and growth.

"And let us not neglect our meeting together, as some people do, but encourage one another, especially now that the day of His return is drawing near." (Hebrews 10:25)

With 95% of Gen Z being fully submerged in a world of mobile devices and social media, they are considered the most connected generation to date, and yet they are also experiencing record-high levels of loneliness. The feeling of being overly connected on a superficial level, and at the same time feeling disconnected from deep, meaningful interactions with other people seems to be humanity's new reality.

Despite the challenge of finding real community in today's modern world, the well from which we draw living water – our congregations, churches and faith gatherings – may be the best place to search for like-minded fellowship, a friend – or even a spouse!

Moses at the well

It was at a well in the Midianite desert where Moses met Tziporah, the woman who was to become his wife. After fleeing Egypt, Moses came across the seven daughters of Yitro[11], the priest of Midian at a well. Moses rescued the girls from the shepherds who were harassing them, drew water for them and watered their flocks. Out of gratitude, Yitro offered Moses his hospitality and gave him his daughter Zipporah in marriage.[12]

Rebekah at the well

It was also at the well where Abraham's servant, Eliezer, found a wife for Isaac. Upon his master, Abraham's instructions, Eliezer traveled to Nahor and waited at a well. **"And he made his camels kneel down outside the city <u>by a well of water</u> at evening time, the time when women go out to draw water."** (Genesis 24:11)

Eliezer presented himself to God beside the well and prayed for the right woman to appear. **"Behold, here I stand by the well of water…"** (Genesis 24:13)

He then immediately met the beautiful Rebekah, who had come to the well to draw water, and knew she was 'the one' for Issac.[13]

---

[11] Yitro is the Hebrew name for Jethro, also called Reuel or Hobab in other biblical passages.
[12] Exodus 2:21-22
[13] Watch YouTube Video <u>How to Find a Good Wife</u>

The well is a meeting place for the community of faith; a place to present ourselves before God and make our prayers and petitions.

If you are searching for a spouse…or even a friend, instead of staying home or even worse, going to bars and clubs, try hanging around the communal well and see who might just show up!

4. Wells Represent Divine Encounters

It is no coincidence that Yeshua, in passing through Samaria, sat down at a well. It was, in fact, Jacob's well where he engaged in conversation with a Samaritan woman. This nameless woman, without wealth, power, or prestige, would become a voice announcing to the world that Yeshua is the Messiah!

Jacob's well still exists in Israel today, in the city of Nablus in Samaria on the grounds of a monastery next to the Balata Refugee Camp. Imagine that you can drink water from the same well where Yeshua asked the Samaritan woman for a drink. How cool is that?[14]

After discussing living water, eternal life, and true worship, the woman said, ***'I know that the Messiah is coming, and when He comes, He will explain all these things.' Yeshua said to her, 'I who speak to you am He.'"*** (John 4:25-26)

Leaving her water jar at the well, the woman went back to the town and said to the people, ***"Come see a man who told me everything I ever did. Could this be the Messiah?"*** The people went to seek Yeshua and many of the Samaritans believed in Him because of the woman's testimony. They urged Yeshua to stay with them, and He spent two days teaching them. Many more believed.[15]

---

[14] Unfortunately, Nablus, a city which also contains the tomb of Joseph, is currently zoned Area A, under the control of the Palestinian Authority and Israelis cannot enter without a military escort.
[15] John 4:28-42

This meeting at the well between the Samaritan woman and Yeshua was a divine encounter. It was not only where Yeshua directly proclaimed himself to be the Messiah, but it was also the place where boundaries and dividing walls were broken down. Yeshua broke down boundaries erected by religion and culture in order to create connection and unity.

Yeshua, a Jew, reached out to have a conversation not only with a Samaritan, but with a woman – behavior that would have been unthinkable in His day. ***"Then the woman of Samaria said to Him, 'How is it that You, being a Jew, ask a drink from me, a Samaritan woman?' For Jews have no dealings with Samaritans."*** (John 4:9)

What is also remarkable about this encounter is that Yeshua chose this particular woman to speak with. Scriptures tell us that it was <u>at the 6th hour</u> when she came to draw water. Why was this unusual? The 6th hour would have been at noontime, the heat of the day, when the rest of the women would have been at home.

No one in their right mind would walk any distance to draw water from a well at noon in the blazing, hot sun. No one except someone trying to avoid running into anyone else.

Why would this woman have wanted to hide from the other women? Yeshua knew the answer, and so He said to her,

"'Go, call your husband, and come here.' The woman answered and said, 'I have no husband.' Yeshua said to her, 'You have well said, "I have no husband," for you have had five husbands, and the one whom you now have is not your husband.'" (John 4:16-18)

Yeshua understood her shame; He understood her unquenchable thirst – for a love that would never let her go, never let her down, never abandon her or fail her.

Have you ever felt that kind of thirst? When I encountered Yeshua, not at a well but in the bathroom of a hotel, I was in a crisis pregnancy, divorced, having been abandoned by a man not my husband, contemplating abortion or suicide.

In this divine encounter, an angel in the form of a Christian woman entered the room and told me that Yeshua loves me, and that He will never leave me or forsake me.[16] After so many broken relationships and disappointments, these are the words I needed

---

[16] Read Hannah's testimony in her book, <u>Grafted in Again</u>

to hear. And I suspect that the Samaritan woman at the well may have felt the same.

Are you a 6th hour person? Do you avoid social encounters and gatherings, believing that if people really knew you, they would reject you? Yeshua accepts us with all our failures and sins; He sympathizes with our weaknesses. In fact it is not the strong and powerful whom God chooses but the weak and the foolish.[17]

Yeshua knows that we are searching for love in all the wrong places, in ways that will never truly satisfy. He comes to offer us a drink of living water – that we will never thirst again.

Yeshua said to the woman at the well, ***"Whoever drinks of this water will thirst again, but whoever drinks of the water that I shall give him will never thirst. But the water that I shall give him will become in him a fountain of water springing up into everlasting life."*** (John 4:13-14)

5. Wells Represent Gifts and Inheritances

God gave a covenant promise to His people to bring them into a good land where houses would already be built, and wells already dug for them. These are God's gifts to the children of Israel.

"So it shall be, when the LORD your God brings you into the land of which He swore to your fathers, to Abraham, Isaac, and Jacob, to give you large and beautiful cities which you did not build, houses full of all good things, which you did not fill, <u>hewn-out wells which you did not dig</u>, vineyards and olive trees which you did not plant.." (Deuteronomy 6:10-11)

God may have wells of supply just waiting for us that someone else has already labored for. These wells can be part of our inheritance from previous generations. In Genesis 26, we see that Abraham's son, Isaac, went back to his father's wells, only to find that the Philistines had stopped up the wells and filled them with dirt.[18]

There was a famine in the land and God instructed Isaac not to go down to Egypt as his father Abraham had done, but to stay in the Land and God would bless him there. We

---

[17] 1 Corinthians 1:27
[18] Genesis 26:15

need to listen to the voice of the Holy Spirit. What worked one time may not be the best course of action the next time it happens.

Isaac headed to the wells – to the place of supply and provision left to him by his father, Abraham. Here we see the generational sins of the father being perpetuated by the son. Just like his father Abraham did, Isaac lied about his wife to Abimelech, saying that she was his sister. And just as before with Abraham, Abimelech took Rebekkah into his harem (some people never learn, or... as a dog returns to his vomit so a fool repeats his folly,[19] or... it's hard for old dogs to learn new tricks).

Isaac dwelt in Grar and tried to re-dig the wells of his father, Abraham:

"And Isaac dug again the wells of water which they had dug in the days of Abraham his father, for the Philistines had stopped them up after the death of Abraham. He called them by the names which his father had called them." (Genesis 26:18)

There may be wells of supply that have been left to us from previous generations that have been stopped up by the enemy, just waiting for us to return and re-dig the wells. It will take hard work, time, and perseverance, but may be well worth the effort.

When the Philistines quarreled with Isaac over the first well, Isaac just walked away and moved on. He was also a peacemaker like his father, Abraham.[20] Isaac kept moving on until he got to a place called Rehovot רחובות, which comes from the root word Rahav רָחַב[21], which means broad or spacious, because here he found a place where God made room for him and he could be fruitful in the Land.[22]

"He brought me out into a spacious place; He rescued me because He delighted in me." (Psalm 18:19)

If we are feeling cramped, crowded or limited, we can ask God to guide us to our place of 'Rehovot' – a broad, spacious place where we have room to grow and can be fruitful. And yet, God has even more....

---

[19] Proverbs 26:11
[20] See Chapter At the Waters of Meribah (Strife)
[21] This was the Hebrew name of Rahab who was a 'broad thinker' to help Israeli spies
[22] Genesis 26:22

Moving on to Be'er Sheva

Even though Isaac had found a good place, God had something even better for him, and so Isaac moved on again – to Be'er Sheva. *"Then he went up from there to Be'er sheva* באר שבע*."* (Genesis 26:23)

Here, God appeared to Isaac, promising to bless and multiply him in the Land as He had blessed his father, Abraham. Isaac built an altar there and called upon the name of Yehovah יְהוָה – <u>and dug a well</u>:

"So he built an altar there and called on the name of Yehovah יְהוָה, and he pitched his tent there; and there Isaac's servants dug a well." (Genesis 26:25)

As good as being in a spacious place is, as gratifying as being in a place where we can be fruitful, God has something even greater in store for us – satisfaction.

Well of Satisfaction - Sheva

We now come to the third meaning of the word, Sheva שבע, and that is 'satisfaction'. It means to be completely satisfied, satiated, and to have one's full, as in to have eaten so much as to be stuffed full or *'filled to the brim'*.

Yeshua said, in the sermon on the Mount, that those who hunger and thirst for righteousness will be filled (satisfied).[23] When we hunger and thirst for the right things, we will be completely satiated; but the flesh is never satisfied, no matter how much we feed it, coddle it, entertain it, indulge it or distract it.

"Hell and Destruction are never full; so the eyes of man are never satisfied." (Proverbs 27:20)

God has a 'Be'er Sheva' for us – a well of abundance – where we can truly say we have been satisfied by the goodness of God. *"We shall be satisfied* שָׂבְעָה *with the goodness of Your house…"* (Psalm 65:4)

---

[23] Matthew 5:6

God satisfies the thirsty soul and those who hunger; He fills with what is good. Oh taste and see that the Lord is good!

To know the love of Messiah which passes knowledge is the way to be filled with the fullness of God (Ephesians 3:19).

Daughters of Sheva

Bat-Sheva (daughter of Sheva) went through terrible heartache that seems to contradict her very name. She committed adultery with King David – a sin which was likely not her choice since she was already married, but then again who can refuse a king? This resulted in the death of her husband through the murderous plot of David, and subsequently, the death of her infant son.

Can you imagine her grief at losing both her husband and her baby? Can we even begin to fathom the guilt and pain of regret she must have felt in watching her infant son die, knowing it was because of her own sin?

And yet, despite all these sorrows and trials, God allowed her to move into the place of her name: Bat בת (daughter of) Sheva שבע (satisfaction). She persevered in life and went on to become a woman of great honor and influence: the wife of King David and the mother of Solomon, the next ruler of Israel.

From Bat-Sheva's example, we can see that we also may come to a place of blessing, contentment and satisfaction in our lives, even after going through times of trial and pain. We must believe and trust in God that even when we walk through valleys of tears (Bacca), we are just passing through:

"As they pass through the Valley of Baca (crying) they make it a spring." (Psalm 84:6)

We have all walked through these valleys of weeping; but despite our human failures and weaknesses, we are still His 'Daughters of Sheva' – meant to live in blessing, abundance, and satisfaction.

The world's blessings in themselves will not bring satisfaction; but the blessing of the Lord adds no sorrow to it.[24]

Some of us have sought satisfaction in finding the perfect relationship; or the right career path, or in degrees, or accomplishments, fat bank accounts, luxury cars or homes, the perfect vacation or place to live, but it has all been in vain. As King Solomon, the wisest man on earth has said, *"It's all vanity – chasing after the wind."*

These things can bring temporary happiness, but do not have the power to ultimately satisfy: **"the eye is not satisfied with seeing, nor the ear filled with hearing."** (Ecclesiastes 1:8)

There are times when we flit from one thing to the next but just feel so lost, empty and unsatisfied. I have a dear relative who travels all over the world, never settling in one place for long. He was recently in the Amazon, then Mexico, then Israel, and last I heard he's moved on to India, trying to find peace in Hindu mysticism and yoga. When we finally realize that our soul is thirsty, we can go to the fountain of living waters to be refreshed in the Spirit of the living God.

Only the Spirit of God can truly quench our thirst. David cried out to God in the wilderness of Judah: **"My soul thirsts for You; my flesh longs for You in a dry and thirsty land where there is no water."** (Psalm 63:1)

David was on the run, being unjustly persecuted by King Saul, desperate to the point of despair; but then He remembered the lovingkindness of God and He praised Him, saying:

"*My soul shall be satisfied* as with marrow and fatness, and my mouth shall praise You with joyful lips." (Psalm 63:5)

---

[24] Proverbs 10:22

> The words used in Hebrew for 'marrow and fatness' are 'halav & deshen' חֵלֶב וָדֶשֶׁן. Halav means '<u>milk</u>' and deshen is a word used for '<u>fertilizer</u>'.
>
> It can also mean manure or fatness. Just like a baby is satisfied with its mother's milk, so too is our soul satisfied with the realization of the lovingkindness of God. It is like 'fertilizer' to our faith! Even situations in life that seemingly 'stink' like manure can eventually lead us to a place of contentment and satisfaction.

My last child, Avi-ad, was born in the city of Be'er Sheva on November 6th 2002. He has brought such delight to my soul; but after twenty-one years together, my last eaglet has flown from the nest. He was released from the IDF and has moved into a new season of independence.

There are those, the Psalmist writes, **"men of the world, who have their portion in this life...they are satisfied with children."** (Psalm 17:14)

As delightful as I find my children, as much as I appreciate the blessing of my family, they are not enough to satisfy my soul. We may find a measure of satisfaction on earth, choosing like Paul exhorted us to be content in all circumstances, but I am reminded that ultimately, the place of Sheva will only be found on that day that we awake in His presence to see His face.

"As for me, I will see Your face in righteousness, I shall be satisfied when I awake in Your likeness." (Psalm 17:15)

We are all on a journey to find our well of living water. Like Abraham, we will go through many times of trial and testing in life, and yet we must still walk onward, trusting in the faithfulness and mercies of God to bring us to our own 'Be'er Sheva' – the well of satisfaction in Yeshua Hamashiach (the Messiah).

"And I will satiate the soul of the cohanim [25] ***with fatness (deshen), and My people shall be satisfied with My goodness, says Yehovah."*** (Jeremiah 31:14)

Prayer: *Dear God, open my eyes to see the well of supply, provision and opportunity that sits right in front of me. Thank you Father for supplying my every need and for the divine appointments You have in store for me. Lead and guide me to the wells of living waters as I sing and praise You. I give You thanks that You are bringing me to the Wells of Sheva where I will be fully satisfied with Your goodness. Amen.*

---

[25] Cohanim are Jewish priests

I Will Arise and Return to the Father - Hozer חוזר

"I will arise and go to my father, and will say to him, 'Father, I have sinned against heaven and before you, and I am no longer worthy to be called your son. Make me like one of your hired servants.'" (Luke 15:18-19)

In this well known parable of the prodigal son, Yeshua described a young man who demanded his inheritance from his father and promptly squandered it all away in 'loose living' in a far off land. Shortly after, there was a famine in the land, and in his lowly state, he was forced into a job feeding the swine.

It must have truly felt like hitting rock bottom for this '*nice Jewish boy*' who had grown up knowing that God called swine 'unclean' and had forbidden His people to eat their flesh or even touch their carcasses.[1]

He was so hungry that he would have gladly eaten the pigs' food but even this was denied to him. Finally, he came to his senses and realized that even his father's servants were treated better than this, so he decided to return to his father and plead for mercy.

---

[1] Leviticus 11:7-8

What we don't realize is that there is a hidden secret here which can only be revealed in the Hebrew; that is, a connection between the swine and the son's returning to the father.

The Hebrew word for **pig, pork, hog, boar** or **swine** is '*hazir*' חֲזִיר

The word for **return** or **come back** is the related word '*hozer*' חוזר.

Both of these words come from the root word, '*hazar*' חזר which means **to repent**.

The Hebrew phrase for **repentance** is '*hazarah b'tshuvah*' חזרה בתשובה

Another related word '*l'hehzir*' להחזיר means **to restore**.

We may easily see how these Hebrew words for return, come back, repent and restore are relevant to the story of the Prodigal son, but what about the swine? What do pigs have to do with returning to the father in repentance and being restored??

Laws of Holiness

The entire book of Leviticus deals with the laws of holiness that pertain to time, place and people. Included are the Biblical dietary laws: animals which God has declared 'clean' and fit to eat for His holy people; and those animals which God considers 'unclean' and unfit for consumption.

These commandments, called the laws of 'kashrut' [2] are not strictly about health, but rather about obedience. The basic rules of kashrut are that a kosher animal is one that has split hooves and chews its cud. A kosher fish has both fins and scales. This rules out pork and shellfish as being acceptable food for consumption by 'holy people'.

The restrictions on our diet is only one way in which God disciplines us into becoming a 'goy kadosh' (holy nation). Rebellion against God's dietary laws goes all the way back to the Garden of Eden when Chava (Eve) and Adam ate the one fruit that God said was forbidden.

---

[2] For a complete discussion of the Biblical Dietary Laws, see Hannah's book, **Kashrut The Biblical Dietary Laws: & Other Elements of a Biblical Lifestyle** on Amazon or as an ebook.

Many of God's people are committing the same sin today in eating those foods that God has said in His Word are abominable and not to be eaten. God is the same today, yesterday and forever. He has not given us His word on this subject and then changed His mind. If we think that God doesn't care what we eat, perhaps we should ask Eve!

Walking in the Fear of the Lord

Our God, the Ancient of Days, is the same in the old as in the new. He is יהוה YHVH – He does not change. *"For I am יהוה YHVH, I do not change."* (Malachi 3:6)

God commands us to be holy as He is holy: *"For I am יְהֹוָה that brought you up out of the land of Egypt, to be your Elohim אֱלֹהִים; you shall therefore be holy (k'doshim) קְדֹשִׁים, for I am holy."* (Leviticus 11:44-45)

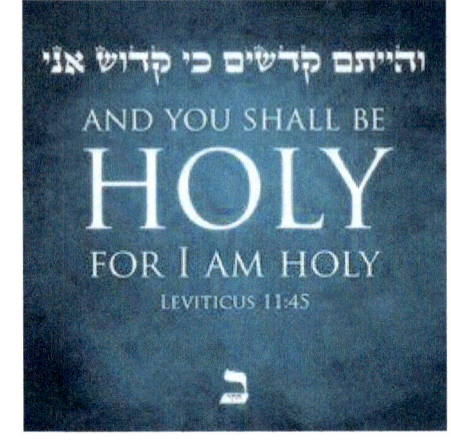

The Hebrew word for holy is 'kadosh' קָדוֹשׁ which means 'set apart for a sacred purpose'. Isn't it interesting that the first thing God deals with in the area of holiness is food!? Perhaps it is because God doesn't want us to be 'once a week' holy people when we meet together in congregations; but to be holy, set apart, sanctified people every moment of every day.

That means that whenever we feel the urge to eat, we must choose to either accept God's way or our own. If Leviticus 11 clearly forbids God's people to eat pork, then why are most Bible-believing Christians still eating it? Good question...

Some say that it is because '*Jesus fulfilled the law*' or that '*we are no longer under the law but under grace*'. Others point to Peter's vision and quote the verse that *seems* to say Jesus declared all foods clean.[3] I would like to challenge some of these assumptions, giving 'food for thought' (excuse the pun).

The Bible gives us instructions on every aspect of our lives: lifestyle, relationships, parenting, work, marriage, birth, death, hygiene, money, attitudes and even sexuality.

---

[3] Mark 7:19 The phrase 'Jesus declared all foods clean' is an addition that not all translations include.

Therefore it only stands to reason that God would also have something important to instruct us about the most basic element of our very survival – food!

This is the meaning of the word, Torah[4]: it is a book of instructions from our Creator – in other words, the human instruction manual. If we were to purchase an expensive machine or vehicle and completely disregard its instruction manual, we would be very foolish indeed, right? Of course right. So too is it foolhardy to ignore the instruction manual for humanity by the One who created us.

God said,**"Speak to the children of Israel, saying, "These are the animals which you may eat among all the animals that are on the earth."** (Leviticus 11:2)

"The swine, though it divides the hoof, having cloven hooves, yet does not chew the cud, *is* unclean to you. Their flesh you shall not eat, and their carcasses you shall not touch. They *are* unclean (Tameh) טמא to you." (Leviticus 11:7-8)

Although little piggies may look cute, pigs are unclean animals who are the garbage eaters of the earth, just as shellfish such as shrimp, crabs, clams, scallops, prawns, oysters and octopus are the water scavengers. They eat garbage, sick creatures, and decaying corpses.

Pigs will eat rats, mice, fecal waste and even maggots. Their bodies are so full of toxins that even poisonous snakes cannot harm them. The parasites that inhabit the flesh of pork have been shown to remain alive and wiggling even after cooking at high temperatures.

God has intelligently designed these unclean animals as environmental cleaners, not as a source of food. Scavengers were created by God to eat dead and diseased things but were not created to be eaten by human beings. They are not 'food' for us.

---

[4] The Torah is a word for the 'Old Testament': the 5 books of Moses, the writings and the Hebrew prophets.

In one example, pigs have been used to eat Philadelphia's garbage and sewage for over 100 years, saving the city $3 million a year in landfill costs. Shellfish can remove cholera, a toxic pollutant associated with raw sewage from the sea. Raw shellfish such as oysters, have been known to carry viral hepatitis which can lead to cirrhosis, liver failure and liver cancer.[5]

Besides the health risks of eating animals that God has forbidden, however, is the more important issue of the defilement of our soul.

Defilement of our Soul

The Hebrew word for 'soul' is 'nefesh' נֶפֶשׁ. God's word specifically states that eating unclean (impure) food defiles not just our body, but our soul. *"You shall not make your soul (nefesh) abominable (detestable – sheketz שֶׁקֶץ) with any creeping thing that creeps; nor shall you make yourselves unclean (impure – tameh) טָמֵא with them, lest you be defiled (tameh) by them."* (Leviticus 11:43)

The Hebrew word used for abominable or detestable is **sheketz** שֶׁקֶץ. This same Hebrew word is used to describe anything without fins or scales: shellfish, catfish, eels, bottom feeders, etc. Likewise, insects, creepy crawly things (except locust and grasshoppers), snails, frogs, lizards, and birds such as eagles, vultures, buzzards, falcons, crows, ostrich, hawks and owls are to be detestable to us and not even considered as food.

"They shall be an abomination to you; <u>you shall not eat their flesh</u>, but you shall regard their carcasses as an abomination (detestable) sheketz שֶׁקֶץ. Whatever in the water does not have fins or scales—that shall be an abomination (detestable) to you." (Leviticus 11:11-12)

In Deuteronomy 14:3, God again reminds His people, *"You shall not eat any detestable thing."* In this Scripture, there is another, even stronger Hebrew word used for detestable, which is *'toevah'* תּוֹעֵבָה – the exact same word used to describe

---

[5] Holy Cow! By Hope Egan, p. 32-33

abominations such as child sacrifice[6] and sexual perversions like homosexuality and bestiality.[7]

So what about Jesus declaring all foods clean? First of all, this phrase is an extra biblical addition to some translations, not included in all Bibles. Secondly, Yeshua was a Torah observant Jew. As such, any animal that God had forbidden him to eat would simply not be considered 'food'. Just as we love our little golden doodle puppy, it would be disgusting in our culture[8] to think of eating her (sorry, Lilly)!

Liat with her new goldendoodle puppy, Lilly.

Daniel was a young man who determined that even while exiled in Babylon, even under adverse conditions in the midst of a people who did not observe God's commandments, he would not defile himself with food that God had declared unfit for His holy people.

"Daniel purposed in his heart that he would not defile himself with the king's food." (Daniel 1:8)

After this trial period of not eating the King's food, not only was Daniel no worse for wear, but he was even healthier and better looking too!

"At the end of ten days their appearances looked better than all the young men who ate the portion of the king's food." (Daniel 1:15)

Unclean foods were permitted to be given to a stranger or foreigner, but were forbidden for God's holy people.[9] So the real question here is, *"What is our identity?"* Are we still foreigners and strangers? Or are we God's holy people? Because if we are a 'holy nation, a royal priesthood, then perhaps we need to act (and even eat) like it.

---

[6] Deuteronomy 18:10-12
[7] Bestiality is sex with animals
[8] The dog meat trade is most widespread in China, South Korea, the Philippines, Thailand, Laos, Viet Nam, Cambodia, Indonesia and Nagaland in northern India. This trade is well-organized, with high numbers of dogs being stolen or taken from the streets, transported over long distances and brutally slaughtered.
[9] Deuteronomy 14:21

Our true identity is this: *"But you are a chosen people, a royal priesthood, a holy nation, God's special possession, that you may declare the praises of Him who called you out of darkness into His wonderful light."* (1 Peter 2:9)

Through the blood of Yeshua, those who were once Gentiles are now part of the commonwealth of Israel – no longer strangers and foreigners.

"Now, therefore, you are no longer strangers and foreigners, but fellow citizens with the saints and members of the household of God" (Ephesians 2:19)

Together, we now make up the 'one new man' – Jew and Gentile in the Messiah. But how can two walk together unless agreed[10] on something as simple and fundamental as what we put in our mouths and stomachs?

There is only one way, one truth, one God, and one Torah. We either choose God's way, the narrow path that leads to life – or we choose to walk the broad path that many walk upon that leads to destruction.

Peter's Vision - Food or People?

The last objection I want to cover is that of Peter's vision. There exists a widespread, gross misinterpretation of this watershed moment in the history of the Church that has led so many of God's people into deception.

In the Book of Acts, in chapter 10, Peter has a vision in which he sees unclean animals being lowered down from Heaven in a sheet. And he hears a voice saying, *"Peter, get up, kill and eat!"* (Acts 10:13)

Peter was greatly puzzled, saying, *"No way, Lord! For I have never eaten anything common or unclean."* (Acts 10:14)

Now, can't we assume that if Yeshua had changed the law (which, btw,[11] is an act of the antiChrist, not the Messiah[12]), he would have let Peter in on this little secret? In all the time they spent together, as one of Yeshua's 'inner circle', Peter never once heard Yeshua say that it's ok to eat unclean animals.

---

[10] Amos 3:3
[11] Btw - by the way
[12] Daniel 7:25

Peter must have thought this was definitely the voice of the devil, tempting him to sin. It would have been as if a sheet descended from Heaven filled with naked women and a voice said, *"Peter, rise up and fornicate!"* This is how shocking the vision was to Peter.

But then the voice of God clarified the meaning of this bizarre vision: **"What God has cleansed you must not call common."** Peter understood that God was talking about people from the nations, Gentiles, not food.

God was calling Peter to go to the house of Cornelius, to share the gospel with the Gentiles – something that would have previously been considered unthinkable. Peter said to them, **"You know how unlawful it is for a Jewish man to keep company with or go to one of another nation. But God has shown me that I should not call any MAN common or unclean."** (Acts 10:28)

Peter received an incredible revelation: Yeshua the Messiah is not exclusively for the Jewish people but also for non-Jews. Peter opened *his* mouth and said: **"In truth I perceive that God shows no partiality. But in every nation <u>whoever fears Him</u> and works righteousness is accepted by Him."** (Acts 10:34-35)

At this amazing moment in history, the gospel began to be preached to the nations! Halleluyah! Peter's vision has everything to do with salvation through Yeshua being available to every person of every tongue, tribe, race, language, ethnicity or nationality – but it has absolutely nothing to do with food.

Setting Boundaries - A Good Father

God, like any good father, sets boundaries for His children; He is a boundary setting God. He told Adam and Eve that they could eat freely of any fruit of any tree in the garden of Eden – except one – the tree of the knowledge of good and evil.[13] He gives us six days to freely work but tells us not to work on the seventh. The problem is that we are boundary breaking people. We look for ways to get around the boundaries, to find a loophole, or to sneak past the gate.

Some Jewish farmers, rather than miss a whole year's worth of planting, harvesting and selling their crops during the year of Shmittah,[14] will put a cover over their tractors so that God can't 'see' that they are working

Hebrew sign says,
'Here we are keeping Shmittah'.

---

[13] Genesis 2:16-17
[14] Shmittah is a commanded year of complete rest for the land every seven years

the land at a time when God had commanded them to give the land a rest.

Too often we see these boundaries as restricting, whereas the limitations are to keep us safe and secure. As a rebellious teenager, I used to sneak out of my window at night to go to wild parties; a foolish act that placed me in physical and moral danger.

Walking in the Valley of the Dry Elephant Bones

In the story of the Lion King, the cubs were told that they could go anywhere in the Kingdom except one place – the Valley of the Dry Elephant Bones.

So where do you think these little cubs went?

Of course they ventured into the Valley of the Dry Elephant Bones – and were immediately surrounded by snarling, drooling, hungry hyenas ready to devour them.

We have an enemy who is like a lion prowling about, the devil,[15] with an entire legion of demons at his command, ready to devour anyone who ventures into his territory. When we transgress God's commandments, we have placed ourselves in his dark kingdom – a very dangerous place – unless we come to our senses, repent and return to the Father.

Of course the Lion King heard their cries and saved his cubs; and so too will our mighty King when we cry out to Him, but we need to keep ourselves safe and secure by staying within the boundaries that God has set for us.

"The fear of Adonai is the beginning of knowledge, but fools despise wisdom and instruction." (Proverbs 1:7)

Wisdom is calling out to us, but the question is whether or not we are listening. The Word tells us that if we will listen to the voice of wisdom, we will be safe and secure without fear of evil. Fools despise wisdom, but, ***"Whoever listens to me (wisdom) will dwell safely, and will be secure, without fear of evil."*** (Proverbs 1:33)

---

[15] 1 Peter 5:8

Devouring Lions

There is an obscure story in the Bible in 2 Kings 17, where the King of Assyria conquered Samaria and carried away the people of Judah & Israel, *replacing them* with foreigners. Then a curious thing began happening – the Lord sent lions among them that began killing some of them.

So they went to the King of Assyria and said:

"The nations whom you have removed and placed in the cities of Samaria <u>do not know the rituals of the God of the land</u>; therefore He has sent lions among them, and indeed, they are killing them because they do not know the rituals of the God of the land." (2 Kings 17:26)

I believe this represents Christians who believe they have replaced Israel, but do not wholly fear the Lord; and do not know how to walk in the ways of the God of Israel. These people either keep a Sunday Sabbath or do not keep it whatsoever; they eat foods that God has called abominable; they celebrate man-made festivals and disregard God's appointed times.

So what did the King of Assyria do to remedy the situation and save the people from being devoured? He sent for the Jewish priests (cohanim) to come back into the Land to teach the people how to walk in the ways of the God of Jacob.

"Many people shall come and say, 'Come, and let us go up to the mountain of the Lord, to the house of the God of Jacob; He will teach us His ways, and we shall walk in His paths.'" (Isaiah 2:3)

I see this as the role of Messianic Jews today who teach the Jewish roots of the Christian Faith. And yet, like the Jewish priests of old, we are only partially successful in our mission; for although the people did fear the Lord, they continued to walk in the customs and traditions with which they were familiar. As it is with many today…

Repentance and Restoration - Return to the Father

Could it be possible that God is calling His Holy people, no matter our background, lineage or nationality, to repent of disregarding His explicit instructions, His Torah, even with regards to our food? God is coming to judge the inhabitants of the earth and those who eat the flesh of swine will be consumed.[16]

God says, **"If you love Me ... keep My commandments."** [17]

Is it perhaps time to rise up out of the pig pen and return to the Father to be cleansed of defilement and to be restored as a son or daughter with a clean, royal robe?

All of Heaven is waiting to throw a party – and we're all invited! Halleluyah!

Prayer: *Dear God, we repent, whether out of rebellion or sheer ignorance, of transgressing Your commandments, even about the foods we eat. We want to return to You, Father, and we ask You to forgive us, cleanse us and restore us to our place as Your children. In Yeshua's name. Amen v'amen.*

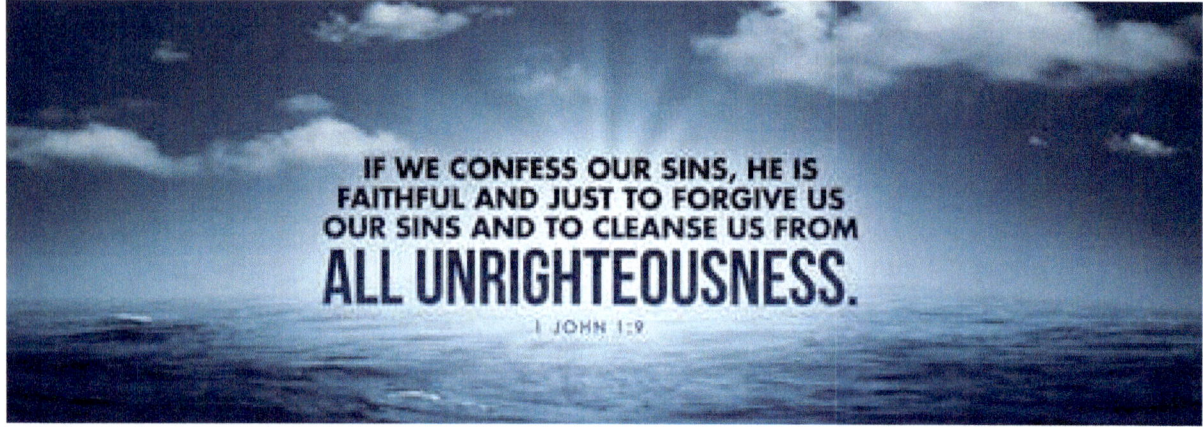

---

[16] Isaiah 66:17
[17] John 14:15

Other Messianic Jewish Materials by Hannah Nesher

Books or eBooks:

Messianic Jewish Commentary (eBooks only)
- Complete Parashot
- B'reisheet - Genesis
- Shmot - Exodus
- Vayikra - Leviticus
- Bamidbar - Numbers
- Devarim - Deuteronomy

Messiah Revealed in the Sabbath
Messiah Revealed in Passover
Messiah Revealed in Shavuot
Messiah Revealed in The Fall Feasts
Messiah Revealed in Chanukah
Messiah Revealed in Purim
Shofar Booklet
Though He Slay Me (eBook only)
Devotionals for an Animal Lovers Heart
Grafted in Again
Journey to Jerusalem
Come out of Her My People
Kashrut: The Biblical Dietary Laws

Online Hebrew Courses:

Shalom Morah I - Hebrew Names of God
Shalom Morah II -
Wisdom in Hebrew Aleph-bet

Digital Viewing:

Exploring the Jewish Roots of the Christian Faith
There is a God in Israel
Walking through the Wilderness
Shalom Jerusalem
Esther's Last Call to the Church
Because He Lives
Passover Lamb or Easter Ham?
Messianic Jewish Passover
Ruth: A Righteous Gentile
Unity In The Messiah
Where is Your Brother Jacob?
Messiah in Chanukah
Blow The Shofar for Zion

www.voiceforisrael.net
nesher.hannah@gmail.com

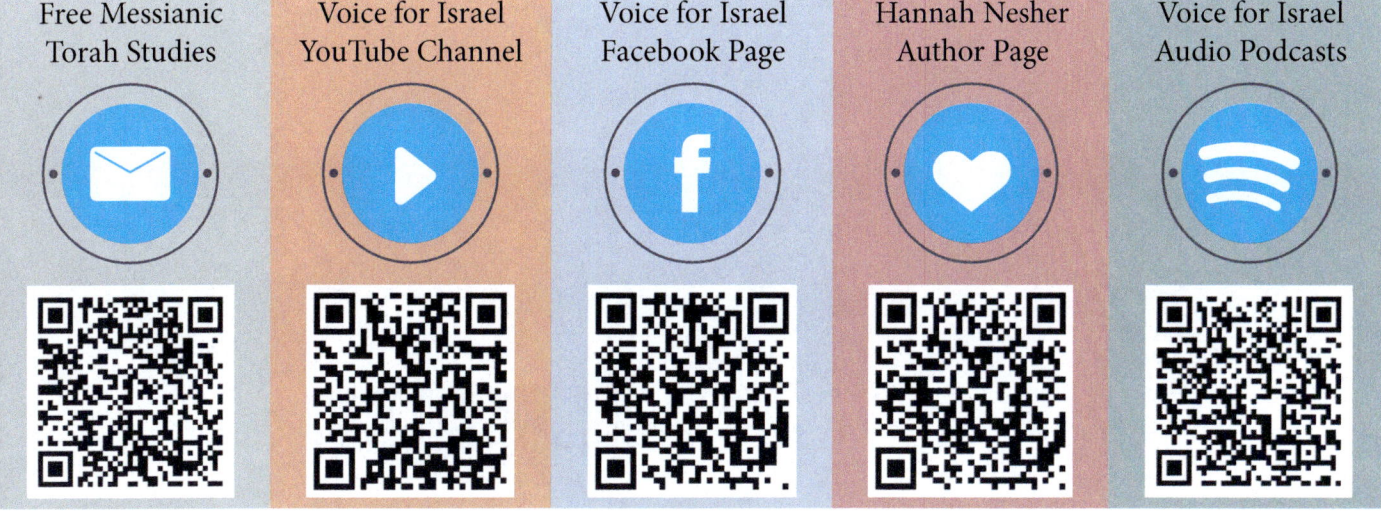

Printed in Great Britain
by Amazon